Naomi Klein –
April 2011

THESE WERE OUR SONS

STORIES FROM
STOCKWELL WAR MEMORIAL

NAOMI LOURIE KLEIN

THESE WERE OUR SONS

STORIES FROM
STOCKWELL WAR MEMORIAL

NAOMI LOURIE KLEIN

ELEFANT
BOOKS

ELEFANT BOOKS
Published by Elefant Books
9 Durand Gardens, London SW9 0PS, England
www.elefantbooks.com

First published by Elefant Books
Copyright © Naomi Lourie Klein, 2010

ISBN 978-0-9565865-0-6

Printed and bound in the United Kingdom
by Antony Rowe Limited

Cover design Lloyd Clater
www.sharpedge.com

www.stockwellwarmemorial.co.uk

Front cover: Jesse Goff, Rifleman, London Regiment, died 1 July 1916
Back cover: the unveiling of Stockwell War Memorial on 3 May 1922

Dedicated to
the men on the Memorial
and to my friend Sheila Dartnell
and all others who work to ensure
that the names of the dead are
not forgotten

These were our sons who died for our lands
In glory will they sleep and endless sanctity
Their name liveth for evermore

Inscription on the Memorial

...the foul wounds of the shells and machine-guns,
the mines, the gas, and the counter-attacks...
But all that wears off and goes away, you don't
know how and you don't know where,
and there's only the names left.

'Under Fire' by Henri Barbusse

Preface

Stockwell War Memorial, which commemorates the deaths of 574 local men who died in the First World War, is marooned on a traffic island at the junction of South Lambeth Road and Clapham Road in south London, encircled by noise and pollution. In 1922 the triangle of common land on which it stands was intended as a place of quiet contemplation of the meaning of war, death and life.

Now, few people take the time and trouble to look closely at the Memorial and the names on it. They have other things to do: rush to the Tube, visit the cashpoint, grab some fish and chips. Most are conspicuously uninterested. An old building, dedicated to unknown men from long ago, is to them of no importance.

I had lived in the area for the best part of 20 years before I looked properly at the Memorial. While passing one day, a name caught my eye: Desaleux. There were three men of that name listed. *Three.* Were they brothers? I walked around the structure, reading the names. For the first time, I appreciated that there were hundreds of them.

Who were these men and what was their story?

The answer is: They were much like me and my fellow residents today – they lived fairly ordinary lives in an area of London that encompassed both comfort and poverty. Many had the misfortune to find themselves in France, Flanders, Gallipoli, Africa and the Middle East in the most dire circumstances, surrounded by destruction and slaughter. Others met their ends through illness, accident or other mishap. They were rich and poor, volunteer and conscript, good soldiers and bad. However, all of these men, who disappeared from Stockwell nearly a hundred years ago, have one thing in common: they deserve to be remembered.

I have tried to tell something of their stories. For some men I found a wealth of information: Service histories, entries in memorial books, letters and photographs. Occasionally I unearthed information of a personal nature – medical conditions, disciplinary matters and punishments – and I have included these.

Some identifications are tentative and I have made this clear in the text. For others, where only scant details are available, I have created a simple biography of each victim based on what is known about that person's occupation, family relationships, age and type and place of residence. In this I have followed the approach used by Yad Vashem, the Holocaust Martyrs' and Heroes' Remembrance Authority in Jerusalem. Each description, however short, adds to our knowledge of that person and increases our understanding of the meaning of their loss.

Others will remain for ever untraceable.

Although some of the sources, including the Memorial itself, contain inaccuracies, any further errors are my own. My aim throughout is not to be wrong, and for this reason I have left out some information. The back section of the book includes explanatory notes on how the research was done and how I have used military and non-military information, as well as other matters.

I am happy to correct errors brought to my attention on my website www.stockwellwarmemorial.co.uk.

Naomi Lourie Klein
Stockwell, July 2010

Introduction

Sixteen million people died in the First World War: 9.7 million military personnel and about 6.8 million civilians. The Allies alone lost 5.7 million soldiers. Nearly 900,000 British and Irish servicemen died. In four years, 10 per cent of the male population under the age of 45 disappeared. The 574 men on Stockwell War Memorial, who had all lived within half a mile of the site, equate to barely six hundredths of one per cent of those who died. These figures are so large, so unimaginable, that it is difficult to appreciate the scale of the loss and what it meant to families and communities.

It might help to think of the streets the men lived in. In Stockwell, the street of greatest loss was South Lambeth Road: 10 men who once lived there died. Eight each went from Clapham Road, Hargwyne Street and Hartington Road; seven from Crimsworth Road; six each from Horace Street (near Wilcox Road) and Larkhall Lane; five each from Aldebert Terrace, Lingham Street, Mordaunt Street, Paradise Road, Portland Place, Stockwell Road, Cottage Grove, Arlesford Road and Edithna Street. To take the exercise one step further, visualise Tradescant Road, a small street off South Lambeth Road, where five men between the ages of 17 and 25 were lost: Edgar Sharman from No. 5; William Mills, No. 8; Frederick Pulsford, No. 10; Ernest Reynolds, No. 20; and Percy Pearce, No. 45. In all, I traced the addresses of 389 men from the Stockwell Memorial. Fewer than 45 came from streets where there were no other casualties listed on the Memorial.

Even before the end of the war, communities throughout the country felt a yearning to honour and remember their dead. In 1916 a wooden "street shrine" was erected in front of St. Mark's Church, Kennington, less than a mile from Stockwell, and there were others at St. Michael's, Stockwell and St. Anne's, South Lambeth Road. Because bodies were not repatriated, these shrines, and the permanent memorials that followed them, took the place of graves, a focus for the families' grief.

There was also, perhaps, a collective guilt – for not appreciating the extreme hardship the men had been through before they died, for encouraging ever more men to join the fight, for not understanding the political forces at work. The Stockwell Memorial, erected by public subscription through the devoted efforts of a few Stockwell citizens, was a permanent reminder of those who had died, a way to help heal emotional wounds, but it was also a way to make amends.

Eight years before the Memorial was unveiled, European nations, one by one, had opted to fight to settle their claims to power and prestige. The German Kaiser, Wilhelm II, had been actively planning for war, and the assassination of Archduke Franz Josef and his wife by Bosnian Serb radicals in Sarajevo on 28 July 1914 proved to be the tipping point.

Britain declared war on Germany on 4 August and recruiting offices were immediately besieged by volunteers. The headquarters of the South London battalions, including the 1/24th (County of London) Battalion of the London Regiment at New Street (now Braganza Street) in Kennington, the 21st Battalion at Flodden Road, Camberwell, and the 5th London Brigade of the Royal Field Artillery in Lower Kennington Road were packed with men eager to join the war effort.

Generally in Britain, despite fears of food shortages and natural anxiety about the risks to their young men, most people felt that this war would be a short, exciting skirmish it would be a shame to miss. There was a patriotic duty to take part and, anyway, it could all be over in months.

This was not a prediction shared by Field Marshall Sir Herbert Kitchener, the great Army recruiter. He knew that Britain's army was tiny compared to Germany's and correctly forecast that the war would last at least three years, and that victory would require the sacrifice of millions.

In south London, as up and down the country, cheered on by the press and government propaganda, families offered up all their sons for service and were congratulated for doing so. The six Charman brothers of Ingleborough Street off Brixton Road joined up. Seventeen-year-old Richard, the youngest, died; remarkably, all the others survived. In nearby Kennington, the six Carpenter brothers, Joseph, William, Thomas, Alfred, George and Stephen, all joined, and appeared in their khaki in *The South London Press*. By July 1915, 175 men living in Trafalgar Street, Bermondsey, had enlisted, the most of any street in London. "They went without being fetched," noted *The Daily Herald*.

The South London Press praised the splendid response to the war and calculated that on 31 August 1914, four weeks after the war started, 652 men from Bermondsey, Camberwell, Lambeth and Southwark had volunteered. But recruitment stalled and by spring 1915 two local heroes, Corporal Frederick Holmes and Lance Corporal Leonard James Keyworth, both Victoria Cross winners, were touring south London to give their

September 1914: Volunteer soldiers march down Brixton Road

encouragement. "Come and show your pluck," was Keyworth's last message to the "shirkers" of south London before he returned to the front and his death at the Battle of Loos a few months later.

Towards the end of 1915, it was clear that voluntary enlistment would not be adequate to feed the engine of war. *The South London Press* estimated that 30,000 men a week were needed, that is 4,286 a day or 178 an hour. The only way forward was conscription. From 2 March 1916, single men aged between 18 and 41 were liable to be called up unless they were widowed with children or were ordained ministers, and in May this was extended to married men. Such was the need for men that the upper age limit was eventually raised to 51.

Once conscription was brought in, men of all types appealed for exemptions. Details of the tribunal hearings were reported in the press. A. Ewing of Railton Road, Brixton, a maker of artificial limbs and crutches, was granted an exemption, but only for a month, a surprising decision given the numbers of maimed and limbless returning home from the front. T. H. Taylor, a professional billiards player living in Fentiman Road, Vauxhall claimed that war work would cause him to lose the delicacy of touch required for his civilian job. His appeal was declined. F. H. Sandy, the manager of slapstick comedy pioneer Fred Karno, was forced to go to war. His occupation was not deemed essential to the Home Front. A chief rat catcher appeared before the tribunal claiming that he could not afford to let his employee go as the place could not be filled by a woman. He was turned down and the next day 500 women applied for the position.

Many other cases concerned men whose many brothers were all serving, fathers caring for bedridden wives and sole breadwinners for widows and siblings, who would otherwise be forced to enter the workhouse.

In the first months of the war, neither *The South London Press* nor *The Brixton Free Press* printed details of casualties. As the war progressed, however, news of noteworthy deaths, always framed in terms of bravery and noble sacrifice, started to appear. There was clearly a class bias – more space was given to local former public schoolboys – but there were also many stories about ordinary men. Whole pages were devoted to the sacrifice of particular schools, parishes or occupations. By the middle of the war, *The South London Press* was printing weekly columns of the names of wounded, missing and dead, often running into the hundreds. *The Brixton Free Press* eventually gave up any attempts at biographies and simply printed lists. Given the fervour for "duty" and the astonishing death rates, it was inevitable that some families would suffer multiple losses. At least two Stockwell families, the Herriotts and the Desaleux, lost three sons each; at least 16 others lost two sons and 15 families an only child.

Some days in Stockwell were, as elsewhere in the country, worse than others. Eleven men on the Stockwell Memorial died on 1 July 1916, the first day of the Battle of the Somme and infamous for being the bloodiest day in the history of the British Army. It produced more than 57,500 casualties, of whom over 19,000 died, most of them cut down in the first hour of the attack. Eight Stockwell men died on 25 September 1915, the first day of the Battle of Loos; six on 7 June 1917, the day of the attack on Messines Ridge; nine on 21 March 1918, the first day of Operation Michael, the German offensive that marked the beginning of the end of the war. The bloodiest month for Stockwell was March 1918 – at least 30 men on the Memorial died.

Of those I have been able to trace, James Clack of Lingham Street was the first to die, on 2 October 1914. His war lasted only 58 days before he succumbed to peritonitis in France. The last was 42-year-old Harry Mead, a house painter from Hartington Road, South Lambeth, who died on 4 November 1920 in England of pulmonary tuberculosis caused by the war.

The Memorial does not distinguish between those who died in the violence of war and those who suffered illness or other misfortune. It includes Victor Corben, an officer who died of complications arising from peritonitis while on leave in London, and whose funeral the Army refused to fund as his illness was not caused directly by war (his grief-stricken father disagreed), and Auguste Cadot, who is not included in the Commonwealth

THESE WERE OUR SONS WHO DIED FOR OUR LANDS

W.A.C.BENSON
W.S.BENSON
P.BIGG
C.F.BILLINGSLEY
S.W.BILLINGSLEY
W.BIRD
A.BLACKER
A.J.BLACKMORE
H.G.BLICK
J.BLINDEN
F.BOWRING
W.BRANSON
M.H.BRIGGS
A.BROOKER
J.F.BROOKS
C.A.BROOM
A.L.BROWN
J.E.BROWN
W.V.BROWN
H.BULL
F.H.BUNCE
S.A.BUNKER
J.BUNN
W.BUNYAN
C.H.BURCHELL
H.C.BURLS
J.BURNS
H.R.BURVILL
A.L.C.CADOJ
F.H.S.CAIGER
S.CAIGER
N.CAIRNS

W.G.CALLEN
A.S.CAMPBELL
A.S.CANDY
C.H.CANHAM
B.H.CAPEWELL
F.H.CAPEWELL
H.CAREY
H.W.CARTER
W.A.E.CARTER
T.C.CAVALIER
F.J.L.HADDOCK
H.W.CHAMBERS
A.E.H CHANCE
A.E.CHANDLER
R.CHARMAN
C.H.CHARNOCK
J.S.CLACK
A.C.CLARKE
J.R.CLARKE
S.W.CLARKE
F.V.CLEMENT
H.CLOUGH
W.R.COLLETT
E.W.COLLINS
C.E.COLLINS
S.H.COMPSON
A.C.COOK
A.T.W.COOK
W.A.COOK
W.W.COOK
A.S.H.COOPER
F.A.J.COOPER

W.G.COOPER
V.L.CORBEN
F.W.COUSINS
E.C.COX
J.COX
W.A.COX
W.CRABB
C.D.CRANHAM
A.CROCKER
H.H.CROCKER
H.A.CROWTHER
A.S.CRUMPLER
J.W.CUMMINS
E.A.CUNNINGHAM
A.CURTIS
C.W.CURTIS
H.CUTMORE
J.C.F.CROSS
C.ON.DAUNT
C.V.DAUNT
C.W.J.DEE
J.J.DERRY
W.DESALEUX
F.J.DESALEUX
J.B.A.DESALEUX
R.P.DICHASON
F.J.DICKER
H.J.DICKTON
S.DIMOND
C.DARTNELL
J.A.DIXON
E.J.DOE

H.R.DOOLEY
A.C.DODSON
R.DOYLE
C.D.T.DREWERY
E.DRISCOLL
H.P.DUDLEY
B.A.M.DUNNING
F.EALES-JOHNSON
H.W.EDNEY
R.C.EDWARDS
C.E.ELRIDGE
A.A.ELLIS
C.ELPHICK
H.ELPHICK
F.T.ELSON
J.ELY
L.C.H.ERDBEER
A.T.EVANS
F.EVERSFIELD
H.J.J.FARRANT
O.P.FARRELL
E.FEDER
F.W.G.FELTHAM
C.E.FENSOME
V.E.FINCH
C.H.A.FISHER
J.M.FRENCH
F.A.FREWER
F.T.FRISBY
H.FROST
W.A.G.FULLER
H.B.GATTON

The Memorial has 574 names of men from the Stockwell area.

War Graves Commission database but whose death in England two years after the end of the war was attributed to his war service.

Most men were killed in action. Of the 387 men whose cause of death I have been able to discover, 276 died this way. Eighty-two died of wounds, presumably in great agony and often after several days of suffering. Twelve died "at home," that is after repatriation, from wounds or illness or, as in one case, even before leaving England. Nine died overseas of illness, including two who suffered pneumonia, with others succumbing to pulmonary tuberculosis, dysentery and malaria. Eight died in accidents, two of them during bombing practice and two while flying; one man fell from his horse, another was run over by a train and another fell down a cliffside. Several died at sea. One man died in the sinking of the S.S. *Belgian Prince,* a notorious maritime atrocity. One died in the bombardment of Lowestoft.

The dead of the First World War are sometimes called the "flowers of youth" and young men certainly predominate on the Memorial. Seventy-two of the 414 for whom I have ascertained age at death were teenagers, the youngest being 16-year-old Frank Mason who, like many others, lied about his age in order to enlist (some older men, such as William Wadmore's father, lied by understating their age). Recruiting officers earned a shilling for every recruit, so they were not given to turning men down, except when they were obviously ill or physically unsuited. Perhaps not surprisingly, the biggest group (236) were in their twenties. However, there were 90 men in their thirties and 12 in their forties. The oldest, William Woodard, was 55.

The Great War was the first in which a professional British army required the services of huge numbers of civilians from all walks of life. Although a few of the men on the Memorial were serving soldiers in 1914 and a handful had previously been professional soldiers, most were leading ordinary lives untouched by war. What kind of people were the Stockwell men? What kind of families did they come from?

The vast majority (52 per cent) of those for whom I found occupations were skilled workers: printers, electrical engineers, apprentice bookbinders, gas meter testers, goldsmiths and cab drivers. Seventeen were in the printing trade, a major employer in the area; five were grocer's assistants; six worked on the railway (some are also named on the memorial at Waterloo Station); three were butchers. There was also a tripe dresser, a baker, numerous shop assistants and messengers, and a player piano maker.

This was, in general, the respectable class, hard-working, steady and settled. They had been educated at least to primary level (free education had been introduced in 1891). Some skilled workers followed their fathers into similar occupations: Walter Ridout was a bootmaker like his father; George Rixton was a brewer's cooper while his father was a brewer's cellarman. Others had branched out or "bettered" themselves: George Fensome was a ticket collector, while his father was a sewer flusher; Henry Dighton was a grocer's assistant but his father was a porter.

The smallest group (three per cent) consisted of those we would see as solidly middle-class: the sons of doctors, lawyers, merchants and academics. There were four sons of doctors. Guy Pearson, a Captain in the embryonic Royal Air Force, who died in an air accident in 1918, grew up in Leighton Buzzard, Bedfordshire. His father was Dr. Spencer Pearson, who lived for a time on Clapham Road, and later became Mayor of Lambeth. Frederick Caiger was the only child of Dr. Frederick Foord Caiger, the long-serving superintendent of South Western Hospital (now Lambeth Hospital) on Landor Road. Conrad and Giles Daunt were sons of Dr. Francis Eldon Horsford Daunt, of 176 Clapham Road. Everard Ridge was the son

August 1914: "Alien enemies" lining up outside the old Brixton Police Station waiting to be registered in accordance with Home Office regulations.

of a solicitor. Reginald Dickason's father was a Professor of Music (and, incidentally, his uncle was an elephant hunter) and Arthur Chance, a Navy officer, was the son of a journalist. Cecil and Percy Philcox's father was a timber merchant. Although the numbers of men from this class were small in comparison to other social groups, they had a higher attrition rate. Taught to lead from the front and imbued at school with a strong sense of duty and the need to set an example, officers were cut down in their thousands.

After the war, the absence of men left women of marriageable age vastly outnumbering men. The lack of career and educational opportunities in all but a few cases, combined with simple loneliness and the impossibility of having children (to do so outside wedlock meant social ostracism), affected the mental wellbeing of thousands. They came to be referred to perjoratively as Surplus Women.

Twenty-five per cent of the men on the Memorial belonged to what I call the clerical classes: booksellers, schoolmasters, chemist's assistants, and sales managers. There were 47 clerks of various kinds, including three bank clerks, four commercial clerks, four civil service clerks, three lawyer's clerks and clerks who worked for the gas company, auctioneers and stonemasons. Had they lived, some of the men in this group may have expected eventually to become officers after serving in the ranks. This was the route taken by railwayman Ernest Alexander Potts, the son of a police pensioner, and possibly also by Frederick Gillard, whose father was a lithographic printer. Of course, these opportunities may have opened up to men of this class simply because so many men of the traditional officer class had already been slaughtered.

Finally, 10 per cent were unskilled. Seven men were general labourers;

two were brewer's labourers; there were also cement workers, packers, potmen and porters.

The regiments the men joined were based all over Great Britain and Ireland and included Australian and Canadian forces. Naturally, London regiments figured highly. Of the 458 men whose military details I was able to trace, 113 joined the London Regiment. The breakdown of the biggest groups is as follows: Royal Field Artillery, 35; King's Royal Rifle Corps, 23; Rifle Brigade and Royal Fusiliers, 21 each; The Queen's (Royal West Surrey) 16; Royal Engineers, 12; East Surrey, 11. Six joined the Royal Air Force (with three in the Royal Flying Corps). Fourteen joined the Royal Navy, with three in the Royal Marines and two each in the Mercantile Marines and Royal Naval Volunteer Reserve.

The highest ranking serviceman I have been able to identify was a Major, Henry Nadaud. Of the officers there were 13 Second Lieutenants, five Lieutenants, and one Captain. Among the "other ranks" were 207 Privates, 79 Riflemen, 33 Gunners and 33 Lance Corporals, 22 Serjeants, 19 Corporals, 12 Drivers.

Service records sometimes reveal the men's vital statistics, although there is not enough data to describe them in a general way. I found information on height for only 77 men. Thirty-five of them were 5 feet 6 inches and under (the shortest, Henry Penn, a brewer's labourer, was 5 foot). There were two officers, Arthur Chance (5 feet 5¼) and Everard Ridge (5 feet 6) in this group. At 6 feet 3 railwayman Ernest Alexander Potts was the tallest.

Men were sometimes weighed when they joined up. I have discovered such information for only 44 of the men. They show a huge variation, with James Stephen Clack and Thomas Albert Pilgrim the heaviest at 11½ stone. The lightest were Samuel James (5 feet 4) and George Starkey (5 feet 6½) – both a mere 7½ stone. Many recruits in the First World War were ill, thin and malnourished. Nationally, almost two in five volunteers were rejected as unsuitable for military service on the grounds of health.

When I collated 1911 census information on the origins of the families, I found that 40 per cent of parents of the men were born in London. Of these 309 families, only 52 included a parent from Lambeth; and only 10 men had parents who were both born in the borough. Seventeen per cent of parents had moved to London from elsewhere in south-east England; 11 per cent came from the West; eight per cent from the East. The rest came from Ireland (three per cent), with a sprinkling from Wales and Scotland. There was a handful of foreign-born parents: four from France, two each from Austria and Germany and one each from Russia and Holland.

Families tended to be large in the days before the widespread use of contraception and confidence in the survival of babies. Having more than 10 children was not considered unusual, and it was also not uncommon for at least some of them to die at or near birth. Harry Nixon had 17 siblings, of whom 11 survived in 1911. The Rance brothers had 16 siblings, but only seven survived. Of the families for whom I found census information, 68 per cent had more than five children born alive, and 32 per cent had four or fewer. Thirty families had lost four or more children who had been born alive. George Fensome's mother Caroline, the wife of a sewer flusher, lost five of her eight children. John Renton's mother Kathrine lost half of her 12. Stillborn babies were not counted in the census, so the extent of this loss is unknown.

Thirty-two of the men on the Memorial for whom I traced census or Service information were married with children. Augustus Cook, Albert Curtis, John Lee and George Barter each left at least five children. Henry Thomas Moss, who died aged 46 in 1917, had 12 children, one of whom, Henry Louis Moss, died in the war in 1915. Uniquely, the names of father and son are inscribed side by side on the Memorial.

The Stockwell Memorial is unusual in the area for being entirely secular and democratic: no ranks are shown and church affiliation was not required. As you might expect, the men were in the main Anglican. A number were remembered at their churches: 35 are on the tiled memorial inside St. Andrew's Church, Landor Road; two are on the stone cross outside St. Mark's, Kennington, for example. There was also a sprinkling of Catholics, Baptists and Methodists, and four men with a Jewish background.

In the early 20th century Stockwell, Brixton and Streatham were "more Jewish" than now. A synagogue, now closed, had opened in 1913 in Acre Lane, Brixton and there was another in Streatham. Jewish tailors and landlords proliferated on the Clapham Road, including Solomon Levy whose student son is on the Memorial.

This community suffered in two ways: from underlying anti-Semitism and from the suspicion that Jews whose family names had been Germanicised by the authorities in Austro-Hungary were enemy Germans. In October 1914 Landy and Berlin, tailors based on Brixton Road, advertised in *The Brixton Free Press*: "Both members of the firm are *naturalized British subjects* under certificates granted by Sir Matthew White Ridley, Bt., in the year 1900," they explained. They even gave birthplaces. "Mr. Landy is

Russian. Mr Berlin [was] born in Kalisch, Poland." Samuel Levy, a Clapham tailor's cutter who survived the war and went on to found a City tailoring company, Ley & Sons, removed the "v" from his name to escape similar suspicions of the alien nature of his origins.

The Brixton Free Press estimated in 1915 that there were 1,500 aliens in the area. When war broke out, all of them were immediately under suspicion. The local newspapers gleefully reported their transgressions. In 1914 Bruno Seybt, a German pastry cook living in St. Michael's Road, Stockwell, was charged with robbing his employers of £3. Rudolf Trager, a German hairdresser and newsagent of Wandsworth Road, and Erich von Springborn, a 54-year-old chemist of St. Michael's Road, Stockwell failed to register with the police as required and were fined. Baker Martin Braun, aged 27, was overwhelmed by it all and committed suicide in Peckham. In October Zoller's bakery shop in Atlantic Road, Brixton became the focus for a hostile crowd of 500. The rioters broke in and destroyed the stock.

Anti-German feeling intensified after 7 May 1915 when the Germans torpedoed a Cunard ocean liner, the *Lusitania*, off the coast of Ireland, killing 1,198 of the 1,959 people aboard. At a German-owned shop in Cold-harbour Lane, all the stock "found a destination in the roadway." A woman inside was alleged to have thumbed her nose at the gathering mob. In August 1915, at 66a Brixton Road, Amelia Schmidt, the English widow of a German baker, had her windows broken and shortly afterwards decided to change the name of her business to Willson's.

Despite anti-German feeling, the Memorial includes several men with German names (Hoft, Erdbeer, Oehring, Geleit, Lippold) who were evidently confident enough to retain them, although the family of Edward Weingartner, were not. They became the Winters.

The war ended, after four terrible years, on the eleventh hour of the eleventh day of the eleventh month of 1918. In London there were joyous, wild and drunken celebrations.

Years later, Ethel, the youngest sister of Christopher Dartnell, who died at Sanctuary Wood in 1917 and whose name is on the Memorial, recalled the day: "We were told to go home at lunchtime. I remember going to see the masses of people gathering in the Strand, London and felt lost in the crowd. People dancing and cheering and drinking. I had to walk home as there were no buses running. When I reached my house my mother was crying because her son Chris had been killed and would not be returning."

After the initial euphoria, the mood darkened. Stockwell, along with

3 May 1922: thousands gathered for official unveiling of the Memorial.

the rest of the country, had suffered immense hardship – uncertainty, fear, deprivation and hunger – and the loss of hundreds of local men. Life was irrevocably altered.

By 11 November 1919 a temporary wooden version of the Cenotaph, whose final design had an influence on the Stockwell Memorial, had been erected in Whitehall. On that day at eleven o'clock, across the city – and across the Empire – all activity ceased. People stood in the streets, their heads bowed. All cars, trains and trams stopped. In London not a single phone call was made. The world remembered the calamity of the war and the lives of the men who had endured it or been sacrificed in it.

In Stockwell, anticipation of Remembrance had started before the war had even ended. In late October 1918 Mr. J. A. Wheeler, who became a stalwart of the Memorial Committee, proposed a permanent tribute to the men of the Stockwell neighbourhood and appealed through the letters page of *The South London Press* for people to come forward to help the effort.

The site – the area known as the Triangle, at the junction of Clapham and South Lambeth Roads, the last vestige of what had once been Stockwell Common – was secured and eventually conveyed to Lambeth Borough Council. It was decided that the design of the monument, a clock tower built of Portland stone, would be chosen through competition by a committee of the Royal Academy.

Raising the money required was a problem and was not completed until after the Memorial was unveiled. It did not help that the price of building materials had rocketed as Europe set about repairing the damage caused by four years of destruction. The Memorial Committee organised numerous fund-raising events: on the first anniversary of Armistice Day, the Stockwell Palladium Cinema at 211 Clapham Road (the building now houses a café) hosted an evening of Mary Pickford and Charlie Chaplin films and Dr. Pearson appealed for donations. There were also fancy dress dances, concerts and fêtes at which local celebrities were encouraged to give their services, as well as their cash. There was even a minstrel show, which was then a popular and acceptable form of entertainment. The troupe, the well-known Police Minstrels, performed in evening dress and blackface.

By March 1920 the design for the Memorial had been selected. There had been 80 submissions, including a number from amateurs, but most of them failed to impress the Royal Academy War Memorials Committee. For them there was only one clear winner. The architect, 31-year-old Frank Twydals Dear, of John Street, Bedford Row, had satisfied the brief to design a simple monument that complemented its surroundings, within a £2,000 budget. The Royal Academy praised his plans for "a tower of excellent proportion and refined detail, depending for its effect on good massing and simple lines."

Benjamin Clemens, a Chelsea-based sculptor, designed the figure of Remembrance adorned with a laurel wreath and a broken sword of war at her feet. Beneath her are the words, "To the Stockwell Men who Served in the Great War, 1914–1919." The stone carving was executed by Greenwich-born Frederick Francis. Dr. Caiger, whose only child Frederick had been

Stockwell War Memorial in 1922, shortly after the unveiling.

Families and friends inspect the names and the wreaths at the Memorial.

killed at the Somme in 1916, donated the four-faced clock. He stepped in after an initial offer from jeweller and clockmaker Sidney Sanders, who wanted his branding on the clock face, was rejected.

By early 1922 the Memorial was ready to be unveiled and dedicated and the date for the ceremony was set for Wednesday 3 May. Hours before it was due to begin, under lowering skies, crowds began to gather in the Stockwell Triangle. People watched from the windows of the surrounding houses; they pressed against the railings. Thousand packed the space from the Underground station to Stockwell Terrace.

As the ceremony started, there was a solemn hush, broken only by the occasional clanking of a passing tram. "Among the onlookers were many ex-Service men and women wearing medals and decorations, and a large number of women in mourning, carrying wreaths or little bunches of flowers, according to circumstances, to place at the foot of the memorial in honour of their fallen," reported *The South London Press*. The crowd sang "O God, our Help in Ages Past" and prayers were read. A host of dignitaries and prominent local figures was in attendance, as well as police and military bands and the choir of Stockwell Orphanage.

Stepping down from the platform, Princess Alice, Countess of Athlone, dressed in deep black, released the Union Jack covering the face of the Memorial, declaring: "To the glorious and lasting memory of the men of Stockwell, who laid down their lives for their King and Country." The notes of the Last Post and the Reveille, sounded by buglers of the East Surrey Regiment, rang out, and simultaneously, at 3.25pm, the clock in the tower was set going. The hymn "For all the Saints" followed. Finally, in a voice heard across the gardens, the tower was dedicated by the Bishop of Kingston. After the site and the Memorial were presented to the Mayor of Lambeth, formal wreaths were laid. People walked round the Memorial, some scanning the names on the panels, others placing their own floral tributes.

Then the storm that had threatened all afternoon burst and dispersed the crowd.

A. E. ADAMS
Not identified.

W. ALEXANDER
Not identified.

F. J. ALLEN
Frederick John Allen, killed in action on 27 September 1915, aged 22.

Second Lieutenant, Devonshire Regiment, "C" Company, 9th Bn.
Remembered at Lapugnoy Cemetery, Pas de Calais, France.

In October 1910 Stockwell bank clerk Frederick John Allen joined the London County & Westminster Bank at its Victoria Street branch and was working there when he enlisted in the Army. After his death, the staff magazine published a short obituary. Allen "was educated at the Westminster City School, and received his earliest military training in their cadet corps. He joined the Artists [Rifles] and was a first rate shot, being in the eight that won the Daily Telegraph Cup for H Company, and later in the sixteen which ran second in the Inter-Battalion Cup. He was the first volunteer to mount guard at the outer gate of the Tower of London. After receiving his commission in the 9th

Devons he became Signalling Officer and was selected for a special job by the Brigadier."

Frederick Allen was born in Brixton, the only child of Frederick Herbert Allen, an assistant elementary schoolmaster for London County Council, and his wife Alice Minta Varney Allen. The 1911 census shows the family living in six rooms at 47 Mayflower Road, Stockwell (they are there in 1901 too). Allen was then 17.

G. H. ALLEN

George Harry Allen, killed in action on 25 March 1918, aged 20.

Private, Middlesex Regiment, 2nd Bn., Service no. G/52892. Enlisted in Camberwell. Remembered at Pozières Memorial, Somme, France.

The 1911 census shows that George Harry Allen, aged 12, lived at 18 Riverhall Street, South Lambeth, where his family occupied two rooms. His father, also called George Henry Allen, a 37-year-old engineer originally from Marchington, Staffordshire, worked "in cold stores". His mother Marceline, 35, was from Kirtling, Cambridgeshire. George Henry was the eldest of five sons. Riverhall Street, now disappeared, was adjacent to Wandsworth Road and ran parallel with Thorncroft Street.

P. D. ANDERSON

Peter D. Anderson, died on 13 February 1919, aged 28.

Private, 9th (Queen's Royal) Lancers, Service no. L/7853. Remembered at Lambeth Cemetery, Blackshaw Road, Tooting, south-west London.

Peter Anderson was born in Glasgow. The 1911 census shows his family lived at 2 Crimsworth Road, off Wandsworth Road. His father, Berwickshire-born Thomas Anderson, 50, was a motor car engineer. His mother, Christina Anderson, 39, was from Ross-shire, Scotland. Anderson himself is not on the census return for this address.

C. C. ANDREWS

Claude Cecil Andrews, killed in action 21 October 1917, aged about 23.

Private, The Queen's (Royal West Surrey Regiment), 7th Bn., Service no. G/11433. Remembered at Tyne Cot Memorial, Heuvelland, West-Vlaanderen, Belgium.

A tentative identification. On the night of the 1911 census a Cecil Andrews, 17, a clerk for a builder's merchant, and his sister, Maud Price, a 23-year-old widow working as a schoolkeeper, along with her two-year-old son George Price, were visiting their parents at 30 Haselrigge Road, Clapham. Charles Thomas Andrews, a 63-year-old schoolkeeper from Shaftesbury, Dorset, and his wife Emma Andrews, 59, from Rendlesham, Suffolk lived there in six rooms with another daughter. The couple had 13 children.

J. A. ANDREWS

James Albert Andrews, killed in action on 12 November 1914, aged 22.

Private, 1st (Royal) Dragoons, Service no. 6703; formerly, 2nd Dragoons (Scots Greys). Remembered at Ypres (Menin Gate) Memorial, Belgium.

James Albert Andrews came from a railway family. In 1911 he was 19 and working as a porter for the London & South Western Railway. He lived at 60 Wilcox Road, South Lambeth with his parents, James Andrews, 48, born in Chelsfield, Kent and working as a foreman porter at L&SWR, and Rose Rebecca Andrews, 44, born at Walton-on-Thames, and three siblings, including a brother, Frederick William, 17, a messenger for L&SWR.

F. A. ANSELL

Frederick Alfred Ansell, killed in action on 21 August 1916, aged 24.

Rifleman, Rifle Brigade (The Prince Consort's Own), 1st Bn., Service no. S/16820. Remembered at Ypres (Menin Gate) Memorial, Belgium and at St. Andrew's Church, Landor Road, Stockwell.

Frederick Alfred Ansell appears on the 1911 census as a 19-year-old apprentice compositor (typesetter) living with his family at 39 Willington Road, Stockwell. His father, Frederick William Ansell, 51, also a compositor, was born in Westminster, as was his mother, Clara Ansell, 48.

A. ASHBY

Not identified.

R. ATKINS

Robert Atkins, died of wounds on 16 September 1917, aged 30.

Rifleman, Rifle Brigade, 8th Bn., Service no. S/23067. Remembered at Trois Arbres Cemetery, Steenwerck, Nord, France.

Printer Robert Atkins lived with his wife Emily Louisa (née Umpelby) and two sons Robert Thomas and Thomas John (born 1913 and 1915) at 14 Horace Road, Stockwell. (Now disappeared, Horace Road, also sometimes called Horace Street, was adjacent to Wilcox Road.)

In December 1915 Atkins joined the Reserve at Lambeth, and in June the following year he was mobilised. He was described as 5 feet 8¼ inches tall, 41 inches around the chest and weighing 10 stone.

Atkins' Army Service file records just one misdemeanour: in November 1916 he was absent without leave from Tattoo for 23 hours, for which he forfeited three days' pay. By the time he died, on 16 September 1917 of gunshot wounds to the neck, legs and left arm at the 2nd Australian Casualty station, he had served one year and 280 days. In January 1918 his widow Emily received his effects: two playing cards, a pipe, a knife, a cigarette box, a pair of scissors, two Rifle Brigade numerals. In May 1919, aged 29, she married 30-year-old Henry Edward Powell.

W. G. AVENILL

William George Avenill, died of wounds on 6 June 1917, aged 40.

Gunner, Royal Garrison Artillery, 1/1st (Wessex) Heavy Bty., Service no. 87965. Remembered at Lijssenthoek Military Cemetery, Poperinge, Belgium.

William Avenill's Army Service record brings to mind a fit, well-made man. Thirty-seven when he attested on 27 May 1916, he stood 5 feet 8¾ inches tall, with a 40-inch chest. His tattoos were noted: an eagle on his left forearm and a tea rose on his right.

In civilian life, Avenill was a head porter at Cadogan Court Gardens, Sloane Square. The records state that he left behind a wife, Edith Elizabeth Avenill (née Robinson), formerly of 141 Sidney Street, King's Road, Chelsea. Edith, 30 when she married Avenill in 1912 at St. Anne's Church, South Lambeth Road, was a manageress (the Parish records give no other detail). Avenill was then living at 52 St. Agnes Place, Kennington. Just a year previously, as shown on the 1911 census, Lambeth-born Avenill was unemployed and living at 53 Hartington Road, South Lambeth with his parents Henry, 65, a street sweeper born in Lambeth, and Jane Charlotte, 58, from Islington, and sister Annie, 40, a laundry hand.

Avenill had served 12 years to 1908 with the Royal Marine Artillery, so he must have known the score when it came to the military. Despite this and while still in England, he transgressed several times. An unknown crime noted on 17 January 1917 led to a forfeit of pay, and his absence for over a week in February was punished with seven days in detention and 10 days' loss of pay. In the same month, he lost a further 10 days' pay and was given five days' detention. We do not know what caused Avenill to be so erratic but perhaps there is a clue in his Service records: the name of his next of kin, his wife, has been scored through and replaced with that of his mother.

On 2 May Avenill was transferred to the Wessex Heavy Battery. His record shows that he was "dangerously wounded" on 5 June and he died the following day at the 10th Ambulance. He was 40. As was usual, the Army set about contacting his widow. A note in the record says: "From Police. 11/6/17 No trace of Mrs. Edith Avenill."

There follows another note: "Miss V. Broughton, 3-0 Block, Sutton Buildings, Chelsea SW states she was living with Private Avenill since Oct 1916 and that he was married and wife died on 5 Dec. She was supported by him and was known as Mrs. Avenill. Asks for his case to be enquired into." It seems that Avenill was having a relationship with Miss Broughton while his wife was still alive.

There are two women in the 1911 census who could be V. Broughton, the most likely being Violet Broughton, a 20-year-old servant from Plumstead who was then working and living at an old people's home at 34 Nottingham Place, Marylebone in central London. Unfortunately, the record does not include the outcome of the Army's enquiry.

Avenill's mother, by now widowed and living at 57 Thorne Road, South Lambeth, received her son's effects: letters, photos, card, disc, pipe, pouch, whistle and, pertinently enough, a marriage certificate. In 1921 she was sent William's war medals and carefully wrote on the receipt she sent back to the War Office: "War medals with very grateful thanks."

F. AVIS

Frederick Avis, died on 9 June 1918, aged 22.

Corporal, Royal Welsh Fusiliers, 4th Bn., Service no. 46278; formerly Wiltshire Regiment. Remembered at Franvillers Communal Cemetery Extension, Somme, France.

Frederick Avis, a 19-year-old single man working for a brewery, joined up on 8 September 1914, barely a month after war was declared on 4 August.

Initially Avis joined the Wiltshire Regiment but he was transferred to the Royal Welsh Fusiliers in May 1916. He rose from Private to unpaid Lance Corporal to paid Corporal. Avis's only transgression was a failure to comply with an order in November 1915, for which he forfeited four days' pay.

Avis stood 5 feet 4½ inches tall, weighed less than 8½ stone, and had a 38-inch chest. He had brown hair and blue eyes. On enlistment he was described as fit, but after three years of gruelling combat he was returned to England and spent at least 60 days in hospital. In September 1917 he was receiving treatment for kidney stones and muscular rheumatism at the Birmingham War Hospital. He spent 38 days there, and a further 22 days in the Convalescent Hospital at Plymouth. And then, on 31 March 1918, he returned to the front.

He died at the Somme in June, after serving three years and 275 days. His widowed mother, Ada Avis, received his effects: letters, photos, a wallet, two religious books and a watch and watchstrap.

B

W. G. BACON

William George Bacon, died on 21 March 1918, aged 33.
Private, South Staffordshire Regiment, 2/6th Bn., Service no. 242252.
Remembered at Arras Memorial, Pas de Calais, France.

William George Bacon was born in Stockwell, lived in Stockwell. He enlisted in Battersea.

L. F. BAILEY

Leslie Frank Bailey, died on 11 March 1915, aged 19.
Midshipman, Royal Naval Reserve, H.M.S. *Bayano*. Previously served on H.T. *Huanchaco,* on which he continued to serve when it was taken over as an Admiralty Transport in the first months of the war. Remembered at Chatham Naval Memorial, Kent.

The *Bayano* was a merchant ship commissioned by the Admiralty in December 1914 as an Armed Merchant Cruiser. On 11 March 1915 the ship was on her way to Liverpool from Clyde to refuel. She sank in under three minutes after she was torpedoed by a German U-boat (U-27) off Carswell Point, Stranraer. Most of the men were asleep below. Four officers and 22 men were saved, but 14 officers and 181 men were lost, including Leslie Frank Bailey.

In 1911 Lambeth-born Bailey, a 15-year-old schoolboy, lived in five rooms at 363 Coldharbour Lane, Brixton with his mother, Maria Bailey, 59, from Croydon, and a sister. He was one of five children.

A. E. BALL

Arthur Edward Ball, killed in action on 23 July 1916, aged 23.

Serjeant, Duke of Cornwall's Light Infantry, 1st Bn., Service no. 10231.
Remembered at Thiepval Memorial, Somme, France.

In 1911 Arthur Edward Ball, then 17, was working as a compositor's (type-setter's) apprentice. He lived at 58 Tasman Road, Stockwell with his father, Charles Ball, 47, a stonemason born in Isleworth, Middlesex and his father's second wife, Sarah, 42, from Chelsworth, Suffolk, and three other family members.

J. BARBER

John Barber, killed in action on 24 March 1918, aged 24.

Driver, Royal Engineers, 47th Signal Coy., Service no. 551983.
Remembered at Beaulencourt British Cemetery, Ligny-Thilloy,
Pas de Calais, France.

Seventeen-year-old John (or Jack) Barber was described in the 1911 census by his father, a 52-year-old butcher also called John Barber, as "at home in business." This opaque description was also applied to his sisters Jessie, 20, and Ethel, 19. The family lived at 92 Landor Road, Stockwell. Barber's mother, Lydia, 46, was from Dymchurch, Kent.

F. BARLOW

Frank Barlow, died in an accident on 17 February 1917, aged 21.

Private, London Regiment, 2/14th Bn. (London Scottish), Service no. 6507. Remembered at Salonika (Lembet Road) Military Cemetery, Greece.

On 17 February 1917 Frank Barlow fell down a precipice, fracturing his skull. He was buried about 10 metres from the road at Katerini, near Thessaloniki, Greece, and his body was moved at a later date.

According to a witness at the Council of Enquiry in the Field, hastily convened by Lieutenant Colonel R. J. L. Ogilby on the day Barlow died, he was killed instantaneously. The handwritten notes from the inquest survive in his Army Service file.

The platoon had been told to make their way down a sharp slope east of their camp and up a hill on the other side. "I came to the edge of a cliff with a drop of about 90 feet to a stream below," related R. C. Hone, who gave evidence. "I told the men to get round [down] the best way they could."

They split into two groups and when Hone got to the stream at the bottom he tried to cross it, but fell in and lost his stick. "I called to the others to catch the stick as it went by," he continued. Then he noticed the body of Private Barlow. "The last time I saw Pte. Barlow was about a quarter of the way down... when I noticed he was carrying a signalling flag," he said.

Meanwhile, Serjeant Souter "saw something in the water, which I first thought was an animal. On looking down I found it was a London Scottish man." They hauled the body out. No one had seen him fall.

"Pte. Barlow was in front of me," said another witness, Private Keech, describing the descent down the slope. "I had to drop out for a few minutes and did not see him any more. I had noticed that he was using his signalling flag as a walking stick." Barlow was examined by Captain J. D. Stubbs of the Royal Army Medical Corps and pronounced dead.

The conclusion was clear: "The court, having considered the evidence [is of the] opinion that the death of 6507 [Private] Frank Barlow was caused by an accident in performance of his duties and that no blame can be attached to any person concerned."

We do not know whether Barlow's family saw the witness statements or received any further explanation of their son's death. Three months after the event, his effects were sent to his mother. On 23 May 1917 she duly completed the paperwork sent to her but added a sad note: "I have not received my son's pay book or will. I have had a copy of the latter sent from the War Office, but I should like his own handwriting."

Barlow had served in France for two months before he was sent to Greece in November 1916. He had enlisted in the London Scottish on 24 January 1916 at Buckingham Gate, London, where he was noted as having "good" physical development. He was 5 feet 8 inches tall, with a chest measurement of 39 inches.

The papers do not include details of Barlow's civilian occupation, but the 1911 census shows that he was then a 14-year-old part-time school student and office boy living with his family at 20 St. Stephen's Terrace, South Lambeth, where they occupied five rooms. His father, Moses Barlow, 52, was a mechanical engineer working in boiler making, originally from Reading, Berkshire. His mother, Frances Barlow, 43, was born in Chelsea. There was a brother, George, who also served in the Army.

A. H. BARNES

Herbert Robert Albert Barnes, died of stomach wounds on
18 September 1918, aged 20.

Private, London Regiment, 2/24th Bn. (The Queen's), Service no. 721131.
Remembered at Epéhy Wood Farm Cemetery, Epéhy, Somme, France.

There is some confusion over Barnes's name. Mike Barnes, who runs the
Barnes Family History website, searched for this casualty, his first cousin
twice removed, after his father showed him a letter written by his aunt
Violet in 1996 in which she mentioned two brothers, one of whom, named
only as "Bob," died in the First World War of stomach wounds. Mike eventually identified Bob as Herbert Robert Albert Barnes of the 24th Battalion,
London Regiment. On the Stockwell Memorial, however, he is listed under
the name A. H. Barnes.

Barnes enlisted at Kennington, probably soon after his 18th birthday.
The 1911 census shows that, then aged 14, Barnes was living at 31 Cobbett
Street, South Lambeth with his father, Thomas George Barnes, 46, a
cellarman from Reading, Berkshire, mother Annie Barnes, 48, from Belfast,
and an elder brother. There were two other children living elsewhere.

T. G. BARNES

Theodore Grace Barnes, died in an atrocity on 31 July 1917, aged 17.

Apprentice, Mercantile Marine, S.S. *Belgian Prince* (Newcastle).
Remembered at Tower Hill Memorial, East London.

Theodore Barnes, a merchant sailor, died in a wartime maritime crime
that shocked the world. On 31 July 1917 he was on board the *Belgian
Prince*, a cargo ship built in 1901, when it was torpedoed by a German
submarine. The 43 crew abandoned ship in two boats, but the Germans
smashed these with axes. They forced the men to stand on the deck of the
U-boat and removed their lifebelts. Then the U-boat was submerged without
warning. All but three were drowned. The Captain survived because the
Germans had taken him below. An Admiralty enquiry concluded: "It was a
cold-blooded murder equalling, if not transcending, the worst crimes that
our enemies have committed against humanity."

Barnes's father, Ernest Henry, was a compositor (typesetter) from
Guernsey, in the Channel Islands; his mother, Alice, 46, was from Camberwell. The family lived in three rooms at 44 Kay Road, Stockwell. There were
four other children..

J. F. BARNSLEY

James Foster Barnsley, killed in action on 1 May 1917, aged 27.

Private, Essex Regiment, 2nd Bn., Service no. 34448. Remembered at Feuchy British Cemetery, Pas de Calais, France. Brother of *William Charles Barnsley.*

In civilian life James Foster Barnsley, one of seven children, was a tailor's packer born in St. Pancras, north London. On the 1911 census he was listed, aged 21, as living with his parents and siblings in five rooms at 10 Henry Street, Vauxhall. His father, William Barnsley, 49, was a cloth shrinker from Marylebone. His mother, Elizabeth, 49, was born in Soho. In October 1915, aged 26, James Barnsley, married Susannah Maria Hurst, 28, at St. Mark's Church, Kennington. He gave his address as 47 Meadow Road.

W. C. BARNSLEY

William Charles Barnsley, killed in action on 22 June 1917, aged about 32.

Driver, Royal Field Artillery, "B" Bty. 103rd Bde., Service no. 55016. Remembered at Woods Cemetery, Ypres, West-Vlaanderen, Belgium. Brother of *James Foster Barnsley.*

In 1911 William Barnsley lived at 11 Glyn Street, Vauxhall (now gone, this street was near the Royal Vauxhall Tavern). Then aged 26, he was married to Emma, 24. They had three children aged five and under.

F. G. BARRETT

Not identified.

H. C. BARTEL

Harvey Charles Bartel, died on 23 October 1918, aged 32.

Private, London Regiment, 1/13th Bn. (Kensington), Service no. 493554. Remembered at Etaples Military Cemetery, Pas de Calais, France.

The 1911 census shows Harvey Charles Bartel as a 24-year-old clerk from Battersea, living in four rooms at 28 Rita Road, South Lambeth, with his father, Charles Joseph Bartel, 57, a carman from Poplar, east London, and mother, Elizabeth Eleanor Bartel, 50, from Faversham, Kent. Harvey was the eldest of three sons.

G. C. BARTER

George Cecil Barter, killed in action on 3 April 1918, aged 38.

Bombardier, Royal Garrison Artillery, 359th Siege Bty., Service no. 130528. Remembered at Voormezeele Enclosures No. 1 and No. 2, Ypres, Belgium. Awarded the *Military Medal.*

When George Cecil Barter died at Ypres in 1918 his widow Mary was left to care for five young children. It was too much for her. "You will notice that my son G. W. B. Barter is not at present living with me as his uncle has undertaken him for me," she wrote to the notoriously strict Army Pension Board in April 1918 from her home at 27 Tunstall Road, Brixton. She had to keep the Pension Board informed because her payments would be affected by the change in her circumstances.

Mary's hands were full coping on her own with four younger children aged from five years to 10 months, she said. Soon afterwards she moved back to her parents' home at 4 Wyvil Road, South Lambeth. Sadly, her burden was reduced a few months later. Ernest, her youngest, died of convulsions and bronchopneumonia. Mary carefully submitted his death certificate to the authorities – the copies are in her husband's Service file.

In civilian life, George Barter was a hotel porter. Before they started their family, the couple lived at 39 Coppermill Row in Walthamstow, east London. Barter was originally from Swindon, Wiltshire, while Mary was a Lambeth girl. They married at St. Anne's Church, South Lambeth Road on 4 December 1910.

Barter, 5 feet 8 inches with a 43-inch chest, according to the Army records, was 36 when he was joined on 19 November 1916. He was in England until June 1917, when he was sent to France.

W. F. BARTLETT

Not identified.

F. C. BASS

Frederick Charles Bass, killed in action on 22 November 1915, aged 30.

Rifleman, King's Royal Rifle Corps, 7th Bn., Service no. R/11906. Remembered at La Brique Military Cemetery No. 2, Ypres, West-Vlaanderen, Belgium. Brother of *Percy Bass.*

P. T. BASS

Percy T. Bass, killed in action on 20 March 1916, aged about 25.

Rifleman, King's Royal Rifle Corps, 10th Bn., Service no. R/4191. Remembered at Essex Farm Cemetery, Belgium. Brother of *Frederick Charles Bass.*

Twenty-two-year-old Percy Thomas Bass stood 5 feet 3 inches tall. He weighed not much more than 8 stone and had dark brown hair, brown eyes and a fresh complexion. In civilian life Bass was a waiter, but he was keen to leave this behind, volunteering for the King's Royal Rifles at Cockspur Street, Westminster on 10 September 1914, only five weeks after war broke out.

On 21 February 1915, while still in England, Bass was docked two days' pay for not turning up for Reveille. He was sent to France in July 1915 and was hospitalised in France for a day in December 1915. He was killed in action on 20 March 1916. Bass's commanding officer listed the effects to be returned to his widowed father, Mr. W. T. Bass, a retired signalman of 6 Nursery Road, Brixton: a packet of letters, postcards and photos, a diary, tobacco pouch, scissors, pipe and lighter and a badge.

Percy's brother Frederick died in November 1915 aged 30. Another brother, Ernest Edward Bass, a porter, survived the war.

A. W. BATHO

Arthur William Batho, died on 25 April 1916, aged 19.

Officer's Steward 3rd Class, Royal Navy, H.M.S. *Conquest*, Service no. L/6439. Remembered at Chatham Naval Memorial, Kent.

Arthur William Batho died on 25 April 1916 during the bombardment of Lowestoft by the German High Seas Fleet. The *Conquest* lost 25 men, with 13 wounded.

The 1911 census shows a 15-year-old Arthur Batho working as a messenger for the General Post Office. He lived at 411 Wandsworth Road with his widowed father, Henry Thomas Batho, a 50-year-old railway porter from Otley, Suffolk, and four siblings.

E. J. BATTERBURY

Ernest James Batterbury, killed in action on 18 August 1916, aged 23.

Lance Corporal, Rifle Brigade, 7th Bn., Service no. S/7006. Remembered at Thistle Dump Cemetery, High Wood, Longueval, Somme, France.

Ernest James Batterbury, aged 18 in 1911, was a hosier's assistant, born in Lambeth. He lived at Buckstone Cottages, Oval Place, with his mother, Sarah Alice Batterbury, 47, who was born in the City, and father, Henry Hooper Batterbury, 47, a theatre attendant originally from Windsor, Berkshire, five siblings and a boarder.

W. BEACHAM

Not identified.

J. E. BEAN

John Edward Bean, died of wounds on 22 August 1916.

Corporal, Royal Field Artillery, "C" Bty. 49th Bde., Service no. 50155. Remembered at Heilly Station Cemetery, Méricourt-l'Abbé, Somme, France.

W. E. BENEY

William Elias Beney, died on 30 November 1917, aged 25.

Private, Machine Gun Corps (Infantry), 36th Coy., Service no. 20342. Remembered at Cambrai Memorial, Louveral, Nord, France.

W. A. G. BENSON

William Albert George Benson, killed in action on 1 September 1918, aged about 19.

Private, London Regiment, "A" Coy., 20th Bn. (Blackheath and Woolwich), Service no. 634829. Remembered at Sailly-Saillisel British Cemetery, Somme, France.

William Albert George Benson, who appears in the 1911 census as an 11-year-old, lived with his family in five rooms at 4 Tandridge Place, Stockwell. His father, William Albert Benson, 36, originally from Bermondsey, was a carman transporting grain and manure. His mother, Rose Louisa, 38, was from Sydenham, south-east London. Benson had four siblings.

W. S. BENSON

William Spencer Benson, died of wounds on 23 April 1917, aged 20.

Private, Royal Army Medical Corps, 17th Field Ambulance, Service no. 35733. Enlisted in Holborn. Remembered at Béthune Town Cemetery, Pas de Calais, France.

The 1911 census shows William Spencer Benson as a 14-year-old paper boy. Born in Brixton, he was the eldest of five children of William Spencer Benson, 43, a general labourer, and Jessie Elizabeth Benson, 35. The family lived at at 62 Ingleton Street, off Brixton Road, and the household included an uncle and a boarder, both working as labourers.

P. BIGG

Percy Bigg, died on 1 January 1915, aged 19.

Private, Royal Marine Light Infantry, H.M.S. *Formidable*, Service no. CH/17624. Remembered at Chatham Naval Memorial, Kent.

Percy Bigg died after H.M.S. *Formidable* was torpedoed at night by a German submarine (U-24) and sank off Portland Bill. Out of a total of 782 on board, 547 crew (35 officers and 512 men) were killed, including the Captain, A. N. Loxley, who remained on the bridge overseeing the evacuation, and his dog Bruce, whose body washed ashore and was buried in a marked grave in Abbotsbury Gardens in Dorset. The *Formidable* was the third British battleship to be sunk in the war, and the second to be sunk by enemy action.

The 1911 census shows Percy Bigg living at 4 Victoria Place, Priory Grove, South Lambeth where his family occupied six rooms. His father, Alfred Bigg, 44, born in Hertfordshire, was a carman for a laundry. His mother, Ellen Bigg, 44, was from Fontmell Magna, Dorset. The couple had six other children.

G. F. BILLINGSLEY

George Frederick Billingsley, died on 29 September 1918, aged 24.

Private, Yorkshire Regiment, 2nd Bn., Service no. 10356. Remembered at Sucrerie Cemetery, Epinoy, Pas de Calais, France. Brother of *Sydney Walter Billingsley* and stepson of *Harry Frank Handel.*

S. W. BILLINGSLEY

Sydney Walter Billingsley, killed in action on 12 September 1916, aged 18.

Rifleman, London Regiment, 1/21st Bn. (First Surrey Rifles), Service no. 4001. Remembered at Thiepval Memorial, Somme, France. Brother of *George Frederick Billingsley* and stepson of *Harry Frank Handel.*

Electrical engineer's assistant Sydney Billingsley, 5 feet 2 inches tall, 8 stone and with a chest measurement of 37 inches, enlisted at Camberwell on 28 May 1915. He claimed to be 19 but he was at least a year younger. His war lasted one year and 107 days.

In 1911, Billingsley was living at 2 Arlington Mansions, Morat Street, Stockwell with his stepfather, Kennington-born Army pensioner Harry Handel, 29, who was working as a cook, and his mother, Ada Harriett Handel (née Mew), 42, from Banstead, Surrey. Ada and Harry had an 11-month son, Robert, a stepbrother to George and Sydney and their siblings. (The Billingsleys' father, Alfred, was listed in the 1901 census as a printer's machine minder, born in Islington, north London. He died in 1903.)

During his Army service, Sydney Billingsley was hospitalised at least four times, each time with "pyrescia" (fever). He was disciplined at least 10 times, his crimes including "breaking out of camp" (twice); having dirty equipment; hesitating to obey an order; and being late for parade.

W. BIRD

William Bird, died on 18 July 1918, aged about 22.

Able Seaman, Royal Navy, H.M.S. *Princess Royal*, Service no. J/24752. Remembered at Lambeth Cemetery, Screen Wall, Blackshaw Road, Tooting, south-west London and at St. Andrew's Church, Landor Road, Stockwell.

In 1911 William Bird was 15 and working as an errand boy. He lived with his family in six rooms at 21 Irving Grove, off Stockwell Road, where the family had been since at least 1901. Bird's father, also called William, was 40 and worked as a butcher's carman. His mother, Mary Ann Bird, 40, was born in Pimlico. They had nine children.

A. BLACKER

Arthur Edward Blacker, died of wounds on 25 June 1918, aged 28.

Rifleman, Royal Irish Rifles, Service no. 44089. Remembered at Wandsworth Cemetery, Magdalen Road, Earlsfield, south-west London.

In 1911, before he married, biscuit factory worker Arthur Edward Blacker lived with his family in three rooms at 7 Lithgow Street, Battersea. His father, also called Arthur, 49, worked as a general builder's labourer and was born in Wandsworth, as was his mother Ellen (Nellie), 46. Arthur Blacker married Charlotte (last name unknown) of 50 Shillington Street.

A. J. BLACKMORE

Albert John Blackmore, killed in action on 30 October 1914, aged 18.

Trooper, 1st Life Guards, Service no. 2966. Remembered at Ypres (Menin Gate) Memorial, Belgium.

A tentative identification. This is the only A. J. Blackmore in the Commonwealth War Graves Commission database and in *Soldiers Died in the Great War 1914–1919*. There was an Albert Blackmore on the 1911 census, living at 1 Kielers Cottages, Clapham Road with his parents, Walter Blackmore and Fanny Blackmore, both 53 and from Devon (Puddington and Sandford). This Albert, then aged 15, was a lift attendant in a mansion block.

H. A. BLICK

Herbert Alfred Blick, died on 21 September 1917, aged 37.

Private, London Regiment, 2/4th Bn. (Royal Fusiliers), Service no. 295157; formerly City Imperial Volunteers (South African Campaign). Remembered at Ypres (Menin Gate) Memorial, Belgium.

In 1911 Herbert Alfred Blick, 31, a ladies and gents tailor born in Stockwell, lived in six rooms at 202 Clapham Road, with his wife, Emily Elizabeth Blick, also 31 and born in Clapham, and eight-month old son, John Herbert Blick.

J. BOWDEN

John Bowden, killed in action on 5 March 1918, aged 19.

Private, Machine Gun Corps (Infantry), 157th Coy., Service no. 118026. Remembered at Cairo War Memorial Cemetery, Egypt.

In 1911 John Bowden, then 12, lived with his widowed mother, Harriet Bowden, 38, a laundress, and two sisters in four rooms at 2 Ely Place, off Dorset Road.

F. BOWRING

Frank Bowring, died of an illness on 26 October 1919, aged 24.

Private, Royal Army Medical Corps, 6th Stationary Hospital (Antwerp), Service no. 115005. Remembered at Schoonselhof Cemetery, Antwerp, Belgium.

The National Roll of the Great War 1914–1919 states that Frank Bowring joined up in 1916 and was sent overseas in that year. He was "engaged on important duties at the 6th Stationary Hospital." He contracted an illness in Antwerp in October 1919 and died there.

The 1911 census shows that Bowring, born in Battersea, was the eldest of three children of Henry John Bowring, 49, a goods porter from Dorchester, Dorset, and Ellen Maria Bowring, 47, from Kent. They lived at 41 Priory Grove, South Lambeth. In 1911 Bowring was 15 and working as an apprentice engineer.

W. BRANSON

Walter Branson, killed in action on 27 August 1918, aged 19.

Private, London Regiment, 1st Bn. (Royal Fusiliers), Service no. 204513; posted to 1/2nd Bn. Remembered at Summit Trench Cemetery, Croisilles, Pas de Calais, France.

Walter Branson was 5 feet 6 inches tall, weighed 9 stone 9 pounds, measured 37½ inches around the chest and had a fair complexion, blue eyes and light brown hair.

He joined the Army twice. First he enlisted in the East Surrey Regiment, but after 180 days' service he was discharged at Witley, Surrey, "having made a mis-statement as to age." He was 17 but had claimed to be 19. Despite his youth, he managed to impress his officers, who judged him to have a good military character. Branson re-enlisted, this time in the London Regiment, some time after he turned 18.

In civilian life Branson was a van guard, and before that an errand boy. In 1911 he lived with his family in four rooms at 71 Dorset Road. His father, John Branson, 51, was a baker from Clapham; his stepmother Emily, 40, was born in Lambeth.

M. H. BRIGGS
Not identified.

A. BROOKER
Arthur Brooker, died of wounds on 24 April 1918, aged about 18.

Private, Devonshire Regiment, 2nd Bn., Service no. 30907. Remembered at St. Sever Cemetery Extension, Rouen, Seine-Maritime, France.

In 1911 Arthur Brooker lived at 36 Rutland Street, South Lambeth with his widowed mother, Annie Brooker, 53, from Wroughton. Wiltshire. She had 10 children, seven of them living at home. The family occupied five rooms.

J. F. BROOKS
Not identified.

G. A. BROOM
George Augustus Broom, killed in action on 30 November 1917.

Corporal, Royal Field Artillery, "D" Bty. 63rd Bde., Service no. 95439. Remembered at Cambrai Memorial, Louveral, Nord, France.

A. L. BROWN
Arthur Leonard Brown, died on 10 April 1917, aged 40.

Rifleman, Rifle Brigade, 8th Bn., Service no. S/26223. Remembered at Arras Memorial, Pas de Calais, France.

Arthur Leonard was the son of Tom and Mary Brown. His widow, Edith Maude May (née Brown) lived at Ellerslie Road, Clapham.

J. E. BROWN

Not identified.

W. V. BROWN

William Valentine Brown, killed in action on 15 November 1916, aged 49.

Lance Corporal, The Queen's (Royal West Surrey Regiment), "B" Coy. 11th Bn., Service no. G/10746. Remembered at Dickebusch New Military Cemetery, Ypres, Belgium.

H. BULL

Henry Bull, died on 14 July 1918, aged 33.

Private, Labour Corps, 179th Coy., Service no. 393397. Remembered at Lapugnoy Military Cemetery, Pas de Calais, France.

OR

Harry Bull, died 21 September 1917.

Queen's Own (Royal West Kent Regiment), 10th Bn., Service no. G/18723. Remembered at Tyne Cot Memorial, Zonnebeke, West-Vlaanderen, Belgium.

There were two men named H. Bull with possible connections to the Stockwell area: Henry Bull was the son of Frederick and Isabell Bull of 3 Tregothnan Road, Clapham; he was born in St. Pancras, central London; Harry Bull, who died on 21 September 1917 and is described in *Soldiers Died in the Great War 1914–1919* as living in "Clapham Common, N.E." He was born in Brighton.

F. H. BUNCE

Frederick Harry Bunce, died on the 20 October 1916, aged 20.

Private, Duke of Cornwall's Light Infantry, "B" Coy. Service no. 19571. Remembered on the Lambeth Cemetery, Screen Wall, Blackshaw Road, Tooting, south-west London.

Frederick Harry Bunce was the son of John and Rosa Bunce, of 7 Victoria Place, Priory Grove, South Lambeth.

S. A. BUNKER

Sidney Alfred Bunker, killed in action on 18 October 1915, aged about 21.

Private, Middlesex Regiment, 11th Bn., Service no. G/8995. Remembered at Loos Memorial, Pas de Calais, France.

In 1911 Sidney Bunker, one of three sons living at home with their widowed father, worked in the printing industry as a press boy. Henry Bunker, 51, from Shepherds Bush, west London cured ox tongues for a living. The family lived at 4 Richmond Street (this street, now gone, was adjacent to Walnut Tree Walk), Kennington.

J. BUNN

John Bunn, died of wounds on 10 August 1917, aged 30.

Rifleman, King's Royal Rifle Corps, "C" Coy. 10th Bn., Service no. R/32876. Formerly TR/13/29465, T.R. Battalion. Remembered at New Irish Farm Cemetery, Ypres, Belgium.

In 1911 John Bunn's widowed mother, Jane Harriett Bunn, 62, was living in four rooms at 35 Meadow Road, South Lambeth with two single daughters. She had six children.

W. BUNYAN

William Bunyan, killed in action on 20 July 1915, aged 34.

Serjeant, York and Lancaster Regiment, 2nd Bn., Service no. 7848. Remembered at New Irish Farm Cemetery, Ypres, Belgium.

In 1911 William Bunyan, then 27, was working as a miller's labourer and living with his widowed grandmother and sister Florence in four rooms at 12 Russell Street, Hertford. Mary Bunyan, 73, was born in Wadesmill, Hertfordshire; Florence and William were born in Bengeo. Some time after 1911, William Bunyan married Ellen Eliza (last name unknown), who after his death lived at 8 Andalus Road, Stockwell.

William Bunyan first joined the York and Lancasters in 1904, when he was about 23. He gave his occupation as "groom". He stood 5 feet 4¼ inches tall, weighed 8½ stone, and measured 38 inches around the chest. The regiment noted his progress after six months' Army service and a "gymnastic course". He had grown a triumphant one-tenth of an inch, gained three pounds and increased his chest measurement by an inch. Generally, he was judged to be of good character and during this period of service gained a good conduct badge. After serving in the Army for over 10 years (with some intervals) Bunyan was killed on 20 July 1915.

C. H. BURCHELL

Charles Henry Burchell, killed in action on 30 June 1916, aged 22.
Private, Royal Sussex Regiment, 13th Bn., Service no. SD/3529.
Remembered at Loos Memorial, Pas de Calais, France.

A tentative identification. The service details above are for the only British-resident C. H. Burchell in the Commonwealth War Graves Commission database. I have not yet found information that links him to Stockwell. Charles Henry Burchell was the son of Thomas and Harriett Burchell, of Mate's Nest, Balcombe, Sussex.

H. G. BURLS

Harry George Burls, died of wounds on 25 October 1918, aged 25.
Gunner, Royal Field Artillery, "B" Bty. 211th Bde. Service no 15147.
Remembered at Romeries Communal Cemetery Extension, Nord, France.

Harry Burls volunteered in April 1915 and was sent to the Western Front soon afterwards. He fought at the Somme, and was wounded. He served in the Retreat and Advance of 1918 but was killed at Cambrai in October.

The National Roll of the Great War has an entry for H. G. Burls as well as for "W. A. Burls" of the same address, 25 Moat Place, Stockwell, and "F. A. Burls" of Combermere Road, a few streets away. Both these men survived the war (the latter being invalided out of the Army) and are likely to have been related to Harry.

The 1911 census shows that Harry George Burls, 18, a labourer, lived with his widowed mother and siblings in five rooms at 25 Moat Place. Elizabeth Burls, 45, was a housekeeper, born in Finchingfield, Essex. She had eight children.

J. BURNS
Not identified.

H. R. BURVILL

Harry Robert Burvill, killed in action on 2 September 1916, aged 24.

Private, Middlesex Regiment, 16th Bn., Service no. PS/1794; also Manchester Regiment, attached 22nd Bn. Remembered at Thiepval Memorial, Somme, France.

Harry Burvill was a 22-year-old storekeeper, living at 15 Hubert Grove, Stockwell. He attested on 27 March 1915 in London (the record is not specific about where). His physical development was judged to be "v. good" he was – 5 feet 9½ inches tall, with a 41-inch chest.

Burvill was posted on 30 March 1915, and again on 18 January 1916. He was admitted to the Countess of Lytton Hospital in London some time after that. His illness or condition is not recorded. On 1 February he was sent to Summerdown Convalescent Hospital, Eastbourne, which had opened in 1915 and could care for up to 3,500 recovering servicemen. Three weeks later, Burvill was granted leave until 3 March, when he was declared fit.

Burvill was killed in action in France on 2 September 1916. He had served one year and 160 days.

Harry Burvill is on the 1911 census as a 19-year-old wharf scaleman living with his parents and brother at 35 Walpole Road, Deptford. His father, also called Harry, 67, was a butcher's scaleman, born at Ramsgate, Kent; his mother, Eliza Burvill, 68, was born in Walworth, south-east London. Harry's brother Charlie, 17, was a draper's assistant. Both boys were born in Kilburn, north London.

C

A. L. C. CADOT

Auguste Cadot, died of illness on 25 January 1920, aged 39.

Gunner, Royal Garrison Artillery, Service no. 127954.

On 11 December 1915 Auguste Cadot, 34 and living at 17 Tregothnan Road, Stockwell, enlisted at Clapham. The Approving Officer noted that he was just over 5 feet 6 inches tall and his chest measured 41½ inches.

The Service records show that Cadot agreed to allot six shillings of his Army pay to his wife Marion whom he had married at St. Stephen's Church, South Lambeth in 1912. Their son Dennis Auguste was born in 1915.

Cadot was one of three children of Laure Erzberger, a Frenchwoman married to Charles Erzberger, a 47-year-old German banker's clerk (Cadot's father had previously died). In 1901 the Erzberger family lived at 63 Gleneldon Road in Streatham. Both Auguste, 20, and his 27-year-old brother Henry were manufacturer's clerks. The household included their 15-year-old sister, Florence, and a domestic servant. Ten years later, in 1911, Auguste was living alone in one room at 261 Clapham Road.

The 1911 census was the first in which householders completed the form themselves. Cadot took the opportunity to describe himself as a "cashier, book-keeper, patentee and manufacturer," but by the time he enlisted in the Royal Garrison Artillery in December 1915, he was merely an accountant and book-keeper.

Cadot served in a Siege Battery of the Royal Garrison Artillery. The records show that he was a signalman, that he passed (1st class) in telephony, that his military character was "good" and that he served in both France and Italy.

However, Cadot was hospitalised several times and sent home on leave; he was discharged on 12 February 1919 after a 16-week stay in hospital, having served three years and 64 days. His health was ruined. "No longer physically fit for war service" was stamped on his Service record. Cadot was diagnosed with chronic nephritis, an inflammation of the kidneys, which the Army accepted was "caused by service". Many soldiers suffered a specific type of the disease known as "trench nephritis", or glomerulone-phritis, caused by living conditions at the front.

Symptoms included breathlessness, swelling of the face or legs, headache and sore throat. The condition affected 1.8 per cent (15,837) of First World War pensioners. Doctors noted Cadot's loss of sight and headaches, traces of albumin in his urine, high blood pressure and cardiovascular changes.

When assessing him for a pension, the medical officer judged him to be 80 per cent disabled, yet optimistically predicted that "he will get work" and that his symptoms were likely to last one year. Alas, the latter proved to be true. Cadot died in Lambeth just under a year later. He was 39.

F. H. S. CAIGER

Frederick Howard Stewart Caiger, killed in action on 11 November 1916, aged 19.

Second Lieutenant, Royal Field Artillery, 92nd Bty. 17th Bde.
Remembered at Caterpillar Valley Cemetery, Longueval, Somme, France and at St. Andrew's Church, Landor Road, Stockwell.

Frederick Howard Stewart Caiger was born on 23 September 1896, the only child of Dr. Frederick Foord Caiger and his wife, Madeline Orr Caiger. The family lived on the premises of South Western Hospital (now Lambeth Hospital) on Landor Road, where Dr. Caiger served as Superintendent for a total of 39 years.

Caiger was educated at Winchester, where he was in the Officer Training Corps. On 1 October 1915 he went up to Gonville and Caius College, Cambridge, and resided there for one term. He was Gazetted (meaning that his Army commission was announced in the official Gazette) in December 1915 and he embarked for France on 23 April the following year. He was attached to the 36th Battery.

Caiger was admitted to the 87th Field Ambulance with a hydrocele (fluid in the scrotum) and later to the General Hospital when he was suffering from scabies, a highly contagious skin disease transmitted by the mange mite. He was discharged on 24 June and posted in September to the 92nd Battery.

On 11 November Caiger was killed near Flers by a high explosive shell and buried at McCormick's Post. His body was moved in 1920 to Caterpillar Valley Cemetery, Longueval.

In 1922 Dr. Foord Caiger donated the four-faced clock on the Stockwell Memorial in memory of his son. "I... shall be very pleased to give it as a tribute to the memory of my only son, who fell in the battle of the Somme at the early age of 19," he wrote to Samuel Bowller, secretary of the Memorial Committee. "The idea of placing a clock... struck me as such a 'live' and appropriate tribute to one who was born and always lived in Stockwell, and who entertained a warm affection for his home."

S. CAIGER

Sidney Caiger, killed in action on 1 July 1916, aged about 23.

Private, Middlesex Regiment, 16th Bn., Service no. P.S.1743. Remembered at Thiepval Memorial, Somme, France.

General labourer Sidney Caiger enlisted at Battersea on 20 March 1915. He was 21. Details of his war service are scant. He gave 1 Bolney Street, Stockwell as his address. He stood 5 feet 5½ inches, and his chest measurement was 38 inches. He weighed just over 8½ stone. There were several scars across his back.

Sidney Caiger was posted on 23 March 1915 and was listed as missing on 8 July 1916. On 15 September he was registered as killed in action. His war had lasted one year and 104 days.

In 1911 Caiger lived with his parents, stonemason Emery Edmund Caiger, 61, from Westminster, and Alice Caiger, 59, from Godalming, Surrey in two rooms at 48 St. Mark's Road, Kennington (this street once ran between Camberwell New Road and Hillingdon Street). There were seven other siblings, all of whom lived elsewhere.

N. CAIRNS

Norman Cairns, killed in action on 26 June 1917, aged 22.

Gunner, Royal Garrison Artillery, 279th Siege Bty., Service no. 76551. Remembered at Vlamertinghe New Military Cemetery, Ypres, West-Vlaanderen, Belgium.

Butcher Norman Cairns's Service history is brief. He joined on 25 April 1916, was posted overseas on Christmas Day; on 14 April 1917 he was hospitalised with a gunshot wound to the shoulder; on 25 April he was invalided back to England; some time after that (the record is too damaged to read) he returned to the field; and on 26 June he was killed.

Cairns stood 5 feet 10 inches and measured 42 inches around the chest.

In December 1917 the Officer in Charge of Records sent Norman's effects to her at 38 Bromfelde Road, Clapham: a coin, an identity disc, a pocket book, a religious book, a penknife and a cigarette holder and case.

Cairns married Florence Penton on Boxing Day 1914 at the Wesleyan Chapel on Clapham Road.

W. G. CALLEN

William George Callen, died on 29 August 1920, aged 24.

Rifleman, King's Royal Rifle Corps, Service no. 12089. Remembered at Lambeth Cemetery, Blackshaw Road, Tooting, south-west London.

The 1911 census return for William George Callen shows that, aged 15, he lived in four rooms at 100 Dorset Road with his father, railway porter William Henry Callen, 45, from Eastleigh, Hampshire, and mother, Ada Elizabeth Callen, 47, from Woolwich, and two siblings.

A. S. CAMPBELL

Archibald Samuel Campbell, killed in action on 26 April 1918, aged about 23.

Private, The Queen's (Royal West Surrey Regiment), 2/4th Bn., Service no. 203096; formerly Royal Army Service Corps. Remembered at Jerusalem War Cemetery, Israel.

Less than a month after war was declared, 19-year-old jeweller's assistant Archibald Samuel Campbell took himself to the recruiting office at Battersea and offered himself to the Wiltshire Regiment. They gave him a number, 13710, and measured him up: 5 feet 2 inches, under 8 stone, with a 34-inch chest. He had a sallow (yellowish) complexion, blue eyes and light brown hair. His overall physical development was judged to be "good." Only 41 days later, however, he was discharged under Para 392 (ii) King's Regulations as "not being likely to become an efficient soldier." Reasons for discharge under this regulation were not recorded in the Service file, so we do not know why he was rejected.

Campbell must have re-enlisted or been called up later. This time he joined the Queen's Regiment and survived to 26 April 1918, when he was killed in action and buried in the war cemetery in Jerusalem.

The 1911 census shows that Archibald Campbell, then 15, was a schoolboy living with his parents and younger brother at 193 Wandsworth Road where the family occupied two rooms. His father, Thomas S. Campbell, 48, originally from Chelsea, was a messenger for the Admiralty; his mother, Humilia, 37, was from Lichfield, Staffordshire. Archibald was born in Langton Herring, Dorset.

A. S. CANDY

Arthur Sidney Candy, died of wounds on 22 October 1917, aged 23.

Private, Rifleman, King's Royal Rifle Corps, 7th Bn., Service no. A/201081. Remembered at Lijssenthoek Military Cemetery, Poperinge, West-Vlaanderen, Belgium.

In 1911 Arthur Sidney Candy, 16, was apprenticed as a compositor (typesetter). He lived with his father, William Robert Candy, 67, an out-of-work plasterer from Southampton, and mother, Amelia Sophia Candy, 59, from Lambeth, at 17 Trevelyan Road, Tooting, where they occupied four rooms. Arthur had five siblings, with two living at home.

G. H. CANHAM

George Herbert Canham, killed in action on 10 September 1916, aged 21.

Rifleman, London Regiment, "D" Coy., 1/16th Bn. (Queen's Westminster Rifles), Service no. 3861. Remembered at Thiepval Memorial, Somme, France.

George Herbert Canham, of 35 Mordaunt Street, Stockwell, enlisted at 58 Buckingham Gate, London on 1 March 1915. He was 20, stood 5 feet 9 inches tall and had a 40-inch chest. His physical development was judged to be "good." Canham's Service file does not include much more than the basic details of his movements. He was in England from the day of his enlistment to 21 April 1916, when he embarked for Rouen. He was deployed in the field from 4 May and survived there until 10 September, when he was killed in action at the Battle of the Somme. Two brothers, William James Canham and Arthur Kitchener Canham, survived the war.

In 1911, the Canham family inhabited five rooms at 4 Tivoli Road, West Norwood. George Herbert, then 16, was a shop porter. There were four siblings. Their father, William, 41, was a brewer's drayman from Wenhaston, Suffolk; their mother, Clara Amy, 43, was from Farnborough, Kent.

B. H. CAPEWELL

Brian Harvey Capewell, died on 21 August 1917, aged 23.

Ship's Steward Assistant, Royal Navy, H.M.S. *Vala*. Service no. M/15985. Remembered at Plymouth Naval Memorial, Devon and at West Norwood Cemetery, south-east London. Brother of *Frederick Harold Capewell*.

Brian Harvey Capewell was the son of Brian Charles and Lily Rosina Capewell, of 35 Union Road, Clapham. He died while serving on the H.M.S. *Vala*, a Q boat sailing from Milford Haven. The entire crew was lost. Q boats were decoy ships, heavily armed merchant ships with concealed weaponry.

F. H. CAPEWELL

Frederick Harold Capewell, died on 1 April 1918, aged 18.

Private, Royal Fusiliers, 17th Bn., Service no. G/75140. Remembered at West Norwood Cemetery and Screen Wall, south-east London. Brother of *Brian Harvey Capewell*.

H. CAREY

Not identified.

H. W. CARTER

Henry W. Carter, killed in action on 24 November 1917, aged 33.

Fitter, Royal Field Artillery, "C" Bty. 93rd Bde., Service no. L/6227. Remembered at Ruyaulcourt Military Cemetery, Pas de Calais, France.

Henry W. Carter was the son of Henry William Carter. His widow, Grace Elizabeth Carter, lived at 25 Aldebert Terrace, Stockwell.

W. A. E. CARTER

William Archibald Edward Carter, killed in action on 31 May 1916, aged 18.

Ordinary Signalman, Royal Navy, H.M.S. *Queen Mary*, Service no. J/25992. Remembered at Portsmouth Naval Memorial.

William Archibald Edward Carter was the son of Archibald and Florence Louisa Carter of 113 South Lambeth Road. H.M.S. *Queen Mary* was sunk by the S.M.S. *Seydlitz* at the Battle of Jutland. Of the 1,266 crew on board, only 21 survived.

T. C. CAVALIER

Thomas Cavalier, killed in action on 20 January 1918, aged 27.

Able Seaman, Mercantile Marine Reserve, R.F.A. *Reliance*, Service no. 468539. Remembered at Plymouth Naval Memorial.

Thomas Cavalier was the son of Mrs. E. Cavalier of 14 Irving Grove, Stockwell. He was killed on H.M.S. *Louvain* after it was attacked by a U-boat in the eastern Mediterranean. The *Louvain* may have been in use as a leave ship when she was torpedoed. Of the 151 men on board, only 10 survived.

F. J. CHADDOCK

Frederick J. Chaddock, died on 31 October 1918, aged about 33.

Corporal, Gloucestershire Regiment, 1st Bn., Service no. 9238. Remembered at Busigny Communal Cemetery Extension, Nord, France.

At the time of the 1911 census, Frederick J. Chaddock was with the 2nd Battalion of the Gloucestershire Regiment at Verdala Barracks, Malta. He was born in Lambeth.

H. W. CHAMBERS

William Henry Chambers, died of wounds on 26 December 1915, aged 34.

Serjeant, Dorsetshire Regiment, 2nd Bn., Service no. 7216. Remembered at Kut War Cemetery, Iraq.

This is a tentative identification. The Commonwealth War Graves Commission database has a William Henry Chambers who was the son of Alfred and Eliza Chambers of 21 Binfield Road, Stockwell.

A. E. N. CHANCE

Arthur Ernest Newton Chance, killed in action on 13 November 1916, aged 24.

Sub-Lieutenant, Royal Naval Volunteer Reserve, Howe Bn., R.N. Div.
Remembered at Thiepval Memorial, Somme, France.

Arthur Ernest Newton Chance, one of four children of journalist Henry Chance and Margaret Anne Chance, joined the Navy on 10 August 1911, aged nearly 20. He was previously an insurance clerk. Chance was commissioned as a Temporary Sub-Lieutenant in November 1915 and joined the British Expeditionary Force in July the following year. He died at the Somme on 13 November 1916.

Chance's military record lists the vessels he served on before the war and after it started, and describes him as 5 feet 5¼ inches, with red hair, blue eyes and a fair complexion. It also gives an outline of his court martial.

On 13 September 1916 he was tried for "1. uttering a forged document (i.e. forged cheque for £3/10/-) on or about 15 July 1916; 2. for ditto on or about 21 July 1916; 3. for behaving in a scandalous manner unbecoming the character of an officer and a gentleman in giving a cheque signed by him in a fictitious name having no account in that name." Found guilty on all three charges, Chance was sentenced to be cashiered and imprisoned "without hard labour" for six months. The record does not divulge where these events took place or how Chance ended up at the Somme.

The 1911 census shows the Chance family living in seven rooms at 24 Winslade Road, Brixton. The household included Chance's sister, Margaret Layder, 28, and her daughter, Margery Florence Layder, 6. Arthur's brother, Harry William Chance, 25, was a "black and white artist" (he produced monochrome illustrations, probably for magazines or newspapers).

A. E. CHANDLER

Albert Edward Chandler, killed in action on 1 July 1916, aged 19.

Private, London Regiment, 1st Bn. (Royal Fusiliers), Service no. 3527.
Enlisted at Handel Street. Remembered at Hubuterne Military Cemetery, Pas de Calais, France and at St. Mark's Church, Kennington, south London.

In 1911 Albert Edward Chandler was a 13-year-old schoolboy. He lived in two rooms at 3 Oval Place, off Dorset Road, with his father, James Walter Chandler, 41, a timber carman from Clapham, mother, Ada Emily Chandler, 39, from Stepney, east London, and an elder sister.

R. CHARMAN

Richard Charman, died of wounds on 23 July 1916, aged 17.

Driver, Royal Field Artillery, "B" Battery, 156th Brigade., Service no. L/21002. Remembered at Heilly Station Cemetery, Mericourt-L'Abbé, Somme, France.

In 1911 Richard (or Dick) Charman's family lived in four rooms at 13 Ingleborough Street, off Brixton Road. His father, Henry Charman, 56, a general labourer, was born in Lambeth; his mother, Mary Charman, 54, was born in Clapham. They had 12 children.

On 25 August 1916, *The South London Press* reported Charman's death:

> He was one of six brothers serving with the colours, all descendants of a fighting race. In a letter to his mother, his company officer says: 'Your son died nobly, doing his duty and as his section commander I can testify to the fine young soldier whom we mourn. He was, for his age, quite exceptional in his work, and beyond praise in the fearless way in which he carried out his dangerous and arduous duties. In him we have lost one who is irreplaceable and who, by his cheerfulness and courage, endeared himself to us all.'

C. H. CHARNOCK

Charles Henry Charnock, killed in action on 14 October 1917, aged about 20.

Gunner, Royal Field Artillery, 120th Bty., 27th Bde., Service no. 195781. Remembered at La Clytte Military Cemetery, near Ypres, Belgium.

The 1911 census shows Charles Henry Charnock, 14, living with nine members of his family, including his grandmother, Mary Ann Varns, 63, in four rooms at 15 Madrid Place, South Lambeth. His parents, Frederick Thomas Charnock, 41, a bricklayer, and Kate Charnock, 36, were both from Southwark. They had seven children.

J. S. CLACK

James Stephen Clack, died of appendicitis and peritonitis on 2 October 1914, aged 29.

Private, Army Service Corps, 1st Div. Supply Col., Service no. MS/775. Remembered at La Ferté-Sous-Jouarre Memorial, Seine-et-Marne, France.

James Stephen Clack stood 5 feet 7¾ inches tall and weighed 11½ stone, with a 40½-inch chest. The statistics bring to mind a strong, well-made man. The Approving Officer gave Clack's physical development a rare accolade: "very good." Clack's sallow (yellowish) complexion, grey eyes and brown hair, and the ganglion on his left wrist were recorded.

Clack was among the first to volunteer, presenting himself on 8 August 1914, a mere four days after war was declared. A lorry driver in civilian life (and before that a motor engineer), he was recruited to the Army Service Corps as a Driver (at this early stage of the war, this may have meant driver of horses rather than of motorised transport). The Army must have been delighted to have such a keen, healthy candidate.

Alas, after only 58 days the war was over for Clack. He was admitted to the 16th Field Ambulance on 28 September 1914 and by 2 October he had died of appendicitis and peritonitis. His widow Annie, living at 10a Lingham Street with their two-year-old daughter Mary Lucy, was sent her husband's effects, along with a handwritten note: "Herewith 70 centimes (French) cash, the property of the late Private James Stephen Clack..." Later she was awarded a pension of 15 shillings a week for herself and her child.

A. C. CLARKE

Alfred Charles Clarke, died on 6 November 1917, aged 22.

Rifleman, London Regiment, 2/11th Bn. (Finsbury Rifles), Service no. 453028. Remembered at Tyne Cot Memorial, Heuvelland, West-Vlaanderen, Belgium.

In 1911 Albert Charles Clarke, 15 and working as a grocer's assistant, lived at 18 Wilkinson Street, Stockwell, where his family shared eight rooms. His father, William Clarke, 52, a plaster model maker at a terracotta works, was born in Burbage, Leicestershire. His mother, Eliza Clarke, 50, was from Whitwick, Leicestershire. They had nine children.

J. R. CLARKE

Joseph Robert Clarke, *died on 1 November 1918, aged 22.*

Private, Royal Fusiliers, 11th Bn., Service no. 15257. Remembered at Tourgeville Military Cemetery, Calvados, France.

Alfred Charles Clarke was the son of Mrs. A. Clarke of 20 Beech Street, Dorset Road, Stockwell.

S. W. CLARKE

Not identified.

F. V. CLEMENT

Frederick Victor Clement, died on 11 June 1916, aged 19.

Private, London Regiment, 1/24th Bn. (The Queen's), Service no. 3538. Remembered at Bruay Communal Cemetery Extension, Pas de Calais, France.

In 1911 Frederick Victor Clement, a 14-year-old schoolboy, his mother Harriett Clement, 58, a widowed charwoman (cleaner) from Clapham, and brother Walter George Clement, 36, a blind chair caner, also from Clapham, boarded with the Faux family at 60 Burgoyne Road, Stockwell.

H. CLOUGH

Harold Clough, died on 31 May 1916, aged 35.

Engine Room Artificer 4th Class, Royal Navy, H.M.S. *Queen Mary*, Service no. M/13358. Remembered at Chatham Naval Memorial, Kent.

Harold Clough's widow Martha lived at 50 Kay Road, Stockwell.

W. R. COLLETT

William Reuben Collett, killed in action on 18 May 1917, aged 19.

Rifleman, Rifle Brigade, 1st Bn., Service no. S/20722. Remembered at Brown's Copse Cemetery, Roeux, Pas de Calais, France.

William Reuben Collett's entry in *The National Roll of the Great War* states that he joined up in June 1916 and after training was sent to the front. He fought at St. Eloi and the Somme, and died at the Battle of Arras. In 1911 Collett, who was born in Battersea, lived with his parents Reuben John

Collett and Helen Eliza Collett in four rooms at 75 Tasman Road, Stockwell. Reuben, 44, was a compositor (typesetter) from Lambeth; Helen, 44, was from Battersea. William had two brothers.

C. E. COLLINS

Charles Edward Collins, died on 28 April 1918, aged 29.

Private, Cameronians (Scottish Rifles), 9th Bn., Service no, 37844; formerly Army Pay Corps. Remembered at Grand-Seraucourt British Cemetery, Aisne, France.

Charles Edward Collins was the son of Walter and Eliza Collins; his widow, Lucy Rebecca Collins, lived at 126 Dorset Road, Stockwell.

E. W. COLLINS

Edwin William Collins, died of wounds on 2 August 1918, aged 26.

Private, London Regiment, 1/24th Bn. (The Queen's), Service no. 479594; then Labour Corps. Remembered at Terlincthun British Cemetery, Wimille, Pas de Calais, France.

Edwin Collins, a railway porter, joined up on 5 September 1914 aged about 22. He stood 5 feet 11 inches tall, and measured 39 inches around the chest. His physical development was judged to be "good". Collins survived almost to the end of the war but on 1 August 1918 he was admitted to 2nd Canadian General Hospital in Boulogne suffering from multiple bomb blast injuries, including a fractured skull. His condition was described as "dangerous" and he died the following day. Collins's effects were sent to his father, a retired policeman also called Edwin, and included a pouch, purse, ring, testament, two leather cases, cards, photos, letters, religious books, four coins and an identity disc. Edwin was the only boy of six children.

S. H. COMPSON

Stanley Henry Compson, killed in action on 23 March 1918, aged about 21.

Private, The Queen's Royal West Kent Regiment, 10th Bn., Service no. G/19059. Remembered at Arras Memorial, Pas de Calais, France, and at St. Mark's Church, Kennington, south London. Awarded the *Military Medal.*

Brixton-born Stanley Henry Compson enlisted on 20 May 1915 at Maidstone, Kent, about five miles from his home in Hunton. Four years previously, as shown on the 1911 census, he was working as an errand boy for a grocer and living with his widowed grandmother, 60-year-old Jane Compson, and other family members at 240 South Lambeth Road. His father, Joseph Compson, was a 37-year-old stockbroker's clerk.

Compson's service record shows that he was 5 feet 7 inches tall, with a 37-inch chest. His physical development was deemed "good." He was posted twice, first on 6 December 1916 and again on the 26th. His death was assumed on 23 March 1918.

A. C. COOK

Augustus Charles Cook, died on 10 July 1917, aged 41.

Private, The Queen's Own Royal West Kent Regiment, 2nd Bn., Service no. G/1381. Remembered at Basra War Cemetery, Iraq.

In 1911 Augustus Charles Cook, then 34, lived with his wife, Mary Ann, 29, and their five children in four rooms at 11 Devonshire Square, Bromley. He was born in Clapham and his father, Matthew John Cook, is found on the 1911 census there. Cook enlisted in Bromley.

A. T. W. COOK

Albert Tom William Cook, died of wounds on 11 July 1916.

Rifleman, Rifle Brigade, 1st Bn., Service no. Z/447. Remembered at Lambeth Cemetery, Screen Wall, Blackshaw Road, Tooting, south-west London.

Cook volunteered in 1914 and was drafted to the front the following year. He fought at Ypres and was severely wounded at the Battle of the Somme. He was invalided home to hospital and soon afterwards died of his injuries.

W. A. COOK

William Arthur Cook, died on 22 September 1916, aged 19.

Rifleman, London Regiment, 1/9th Bn. (Queen Victoria's Rifles). Remembered at Etaples Military Cemetery, France.

William Arthur Cook was the son of John and Rhoda Cook of Stockwell.

W. W. COOK

Walter William Cook, killed in action on 28 April 1917, aged 22.

Private, Middlesex Regiment, 4th Bn., Service no. G/43050. Remembered at Arras Memorial, France and at St. Andrew's Church, Landor Road, Stockwell.

In 1911, 10 people shared the four rooms of the Cook household at 3 Priory Buildings on Southville, off Wandsworth Road. Walter William Cook, 15, who worked in a box factory, lived with his brother Edward Cook, 42, Edward's wife Alice, 39, and their six children, as well as his widowed father, Edwin Cook, 67, a retired greengrocer.

A. S. H. COOPER

Not identified.

F. A. J. COOPER

Frank Arthur John Cooper, killed in action on 7 November 1917.

Lance Serjeant, London Regiment, 2/14th Bn. (London Scottish), Service no. 511407. Remembered at Jerusalem Memorial, Israel.

Frank Cooper enlisted in London and lived in Clapham.

W. C. COOPER

Not identified.

V. L. CORBEN

Victor Leslie Corben, died of complications arising from appendicitis on 22 July 1918, aged 23.

Second Lieutenant, Royal Fusiliers; also Rifle Brigade, attached 52nd Bn., Remembered at Lambeth Cemetery, Blackshaw Road, Tooting, south-west London.

In July 1918 Victor Leslie Corben, a Second Lieutenant attached to the Rifle Brigade, was on leave in London when he started to suffer headaches and fever. He was admitted to the 3rd London General Hospital (this building, now known as the Royal Victoria Patriotic Building, sits opposite Wandsworth Prison). Appendicitis was diagnosed and on 7 and 13 July he was operated on by an Army surgeon. On 21 July he had further surgery but died the next day at 10.40am. Corben's effects, a suitcase and a small parcel of personal property, were sent to his father, Fred Corben, a stone merchant of Hillside, 51 Union Road, Clapham. Buried at Lambeth Cemetery with full military honours, Corben was also remembered at a service at the United Methodist Church in Fentiman Road, Oval, where he had been a worshipper.

"The loss of the boy is indeed a severe blow to us," Fred wrote in August to Major Bright of the Rifle Brigade at Colchester, thanking him for his sympathy and for the settlement of Victor's accounts.

However, when Fred applied to the Army for funds to cover his son's funeral expenses, he was turned down. Your son died in England, of an illness not related to his service, the authorities said. Fred was outraged, barely concealing his anger in a note written on 10 December 1918. For him, the appendicitis was clearly connected with the wounds Victor had sustained the previous year, and also with a bout of trench fever.

"I was never consulted in reference to the operations which were performed on him at the hospital," he complained. "[Yet] as soon as he had passed away in his country's service I was called upon to pay for the coffin in which he was to be buried. [...] This seems to me a gross injustice." The Army was intransigent: "No grant for Army funds is admissible," it stated.

Victor Corben was born in Clapham on 23 February 1895, and after boarding at Cranleigh School, Surrey, worked at the London and South-western Bank.

He joined the East Surrey Regiment on 20 January 1916, was wounded in Flanders in May 1917 and later suffered from trench fever. However, he recovered well and was made musketry officer to a battalion in the Rifle Brigade. According to a report in *The South London Press*, he volunteered to return to active service but was refused on medical grounds.

Corben was 5 feet 10 inches tall and weighed just over 10 stone.

The 1911 census shows the Corben family living in 10 rooms at 51 Union Road. Fred, then 49, was born in Lambeth; his wife, Esther Margaret, 48, was from Chelsea. Their daughter Florence, 25, was "assisting in the business", as was Leslie's brother Frank H. Corben, 20. Domestic servant Mary Bower, 26, from Langton Matravers in Dorset, had been with the family for at least 10 years (she appears on both the 1901 and the 1911 censuses). Later, Fred and Esther moved to Bournemouth.

F. W. COUSINS

Frederick William Cousins, died of wounds on 1 September 1917.

Gunner, Royal Field Artillery, "L" Bty. 112th Bde. Service no L/13154. Remembered at The Huts Cemetery, Ypres, West-Vlaanderen, Belgium.

Frederick William Cousins was the son of Mrs. S. A. Cousins of 82 Dorset Road, Stockwell.

E. C. COX

Not identified.

J. COX

Not identified.

W. A. COX

This name is also listed on Waterloo Station War Memorial, London SE1.

W. CRABB

William Edward Crabb, died of cerebral malaria on 23 May 1917, aged 39.

Private, Army Service Corps, 618th M.T. Coy., Service no. M2/150639. Remembered at Morogoro Cemetery, Tanzania.

William Edward Crabb died on 23 May 1917 in the 15th Stationary Hospital at Morogoro, Tanzania. He had cerebral malaria "caused by field opera-tions". Crabb's file offers few details on this, other than to note that he was dangerously ill when admitted and subsequently died.

Malaria is transmitted by infected mosquitos and its presence in sub-Saharan Africa was and still is endemic. Only some cases develop into cerebral malaria, an acute disease of the brain that is accompanied by high fever and whitening of the retina. The mortality rate is currently between 25 and 50 per cent, and was probably greater in 1917.

Crabb left a widow, Alice Beatrice (née Stout), and four children, the youngest born in 1915.

Born in Southampton, Crabb was an engineer's fitter in civilian life. He stood 5 feet 2 inches tall, with a 38-chest, and weighed under 8½ stone. In 1911 Crabb, then 32, and Alice, 24, lived at 44 Union Grove, Clapham, where the family had three rooms, along with their two children, Alice Marie, 2, and Elsie Amelia, 1.

G. D. CRANHAM

George David Cranham, killed in action on 17 August 1917, aged 24.

Private, Duke of Cornwall's Light Infantry, 7th Bn., Service no. 11179.
Remembered at Sanctuary Wood Cemetery, Ypres, Belgium.

George David Cranham's widow, Ellen Kate Trumper (she remarried after his death), lived at 6 Horace Street (near Wilcox Road), South Lambeth.

A. CROCKER

Abraham Crocker, killed in action on 1 October 1916, aged about 33.

Private, London Regiment, 1/20th Bn. (Blackheath and Woolwich), Service no. 5308. Remembered at Thiepval Memorial, Somme, France.

In 1911 Abraham Crocker, from Crewkerne, Somerset, was employed as a carman for a building contractor. He lived at 2 Layham Cottages (near Bolney Street), Stockwell with his brother John, 45, a labourer at a brewery, and his sister-in-law Annie, 46, also born in Crewkerne, and their three children. The family lived in four rooms.

H. H. CROCKER

Herbert Howard Crocker, killed in action on 7 April 1917, aged 29.

Private, London Regiment (Royal Fusiliers), 1st Bn., Service no. 203662; formerly 2nd London Regiment. Remembered at Arras Memorial, Pas de Calais, France.

In 1911 Herbert Howard Crocker, then 23, was working as a dairy manager and living in four rooms at 2 Myrtle Cottages, Park Road in Hillingdon, west London. He and his wife, Edith Maud, 21, had been married for a year and had a one-month-old baby, Evelyn Elsie. Herbert was from Paddington, west London and Edith was from Halesworth, Suffolk. His parents, Horace Howard and Clara Sophia Crocker, were living at 8 Moat Place, Stockwell where Horace was a dairy manager and Clara was "assisting in the business." Their remaining four children lived with them. After the war, Herbert's widow Edith lived at 13 Tregothnan Road, Stockwell.

J. C. F. CROSS

James Charles Frederick Cross, killed in action on 29 September 1918, aged 26.

Private, Duke of Wellington's (West Riding Regiment), 13th Bn., Service no. 27166; formerly King's Royal Rifle Corps. Remembered at Vieille-Chapelle New Military Cemetery, Lacouture, Pas de Calais, France.

James Charles Frederick Cross, a warehouseman, joined up in St. Paul's Churchyard, London on 14 September 1914, just over a month after war was declared. He died barely six weeks before hostilities ceased.

Cross's badly damaged Service records document his many movements and transfers. He was first assigned to the Army Service Corps; he landed in France on 25 March 1915 and was wounded in action two months later; in June 1916 he was given 10 days' detention for neglecting to comply with an order; he joined the King's Royal Rifle Corps at Etaples on 22 June; and he was transferred to the Duke of Wellington's (West Riding Regiment) later that same month. He was wounded again in September and classed "P.B." (that is, assigned to Permanent Base at Etaples, which was a welcome relief to most soldiers and almost as good as being sent home to "Blighty"). On the 16 October he came down with "ear disease."

Cross was killed in action on 29 September 1918.

In 1911 James Cross lived at 22 Larkhall Lane, Clapham. The family occupied three rooms. James's father, Charles Cross, 67, was a milkman from Devon; his mother, Georgina Cross, 47, was from Oxfordshire. They had two children. Beatrice Emily Cross, 36, a child of Charles's first marriage, was a boot saleswoman. James Charles Frederick Cross was a warehouseman. On Army Form W.5080, on which the next of kin listed the dead soldier's relatives, Georgina signed her name with a mark.

W. A. CROWTHER

William Alfred Crowther, killed in action on 9 July 1917, aged 19.

Stoker 1st Class, Royal Navy, H.M.S. *Vanguard*, Service no. K/27519. Remembered at Chatham Naval Memorial, Kent.

At Scapa Flow in the Orkney Islands, off the north-east coast of Scotland, just before midnight on 9 July 1917, the *Vanguard* suddenly exploded, taking over 800 of her crew down with her.

There were only two survivors. A definitive cause was never found but the most likely scenario was that a fire smouldered undetected, long enough for nearby cordite to overheat. Able Seaman Charles William Tidnam, who is also remembered on the Stockwell Memorial, was also among the dead (see page 204).

In 1911 William Alfred Crowther, then working as an errand boy, lived at 48 Cottage Grove, Stockwell, with his parents, George Crowther, 39, a coal porter, and his mother, Elizabeth Crowther, 38, and four siblings, where they occupied four rooms.

A. S. CRUMPLER

Arthur Stephen Crumpler, died on 9 January 1917, aged 22.

Leading Stoker, Royal Navy, H.M.S. *Cornwallis*, Service no. SS/112057. Remembered at Chatham Naval Memorial, Kent.

Crumpler was one of 15 men who died when the *Cornwallis* was torpedoed by the German U-boat (U-32) off Malta. He had previously survived the sinking of the *Cressy*, which went down in the North Sea in less than 30 minutes on 22 September 1914 after an attack by the U-boat U-9.

In civilian life, Crumpler was a plumber's mate working in the building trade. One of five children, he was born in Charminster, Dorset. In 1911 he lived with his family in five rooms at 41 Dorset Road, Stockwell. Crumpler's widowed mother, Mary Ann, 53, was a newsagent and tobacconist, from Martinstown, Dorset.

J. W. CUMMINS

James William Cummins, died on 20 May 1916, aged 31.

Corporal, London Regiment, 22nd Bn. (The Queen's), Service no. 2033. Remembered at Bruay Communal Cemetery Extension, Pas de Calais, France.

In 1911 Lambeth-born James William Cummins, then 26, was married and living with his family in two rooms at 191 South Lambeth Road. He was a foreman in a coffee husking mill. His wife, Edith, 25, was born in Battersea. They had a four-month-old son, Leslie.

E. A. CUNNINGHAM

Not identified.

A. CURTIS

Albert Curtis, died on 30 August 1915, aged 35.

Private, Army Service Corps, Service no. SS/8149. Remembered at Wandsworth Cemetery, Magdalen Road, Earlsfield, south-west London.

Albert Curtis died on 30 August 1915, was buried at Wandsworth Cemetery and is remembered on a memorial plaque there. He left a widow, Florence Maud Curtis, living at Paradise Road, Stockwell, and five young children.

Albert married Florence Maud Skinner in 1906, and worked as an upholsterer and maker of portmanteaux (suitcases and travelling bags). The 1911 census shows that Albert, then 32, and Florence, 22, had been married for five years, and lived with their two young children in one room in Speke Road (this street has now gone but once ran parallel with Grant Road), Clapham Junction.

Albert's medal card shows that he served in France from 26 April 1915. He died in the Royal Victoria Hospital, Southampton on 30 August 1915, three weeks after Florence gave birth to her fifth child. There is a family story that a sack of flour fell on him from a crane and his death certificate appears to back this up – it gives fracture of the spine among the causes of death. Florence remained in Paradise Road, remarried and had three further sons who all served in World War Two.

C. W. CURTIS

Charles William Curtis, killed in action on 12 April 1918, aged 34.

Lance Serjeant, Worcestershire Regiment, "D" Coy. 3rd Bn., Service no. 8672. Remembered at Ploegsteert Memorial, Comines-Warneton, Hainaut, Belgium.

In 1911 Charles William Curtis, a blacksmith's striker, lived with his family at 37 Union Street, Clapham, where nine people shared four rooms His father, Charles Henry Curtis, 48, was a laundry carman married to Harriet Emily, 44, an ironer. Curtis had six siblings.

H. CUTMORE

Harry or Henry Cutmore, died on 2 January 1917, aged 36.

Lance Corporal, London Regiment, 24th Bn. (The Queen's), Service no. 720754. Remembered at Lijssenthoek Military Cemetery, Poperinge, Belgium.

Harry Cutmore was a house decorator. In 1911, aged 31, he was working in the family's decorating business and living with his parents, William Cutmore, 60, and Annie Cutmore, 61, both from Lambeth, and three siblings in a nine-roomed house at 13 St. Martin's Road, Stockwell.

D

C. DARTNELL

Christopher Dartnell, killed in action on 16 October 1917, aged 20.

Lance Corporal, Duke of Cornwall's Light Infantry, 6th Bn., Service no. 19561. Remembered at Hooge Crater Cemetery, Ypres, West-Vlaanderen, Belgium.

Chris Dartnell enlisted at Camberwell shortly after the start of the war. He was part of what was known as "Kitchener's Army" formed from volunteers in 1914 and 1915.

According to the War Diary of the 6th Duke of Cornwall's Light Infantry his battalion was at Ypres supporting the 10th Battalion of the Durham Light Infantry, who were in the frontline trenches. They were quartered in dugouts and shelters behind the front line, in the ironically named Sanctuary Wood.

During the night of 15 October 1917 the Germans bombarded the area with high explosives and gas shells, continuing the next day from nine in the morning until dusk. Seven men were wounded

and four were killed, one of whom was Christopher Dartnell. The head-stones of the three other N.C.O.s who were killed lie next to his at Hooge Crater Cemetery.

Dartnell had 11 siblings. Shortly before she died in 1980, the youngest, Ethel Florence, who was born in 1903, wrote this reminiscence:

> My brothers Roger, Jim and Fred were called up [conscription did not start until 1916, so they probably volunteered] and transported to France and India. My father was called to repair the hospital ships and was often in France for a month at a time. His trade was plumbing. It was frightening when the Zeppelins came over and dropped bombs and you wondered if you might be killed when they came your way. We very often stayed and sheltered in the Underground where the trains were stationary until the All Clear was sounded.
>
> Next to be called up was my brother Chris, when he was 18 [again, he probably volunteered]. He hated war and violence and often wished he was not in the Army. When he had leave from France he never wanted to go back and the last break he had from the trenches he didn't go back until after another day had passed. That was in May 1917. We then had a telegram to say he was killed in action in October – he was just 21 [he was probably 20]. We all were very shocked because of this and the news that my brother Bill had been wounded in German East Africa and was on his way home having been shot in his right hand and had lost a thumb and was also wounded in the right hip. So he was out of soldiering for good. He became a Commissionaire for a firm in the City of London.
>
> My last brother, Reg, was called up when he was 18, in January 1918 and sent to France for the big push in May 1918. We had a couple of cards from him the first few weeks and then no more news until August when we heard that he was a prisoner of war. Thank goodness they all arrived home except Chris, safe and well after the war ended in November 1918.
>
> Then Armistice was declared in November 1918 and we were told to go home [from work] at lunchtime. I remember going to see the masses of people gathering in the Strand, London and felt lost in the crowd. People dancing and cheering and drinking. I had to walk home as there were no buses running. When I reached my house my mother was crying because her son Chris had been killed and would not be returning and my other brother Reg was a prisoner of war and we were still waiting to hear if he was alive.

C. O'N. DAUNT

Conrad O'Neill Daunt, died on 29 September 1918, aged 27.

Lieutenant, Royal Air Force, South Lancashire Regiment, 8th Bn.
Remembered at Bronfay Farm Military Cemetery, Bray-sur-Somme, France.
Brother of *Giles Vellacott Daunt.*

Conrad O'Neill Daunt, born in 1891, and his brother Giles Vellacott Daunt, born in 1895, were two of five children of Irish physician and surgeon Francis Eldon Horsford Daunt and Annie Elizabeth Daunt (née Vellacott) of 176 Clapham Road. Both boys were educated at City of London School.

Conrad returned to England from Canada to fight in the war and initially served as a Private with the Second Canadian contingent. He was offered a commission with the South Lancashires, and served with them through 1917. In 1918 he was transferred to the Royal Air Force (established in April) and promoted to Lieutenant.

In 1911 the Daunts lived at 118 Newington Causeway, Borough but at this time Conrad, then aged 20, was working as a "farm pupil" at the house of his uncle, Walter John Vellacott, at Tunnel House, West Thurrock, Essex. There was a visitor on the night of the census: Moss T. Reick, 44, an evangelist from Berlin.

G. V. DAUNT

Giles Vellacott Daunt, killed in action in Mesopotamia on 9 April 1916, aged 19.

Second Lieutenant, South Lancashire Regiment, 10th Bn., attached 6th Bn.
Remembered at Basra Cemetery, Iraq. Brother of *Conrad O'Neill Daunt.*

On 20 August 1914 Giles Vellacott Daunt, aged 18 and working as a clerk, joined the Royal Fusiliers as a Signaller. He was almost immediately offered a commission in the South Lancashires (with whom his brother Conrad also served). Quite apart from his middle-class background – he was a son of the physician and surgeon Francis Eldon Horsford Daunt – he must have looked the part. Six feet tall, over 11 stone and with a 41-inch chest, blue eyes and fair hair.

In February 1916 Daunt embarked on the H.M.S. *Ionic*, headed for Port Said, Egypt and then Basra, Iraq. He was reported missing in action on 9 April 1916. His death was later confirmed. A memorandum of 6 August states that his body was buried at Sanniyat.

C. W. J. DEE

Not identified.

J. J. DERRY

John James Derry, killed in action on 9 April 1917, aged 26.

Private, Essex Regiment, 2nd Bn., Service no. 41051. Remembered at Fampoux British Cemetery, Pas de Calais, France.

John James Derry was the son of Lionel and Sarah Derry. His widow remarried, becoming Mrs. M. L. Eaton. She lived at 5 Irving Grove, Stockwell.

E. W. DESALEUX

Ernest William Desaleux, killed in action on 15 April 1917, aged 23.

Rifleman, Rifle Brigade, 1st Bn., Service no. S/14522. Remembered at Arras Memorial, Pas de Calais, France. Brother of *Frederick J. Desaleux* and *Jules Benjamin Alfred Desaleux.*

F. J. DESALEUX

Frederick J. Desaleux, killed in action on 25 February 1917, aged about 20.

Rifleman, London Regiment, 21st Bn. (First Surrey Rifles), Service no. 653511. Remembered at Railway Dugouts Burial Ground, near Ypres, Belgium. Brother of *Ernest William Desaleux* and *Jules Benjamin Alfred Desaleux.*

J. B. A. DESALEUX

Jules Benjamin Alfred Desaleux, killed in action on 25 May 1917, aged 29.

Gunner, Canadian Field Artillery, 76th Bty. Reserve Bde., Service no. 1250216. Remembered at Shorncliffe Military Cemetery, Kent. Brother of *Ernest William Desaleux* and *Frederick J. Desaleux.*

Shorncliffe Barracks, on the Kent coast close to Folkstone and Dover, was subject to airborne attacks by German bombers. The most devastating came on 25 May 1917 when two bombs fell on the huts occupied by 18 soldiers, of whom 16 were Canadian. Jules Desaleux was killed, along with 70 other military and civilian casualties.

Jules had emigrated with his wife to Canada and lived at 253 Park View Street, St. James, Winnipeg. He attested on 8 January 1917, stating that he had previously served in the Territorials with the Royal West Surreys. He was described as brown-eyed with dark brown hair and a fair complexion, and 5 feet 9 inches tall with a 38-inch chest.

In 1911 the Desaleux family lived at 20 Fountain Street, off Wandsworth Road, Stockwell. Jules Desaleux, Jules Benjamin Alfred's father, 45, was a map publishing assistant who was born in London's West End. His wife Edith (née Barton) was from Dover, Kent. They had 12 children.

On the night of the 1911 census Alice Eleanor Desaleux, 20, wife of Jules Benjamin Alfred Desaleux, and their six-month-old son Alfred Hugh were listed as visiting Henry James Kemp and his wife Alice and their five children at 8 Pownall Terrace, Kennington Road. (Pownall Terrace, now gone, was one of the many residences of Charlie Chaplin – he had lived for a time at No. 3.)

The Desaleux brothers' grandparents, Benjamin, a journeyman lamp-maker, and Maire, a corset-maker, had emigrated to London from France some time before 1861.

R. P. DICKASON

Reginald Percy Dickason, killed in action on 14 February 1917, aged 20.

Second Lieutenant, Middlesex Regiment, 6th Bn., attached 1st Bn.
Remembered at Péronne Communal Cemetery Extension, Somme, France.

Reginald Percy Dickason, an only child, was educated at King's College School and Pitman's Metropolitan School. Pitman's, the world's first school of business education (it opened in 1870), had a branch at 65 Brixton Hill and regularly advertised in *The South London Press*. It offered training in office routine, accounting and law, and shorthand and typing.

Possibly Dickason was training to be a court reporter – he transferred out of the 3/25th London Cyclists, which he joined as a Private on 1 April 1915, to the Inns of Court Officer Training Corps at Berkhamsted, Hertfordshire. This corps was originally part of the London Territorial Force and consisted mainly of men connected with the law courts.

On 4 August 1916 Dickason was accepted for admission to No. 8 Officer Cadet Battalion at Lichfield, Staffordshire and a little over three months later he left for France, serving with the Middlesex Regiment. He survived for just under four months, dying near Cléry-sur-Somme on 14 February 1917. In July 1920 the Army wrote to his father, Harold Burfield Dickason, to tell him that his son's body had been moved to the cemetery at Péronne and assuring him that the removal was done "carefully and reverently."

The Army Service record gives Dickason's vital statistics: he was 5 feet 8 inches tall, weighed over 10½ stone and measured 42½ inches around the chest.

The 1911 census shows Dickason's family living at 155 Clapham Road (the building has been replaced by a job centre). Reginald's father, then 36, was an orchestral musician (by 1916 he was a Professor of Music) from Highgate, north London. Reginald's mother, Esther, 35, was from Lambeth. The household included a great-aunt, a boarder, a live-in servant and an uncle, Percy Dickason, who was an elephant hunter.

On 17 November 1918, 22 years after Reginald's birth, Harold and Esther, now in their early forties, had another baby, Lloyd Aubrey Dickason. Lloyd's daughter, Jane Skellam, writes: "My grandfather [by then widowed, Esther having died in 1933] had to go through the same anxiety when World War Two started and Lloyd was called up. Luckily, he survived."

F. J. DICKER

Frederick John Dicker, killed in action 19 August 1917, aged about 37.

Private, London Regiment, 1/4th Bn. (Royal Fusiliers), Service no. 295165. Remembered at Ypres (Menin Gate) Memorial, Belgium.

Frederick John Dicker joined the Army in April 1917 and, after training, was drafted overseas in July. During his brief service on the Western Front he was engaged in heavy fighting at Ypres, where he was killed in action.

The 1911 census shows that Frederick John Dicker, 31, lived in four rooms at 8 Beech Street, Dorset Road with his wife, Susan, 30. He was born in South Lambeth and was working as a general labourer. Susan was from Battersea. They had previously had one child, who had died.

H. J. DIGHTON

Henry or Harry James Dighton, died of wounds on 29 April 1918, aged about 22.

Private, Lincolnshire Regiment, 2/5th Bn., Service no. 8159. Remembered at Arneke British Cemetery, Nord, France.

In 1911 Henry Dighton was 15 and working as a grocer's assistant. He lived with his family in four rooms at 35 Crimsworth Road, off Wandsworth Road. His father, James Dighton, 46, who was born in Pimlico, worked as a caterer's porter. His mother, Clara, 47, was born in Paddington. Dighton had five siblings.

G. DIMOND

George Dimond, died of wounds on 9 November 1914, aged 18.

Private, The Queen's Own Royal West Surrey Regiment, 2nd Bn., Service no. L/6478. Remembered at Poperinghe Old Military Cemetery, Belgium.

On 27 April 1914, a few months before the war started, George Dimond, 18, a sawyer's assistant, joined the Army. He lived for only 194 days after that, dying of wounds to the legs on 9 November at Poperinge.

Dimond was blue-eyed with dark brown hair, stood 5 feet 7½ inches tall and weighed 8¼ stone, with a 35½-inch chest.

In 1911 his mother Clara, then 50, was listed as a boarder at 104 Hartington Road, South Lambeth. She worked as a charwoman (cleaner) and was described as "married but separated." Dimond's father, Charles, 49, was boarding at 27 Dawlish Street (near Wilcox Road). Between them they had five daughters and George.

J. A. DIXON

James Albert Dixon, died on 13 August 1916, aged 27.

Private, East Surrey Regiment, 7th Bn., Service no. 9159. Remembered at Thiepval Memorial, Somme, France.

James Albert Dixon was the son of Mr. and Mrs. Browell of 69 Stewart Road, Battersea. His widow, Isabel Constance Dixon, lived at 17 Camellia Street, South Lambeth.

F. J. DOEL

Frederick or Fredrick John Doel, killed in action on 3 May 1917, aged about 20.

Private, East Surrey Regiment, 8th Bn., Service no. 31188. Remembered at Arras Memorial, Pas de Calais, France and at Waterloo Station War Memorial, London SE1.

In 1911 Frederick John Doel, one of three sons of Ada J. Doel, 33, a washer and ironer, lived in three rooms at 29 Fountain Street, off Wandsworth Road.

H. R. DOOLEY

Henry Richard Dooley, killed in action on 16 September 1916, aged 22.

Private, London Regiment, 1/23rd Bn., Service no. 701393. Remembered at Thiepval Memorial, Somme, France.

Henry Richard Dooley, a plumber's mate, joined the Army at Clapham Junction on 25 May 1915. The Army described him as 20 years old, 6 feet and a half-inch tall, and 11½ stone with a 38½-inch chest. His physical development was judged to be "good." The Army must have been delighted to receive into its ranks such a fit and healthy young man.

The Army was probably was not so pleased when Dooley started to go sick and then to challenge his superior officers' authority. On 26 October, he was shipped to France. On the 5 February 1916 he reported sick with pyrexia (fever) and lumbago (lower back pain). Just two days later he was complaining of an ailment "N.Y.D." (not yet diagnosed), and on 24 February he had myalgia (muscle pain), after which he rejoined his unit on 15 April By 25 June he was accused of using "improper language to an N.C.O."

On 2 August Dooley was again in trouble, this time more seriously. He was tried by a Field General Court Martial on two counts: using insubordinate language to his superior officer and disobeying an order given by his superior officer. He was found guilty and sentenced to a year's hard labour, almost immediately commuted to three months. The Army, after all, needed all available men at the front. On 16 September he was missing, "death being presumed". He had served a total of one year and 115 days.

The 1911 census shows that Henry Dooley was one of two children of Richard Dooley, 64, a pensioner from Ireland, and Mary Dooley, 57, a charwoman (cleaner) also from Ireland. The family lived in three rooms at 153 Larkhall Lane, Stockwell.

A. C. DOPSON

Alfred Colin Dopson, killed in action on 23 September 1917, aged about 20.

Rifleman, Rifle Brigade, 10th Bn., Service no. P/200377. Remembered at Tyne Cot Memorial, Zonnebeke, West-Vlaanderen, Belgium.

Alfred Colin Dopson, aged 15 on the 1911 census, lived with his family at 33 Ely Place, Stockwell. He and his brother Edward, 16, were apprentices in the printing trade. Their father, George Dopson, 47, was a railway porter from Newbury, Berkshire, and their mother, Elizabeth Dopson, 46, was from Shipnal, Shropshire. There were three other children.

R. DOYLE

Robert Doyle, killed in action on 23 October 1916, aged 21.

Private, Lincolnshire Regiment, 2nd Bn., Service no. 8024. Remembered at Bancourt British Cemetery, Pas de Calais, France.

In 1911 Robert Doyle's family lived at 105 Hartington Road, Stockwell. His parents, Lawrence Doyle, 38, a house painter and builder from Pimlico, and Deborah Doyle, 39, born in Lambeth, had five children.

G. D. T. DREWERY

George Daniel Talbot Drewery, killed in action on 12 December 1917, aged 21.

Officer's Steward 2nd Class, Royal Navy, H.M.S. *Partridge*, Service no. L/5032. Remembered at Portsmouth Naval Memorial.

George Daniel Talbot Drewery, the son of George Talbot Drewery and Louisa Emma Drewery, of 25 Lansdowne Road, died on board the *Partridge*, which was sunk in the North Sea by four German destroyers with the loss of 74 men. She had been escorting a convoy.

The 1911 census records George Drewery, then a 15-year-old office boy, living with his aunt and uncle, Mary Ann Elizabeth and Robert White, both 53, and their family at 62 Landor Road, Stockwell.

E. DRISCOLL

Edward Driscoll, killed in action on 21 October 1917, aged 24.

Gunner, Royal Field Artillery, 12th Bty. 35th Bde., Service no. 216940. Remembered at The Huts Cemetery, Ypres, Belgium.

In 1911 Edward Driscoll, 18, was working as an acetylene driller and living with his family in four rooms at 26 Madrid Place, South Lambeth (now disappeared, this road was off Carroun Road). His father, Michael Driscoll, 56, a road sweeper for the borough council, was originally from the City of London; his mother, Ellen, 55, was also born in the City. The couple had three other children.

H. P. DUDLEY

Harold Putnam Dudley, killed in action on 1 July 1916, aged 29.

Rifleman, London Regiment, "C" Coy., 1/5th Bn. (London Rifle Brigade), Service no. 2460. Remembered at Thiepval Memorial, Somme, France.

Harold Dudley was a commercial clerk. In 1911, aged 24 and an only child, he was living at 298 South Lambeth Road with his parents, James Robert, 53, also a commercial clerk, and Charlotte Emily, 50, plus three boarders.

B. A. M. DUNNING

Bernard Allen Miller Dunning, died on 6 December 1918, aged 39.

Driver, Royal Engineers, Army Signal Company, Service no. 558257. Remembered at Baghdad (North Gate) War Cemetery, Iraq.

Devon-born Bernard Allen Miller Dunning of 56 Edithna Street, Stockwell, joined the war effort on 5 December 1914. In civilian life he was a tram conductor for London County Council. He was 5 feet 7 inches tall with a 37-inch chest and his physical development was assessed as "fair."

Dunning served in France between 12 February and 7 November 1916, but was admitted to hospital in England suffering from haemorrhoids. Later he was deployed in the Middle East, where he was admitted to hospital, again with haemorrhoids. Dunning survived military action, but on 10 November, the day before the Armistice, he was admitted to the 31st British Stationary Hospital; by 24 November he was described as danger-ously ill with dysentery. He died on 6 December, leaving a widow, Rosina Harriet, and a 12-year-old son, Herbert William.

E

F. EALES-JOHNSON

Fredrick Eales-Johnson, died on 17 June 1917, aged 22.

Gunner, Royal Field Artillery, "A" Bty. 235th Bde., Service no. 950162. Remembered at Reninghelst New Military Cemetery, Poperinge, Belgium.

Fredrick Eales-Johnson was the son of Fredrick and Mary Eales-Johnson, of 37 Portland Place North, Clapham Road. This street, now gone, has been replaced by the Mursell Estate, although a few houses remain, renamed Portland Grove. Eales-Johnson was born in Lambeth.

H. W. EDNEY

Henry or Harry Wilfred Edney, died on 17 October 1917, aged 21.

Lance Corporal, London Regiment, 5th Bn. (London Rifle Brigade), Service no. 315081; formerly 12th London Regiment. Remembered at Longuenesse (St. Omer) Souvenir Cemetery, Pas de Calais, France and at St. Andrew's Church, Landor Road, Stockwell.

In 1911 Henry Wilfred Edney was working as a messenger and living with his widowed mother, Elizabeth Edney, 47, four siblings and a boarder at 50 Stockwell Green, where the family occupied seven rooms.

J. R. C. EDWARDS

John Reginald Charles Edwards, killed in action on 7 June 1917, aged 21.

Lance Corporal, London Regiment, 1/23rd Bn., Service no. 701405. Remembered at Ypres (Menin Gate) Memorial, Belgium.

The 1911 census shows 15-year-old John Reginald Charles Edwards working as a "page boy in private houses" and living with his family in four rooms at 37a Crimsworth Road, South Lambeth. His father, John Edwards, 48, was from Kington Magna, Dorset and was employed as a coke porter at the gasworks. His mother, Louisa Edwards, 43, was from Dorchester, Dorset. The couple had seven children.

L. ELDRIDGE

Leonard Eldridge, killed in action on 9 October 1916, aged about 19.
Rifleman, London Regiment, 1/5th Bn. (London Rifle Brigade), Service no. 304022. Remembered at Thiepval Memorial, Somme, France.

In 1911, Leonard Eldridge worked as a messenger for the General Post Office. He lived with his parents and five of his eight siblings at 14 Aldebert Terrace, South Lambeth where the family occupied five rooms. Leonard's father Harry Eldridge, 51, was a carman, transporting milk for a dairy. He was originally from New Cross, south-east London. His mother, Martha Eldridge, 50, was from Norfolk.

A. A. ELLIS

Died on 27 July 1917, aged 22.
Driver, Royal Field Artillery, "C" By. 76th Bde., Service no. 201091. Remembered at Mendinghem Military Cemetery, Poperinge, Belgium.

A. A. Ellis was the son of John and Emily Ellis of Clapham. His widow, Annie May Ellis, lived at 25 Haines Street, Battersea. His first and middle names are not recorded in the Commonwealth War Graves Commission database.

C. ELPHICK

Cecil Herbert Elphick
This is a tentative identification. C. Elphick and H. Elphick may have been brothers Cecil Herbert Elphick, 30, a clerk in the Comptroller's Department of London County Council, and Henry James Elphick, 34, a civil servant working for the secretariat of the General Post Office, who are on the 1911 census sharing three rooms at 14 Kellett Road, Brixton.

H. ELPHICK

Henry James Elphick
See C. Elphick

F. T. ELSON

Frederick Thomas Elson, died of wounds on 11 May 1917, aged 32.

Lance Corporal, Royal Fusiliers, 4th Bn., Service no. 62188; formerly 3/1st County of London Yeomanry. Remembered at Etaples Military Cemetery, Pas de Calais, France.

In 1911 railway clerk Frederick Thomas Elson, 25, was living with his widowed mother, Louisa Elson, 56, and five siblings at 74 Victoria Avenue, Plashet Lane, East Ham, in east London, where the family had six rooms. On 21 November 1915 Frederick married Laurel James at St. Michael's Church, Stockwell. Laurel lived at 5 Grove Road, Stockwell.

J. ELY

Jeffrey Ely, killed in action on 25 September 1915, aged about 25.

Private, The Queen's Own Royal West Surrey Regiment, 2nd Bn., Service no. C/276. Remembered at Loos Memorial, Pas de Calais, France.

Jeffrey Ely, a labourer, lived with his parents and siblings at 95 Paradise Road, Stockwell, where the family had four rooms. His parents, Charles Ely, 47, a sewer flusher from Horseheath, Cambridgeshire, and Alice Ely, 50, born in Lambeth, had eight children. On 22 December 1912 Jeffrey Ely married Rose Leeves at St. Anne's and All Saints Church, South Lambeth Road.

L. G. H. ERDBEER

Leonard George Henry Erdbeer, killed in action on 13 April 1918, aged 21.

Private, Grenadier Guards, 4th Bn., Service no. 30085. Remembered at Merville Communal Cemetery Extension, Nord, France.

In 1911 Leonard George Henry Erdbeer, 13 and still at school, lived at 9 Stockwell Grove with his father, Henry Erdbeer, 43, a tinsmith born in Poplar, east London; his mother, Ellen Elizabeth Page Erdbeer, 34, born in Brighton; his maternal grandfather, Charles Morris, 72, a retired tram conductor from Guestling, Sussex; and two younger siblings. The family occupied six rooms. Erdbeer means strawberry in German.

A. T. EVANS
Not identified.

F. EVERSFIELD

Frederick Eversfield, died on June 1918, aged 24.

Able Seaman, Royal Navy, H.M. S/M *D6*, Service no. J/12826. Remembered at Chatham Naval Memorial, Kent and at St. Andrew's Church, Landor Road, Stockwell.

In 1911 Frederick Eversfield, a 16-year-old stores porter, lived at 6 Emily Mansions, Landor Road, Stockwell with his family: his parents Harry Eversfield, 46, a stonemason born in Wrotham, Kent, and Mary Eversfield, 45, from Dover, plus two sisters. After the war, his widow, Kathleen Christina Eversfield, lived at 19 St. James Road, Carshalton, Surrey.

H. J. J. FARRANT

Henry Joseph John Farrant, killed in action on 28 August 1918, aged 18.
Private, London Regiment, 3rd Bn. (Royal Fusiliers), Service no. 254446.
Remembered at Bronfay Farm Military Cemetery, Bray-sur-Somme, Somme, France.

Henry Joseph John Farrant was born in Stoke Newington, north London, and lived in Tottenham, where he attested in November 1917. After his training he was drafted to France, where he took part in the Second Battle of the Somme. On 28 August 1918 Farrant was killed in action at Albert. A connection between Henry Joseph John Farrant and the Stockwell area is yet to become apparent, which means that this identification remains somewhat tentative. However, as there is only one H. J. J. Farrant in the military records, this is likely, if not certain, to be the correct one.

In 1911 Henry J. J. Farrant, one of two children, was 11 and living with his family at 51 Abbotsford Avenue, South Tottenham, where the household occupied eight rooms. His father, Henry John Farrant, 54, a former ironmonger now working as a "commission agent," was born in Limehouse, east London. His mother, Alice Jane Farrant, 52, was born in Kingsland, Hackney, east London.

C. B. FARRELL

Charles Bernard Farrell, died after a fall from his horse on 15 April 1916, aged 26.
Colour Serjeant, South Lancashire Regiment, 2nd Bn., Service no. 8272.
Remembered at Streatham Park Cemetery, Rowan Road, Streatham Vale, south-west London.

Warrington-born Charles Bernard Farrell was a serving soldier when war broke out. He was mobilised and embarked for France in November 1914.

He fought in the first and second Battles of Ypres but broke his thigh in a fall from his horse and was invalided back to England after complications arose. He died at Edmonton Hospital, north London, on 15 April 1916.

The 1911 census shows the Farrell family living at 66 Dalyell Road, Brixton. Charles's father, Michael Farrell, 56, was a former Army musician now living on his pension, born in St. Mary's, Cork, Ireland. His mother Elizabeth, 54, an attendant in an art gallery, was born in Jersey, Channel Islands. Of their seven children, two lived at home.

E. FEDER

Emanuel Feder, killed in action on 1 September 1918, aged about 28.

Private, London Regiment, 7th Bn. (City of London), Service no. 354910; also London Regiment, posted to 1/19th Bn. Remembered at Vis-en-Artois Memorial, Pas de Calais, France.

The 1911 census has a match for a "Manny Feder," born around 1890, and living in three rooms at 58 Wardour Street in the Borough of Westminster with his parents, Wolf Feder, 58, a clothes dealer who had emigrated from Litin, a Jewish shtetl in Russia (the town is now in the Ukraine), and Dina Feder, 44, who had emigrated from the Austro-Hungarian Empire. According to the 1901 census, Wolf and Dina were naturalised British subjects. Manny, 21, and his brother David, 18, were born in the West End of London and worked in the family business.

Soldiers Died in the Great War 1914–1919 gives Emanuel Feder's residence as Brixton. His brother David served as a Driver in the Royal Field Artillery and survived the war.

F. W. G. FELTHAM

William George Frederick Feltham, killed in action on 23 October 1917.

Private, Lancashire Fusiliers, 18th Bn., Service no. 32204; formerly Royal Engineers. Remembered at Tyne Cot Memorial, Heuvelland, West-Vlaanderen, Belgium.

A tentative identification. *Soldiers Died in the Great War 1914–1919* includes a William George Frederick Feltham, who lived in Clapham. His details are given above.

G. E. FENSOME

George Edward Fensome, died on 15 March 1919, aged about 24.

Gunner, Royal Field Artillery. Service no 955621. Remembered at Lambeth Cemetery, Blackshaw Road, Tooting, south-west London.

In 1911 George Fensome, then aged 16, was working as a ticket collector for the City & South London Railway and living with his family at 38 Osborne Terrace, Clapham Road (this street was later merged with Richmond Terrace to become Richborne Terrace). The family occupied three rooms. George's father, Mark Fensome, 52, from Harpenden, Hertfordshire, was a sewer flusher for the borough council. His mother, Caroline, 51, was born in Lambeth. The couple had three children.

V. E. FINCH

Victor Edwin Finch, killed in action on 25 May 1915, aged about 21.

Rifleman, London Regiment, 1/8th Bn. (Post Office Rifles), Service no. 2829. Remembered at Le Touret Memorial, France and at St. Andrew's Church, Landor Road, Stockwell.

In 1911 Victor Edwin Finch, 17, was working as a telegraph messenger for the General Post Office and living with his family in two rooms at 11 Stockwell Green. His father, Frederick James Finch, 46, was a brewer's drayman from Surrey. His stepmother, Elizabeth, 45, was from Headley, Surrey. Finch had four half-siblings.

G. H. A. FISHER

Not identified.

J. M. FRENCH

John Morgan French, died of wounds on 31 August 1916, aged 25.

Gunner, Royal Garrison Artillery, 1/5th Glamorgan Bde., Service no. 668. Remembered at Richmond Cemetery, Grove Road, Richmond, Surrey.

John Morgan French was the son of John W. French, of 282 South Lambeth Road. He was born in Lambeth and enlisted in Cardiff.

F. A. FREWER

Frederick Amos Frewer, killed in action on 30 October 1918, aged 25.

Gunner, Royal Field Artillery, "A" Bty. 290th Bde., Service no. 926373. Remembered at Tournai Communal Cemetery Allied Extension, Hainaut, Belgium.

In 1911 Frederick Amos Frewer, 17, an apprentice letterpress machine minder, lived at 40 Chantry Road, Brixton where his family had six rooms. His father, James Frewer, 49, was also in the book production trade (he was a vellum binder); both he and his wife, Elizabeth, 44, were from Marylebone, central London. Frederick had a younger sister.

F. T. FRISBY

Frank Thomas Frisby, died on 12 October 1917.

Private, Grenadier Guards, 1st Bn., Service no. 26192. Remembered at Tyne Cot Memorial, Heuvelland, West-Vlaanderen, Belgium.

H. FROST

Not identified.

W. A. C. FULLER

William Bert Fuller, died on 9 September 1916, aged 20.

Rifleman, London Regiment, 1/12th Bn. (The Rangers), Service no. 474078; formerly 7th London Regiment. Remembered at Thiepval Memorial, Somme, France.

This is a tentative identification. As a 12-year-old schooboy Kennington-born William Bert (possibly Albert) Fuller and his brother boarded with Edith Ruddick, a widow, at 37 Kay Road, Stockwell. At the time of enlistment Fuller lived on Clapham Road. After the war, William's father lived at 38 Dumbarton Road, Brixton Hill.

G

H. B. GAYTON

Harry Bird Gayton, died on 18 December 1917, aged 24.

Private, The Queen's Own Royal West Kent Regiment, 7th Bn., Service no. 6172. Remembered at the Dozinghem Military Cemetery, Poperinge, West-Vlaanderen, Belgium. Awarded the *Military Medal.*

Harry Bird Gayton, one of five sons of Finetta and Robert Gayton of 51 Clifton Street, Clapham, was born in Battersea in about 1894. He volunteered on 12 April 1915 and was enlisted into the Queen's Own Regiment. He gave his age as 21 years and 194 days and his occupation as "tripe dresser" (on the 1911 census he was described as a shop assistant). Gayton stood 5 feet 5 inches tall, with a 36½-inch chest. He had a small scar on the left side of his forehead and he wore upper dentures.

While with his regiment at Chatham, Kent in July 1915, Gayton was punished for failing to comply with an order with seven days' confinement to barracks. He was posted with the British Expeditionary Force on 1 November 1915 and took part in the Battle of Ypres, where on 28 February 1916 he was wounded – he received a gunshot wound to the right arm. He was not admitted to hospital until 10 March and he was operated on a week later. He remained in hospital for four weeks, after which he rejoined his unit.

Gayton received the Military Medal for actions on 15 September 1917 (it is not clear what these were), and on 15 December he sustained shrapnel wounds to his knee and right leg. He was admitted to 61 Casualty Clearing station but died of his wounds four days later. His effects included letters, cards, photos and religious books, a wallet, a cap badge and his false teeth (listed as "broken").

In May 1918 the Infantry Record Office wrote to Gayton's mother Finetta asking how she would like to receive her son's Military Medal, privately by post or at a presentation. She opted to have it sent and she later acknowledged its receipt: "Sir, received the medal quite safe and thank you very much. I only wish the dear Boy [sic] was here to wear it."

The 1911 census shows Harry's family living at 51 Clifton Street, Clapham, where they occupied four rooms. His father, Robert Gayton, 44, originally from Fenny Stratford, Buckinghamshire, was an engine driver for the London & South Western Railway; Finetta Gayton, 45, was from Marks Tey, Essex.

G. F. GELEIT

George Frederick Geleit, killed in action on 29 May 1917, aged about 33.

Rifleman, Rifle Brigade, 13th Bn., Service no. B/20079. Remembered at Arras Memorial, Pas de Calais, France.

In 1911 George Geleit, who was born in Bermondsey, was 27 and married to Clara, 25, from Walworth. They had two children whom they had named after themselves: George, 2, and Clara, 1, both born in Brixton. The family lived in two rooms at 87 Hackford Road, Stockwell. George described himself as a "housekeeper." George's grandfather, August Geleit, a tailor, emigrated to London from Germany some time before 1871. Geleit means escort or convoy in German.

A. H. GEORGE

Arthur Henry George, killed in action on 1 July 1916, aged 23.

Private, London Regiment, 1/2nd Bn. (Royal Fusiliers), Service no. 230638. Remembered at Gommecourt British Cemetery No. 2, Hebuterne, Pas de Calais, France.

In 1911, then aged 17, Arthur Henry George was working as a messenger in a newspaper office. He lived with his parents and brother at 11 River-hall Street (now disappeared), off Wandworth Road. John Daniel George, 57, was an unemployed general labourer, born in Middlesex; Elizabeth George, 57, was from Billericay, Essex. The couple had five children. Arthur enlisted at Tufton Street, London SW1.

B. J. GEORGE

Benjamin James George, died of wounds as a prisoner of war on
15 July 1916, aged 25.

Private, Middlesex Regiment, 16th Bn., Service no. PS/2124. Remembered at Hamburg Cemetery, Germany.

The file for Benjamin James George notes his status as "Missing" on 1 July 1916, the first day of the Battle of the Somme. His status changed to "Killed in action" two weeks later. However, he was actually a prisoner of war in Germany, captured on 1 July, and he was suffering from gunshot wounds to the left side of the chest as well as from pneumonia. He died in the hospital of a German prisoner of war camp at Minden, a city west of Hanover and over 375 miles from the front.

A document passed to the War Office through the Red Cross gave the date and time of George's death (15 July 1916 at 12.30am) and stated that he was visited by a clergyman and buried in the French Cemetery at Minderheide. In 1923, 55 bodies from this cemetery were moved to Hamburg when it was decided that the graves of Commonwealth servicemen who had died in Germany should be relocated to four permanent cemeteries.

After his death, George's effects were sent to his family: a French dictionary, a torch, a holdall, a notebook and a steel mirror.

George's Service record shows that in October 1915 he was hospitalised for over three weeks with impetigo on the chin. This highly contagious skin disease was common in soldiers, although rarely reported in the field, as soldiers would wait until it became badly infected before seeking help, perhaps to boost their chances of some "Blighty leave". An article in the *British Medical Journal* of 2 February 1918 claimed that of 1,800 military patients in one of the London General Hospitals over 1,400 had impetigo.

The file on George includes these details: he was 5 feet 6 inches, with a 37-inch chest; he weighed just over 9½ stone; there were small moles on the left side of his neck; he had fair hair; he gave his address as 46 Hemberton Street, Stockwell and his occupation as salesman (the 1911 census describes him as a bookshop assistant); he was 25 years and nine months old on enlistment at Lambeth; he was born in Thornton Heath.

The 1911 census shows Benjamin James George, then 21, living with three brothers and sisters at 71 Stanley Street (now Stanley Grove), off Queenstown Road, Battersea. His father, David Gingell George, was a police sergeant. He and his wife Emily lived in Southwick, Sussex.

F. C. GEORGE

Frederick Charles George, died on 31 July 1917, aged 19.

Rifleman, Rifle Brigade, 3rd Bn., Service no. S/31588. Remembered at Ypres (Menin Gate) Memorial, Belgium.

Frederick Charles George, born in South Lambeth, enlisted in Wandsworth in 1917 and in March of that year was sent overseas. He died near Hill 60, a battle site about three miles south-east of Ypres. The hill acquired its name from its height: 60 metres above sea level. Because its slight incline provided a valuable vantage point, it was some of the most fought-over territory of the war. The Battle of Messines, which started in June 1917, took place there.

The 1911 census shows Frederick Charles George, 13, living with his family at 27a Goldsborough Road, Wandsworth. His father, William George, 41, was a railway porter from Old Basing, Hampshire; his mother, Sarah George, 39, was from Battersea. The household included an elder sister and an uncle.

F. W. GIBBINS

Frank William Gibbins, died on 21 March 1918, aged 28.

Rifleman, Rifle Brigade, 7th Bn., Service no. S/32220. Remembered at Pozières Memorial, Somme, France.

In 1911 Frank Gibbins, a 21-year-old railway guard, was living at 161 Hartington Road, South Lambeth with his parents William Gibbins, 57, a railway guard born in Sussex, and Charlotte Gibbins, 47, also born in Sussex, and three siblings.

J. W. GILBERT

James William Gilbert, died on 10 January 1918, age 19.

Stoker 2nd Class, Royal Navy, H.M.S. *Cornwall*. Service no. K/42535. Remembered at Plymouth Naval Memorial.

In 1911 James William Gilbert, then aged 12, lived at 74 Thorparch Road, South Lambeth with his father William, 52, a railway guard originally from Frampton, Dorset and mother, Annie, 48, born in London. They had six children.

W. H. M. GILES

William Henry Murray Giles, died on 9 May 1915.

Private, Royal Fusiliers, 2nd Bn., Service no. G/4952. Remembered at Helles Memorial, Turkey.

William Henry Murray Giles was born in Lambeth and lived in Stockwell. He enlisted in London.

F. GILLARD

Frederick Gillard, died on 24 August 1918, aged 20.

Second Lieutenant, King's Own Yorkshire Light Infantry, 9th Bn. Remembered Vis-en-Artois Memorial, Pas de Calais, France.

In 1911 Frederick Gillard, 12, lived in five rooms at 48 Akerman Road, near Myatts Fields, with his parents Frederick Gillard, 41, a lithographic printer, and Harriet Gillard, 34, both from Blackfriars, three sisters and a boarder.

E. GIRDLESTONE

Ernest Arthur Girdlestone, killed in action on 17 September 1916, aged 38.

Private, Oxford and Bucks Light Infantry, 6th Bn., Service no. 16374. Remembered at London Cemetery and Extension, Longueval, Somme, France and at St. Andrew's Church, Landor Road, Stockwell.

In 1911 Ernest Arthur Girdlestone, 30, was working as a painter's labourer and living with his brother, Percy James Girdlestone, 28, a widowed upholsterer, and Percy's son, William Girdlestone, 6, at 188 Icknield Port Road, Birmingham, where they occupied two rooms. All were born in Brixton. Girdlestone enlisted in Lambeth.

G. H. GLOVER

George Harry Glover, died of wounds on 31 March 1915, aged 20.

Private, Border Regiment, 2nd Bn., Service no. 11773. Remembered at Wimereux Communal Cemetery, Pas de Calais, France.

At 6 feet 2 inches, George Harry Glover was one of the tallest men on the Memorial. He was reasonably well built, too – 10 stone, with a 38-inch chest. Hazel eyes, brown hair and a fresh complexion complete a picture of an attractive, fit and healthy young man. He enlisted, aged 20, on 4 September 1914, a mere month after war was declared.

In civilian life Glover was a furniture salesman and he had spent two and a half years in the National Naval Cadets (Wandsworth Battalion), leaving the service in 1910.

Glover was on the Home Front until 17 February 1915 when he joined the British Expeditionary Force. He sustained a gunshot wound to the shoulder on 15 March and was transferred to a hospital in Boulogne where, a week later, he was deemed to be "improving", but he died on 31 March. He had lasted only 210 days. Glover's effects, sent to his parents, included two leather purses, a keyring and five keys, a chain, a broken watch key, a combination lock, a cigarette case with seven cigarettes, the St. John's Gospel, letters, postcards and photos.

Two weeks after he had died, Glover's mother, Mary Jane, wrote to the Officer in Charge at the Record Office in Preston from her home at 19 Hargwyne Street, Stockwell: "Sir, I beg to ask if you can give me any information as to the whereabouts of Private G. H. Glover, No. 11773, A Company, 2nd Batt. Border Regt, with the Expeditionary Force…"

She wrote again a week later, having since heard of his death: "I beg most respectfully to ask as I am his mother would you kindly say when I can have any further news regarding his death." The Army directed her to write to the Officer in Charge at the hospital where her son died. His replies, if any, are not in the file.

P. W. GOFF

Jesse William Goff (right), killed in action on 1 July 1916, aged 19.

Rifleman, London Regiment, 1/5th Bn. (London Rifle Brigade), Service no. 300319. Remembered at Thiepval Memorial, Somme, France.

Jesse William Goff is consistently misnamed as P.W. (Percy William) Goff – in his Army records, on his medals cards, in the Commonwealth War Graves Commission database, on the Thiepval Memorial, and at Stockwell. Why this should be is still a mystery to his family. They have his medals and plaque, which give his Army number, so there is no question that this is the correct man.

Two letters Jesse wrote to his maternal Aunt "Op" (Annie Margaret Carroll), who lived in Weald Village, Middlesex, provide a vivid portrait of the hard work required of soldiers at the front and point up their dry good humour. In the first, dated 28 May 1916, Jesse mentions the fact that Op's husband Jim may be called up. By January 1916 conscription was in place. Initially it applied to unmarried men between 18 and 41 or widowers without children, but from 25 May 1916 married men were included.

> ... Well I am out here again & very near where I was before. In fact we pass some of our old billets daily. It is rather warmer than before in more ways than one. Nevertheless by dint of hard work & fresh air we manage to keep ourselves alive & fit. Mind you it's not all cakes & ale but our various little "grouses" would fill a book. We go out & work every day with picks & shovels just like navvies (the only difference is that the latter get about three times the pay). Sometimes we get a little shelling or "strafing", sometimes not, usually the former but we have managed without any casualties so far. Our week usually consists of seven days (working) & after a lengthy discussion today we have come to the conclusion that the man who could put forward an invention that would get another 24 hrs out of a week, would make his fortune. I have heard

from Ma about Uncle Jim & the "garrison duty abroad" business. Really I should not think that he would be called up at all. I'm sure I don't know how our "boss" [possibly a reference to Jesse's mother] will get on if the age limit extends much more... Let's hope it will be all over soon.

The second letter was written on 23 June, a week before he was killed, along with nearly 20,000 others, on the first day of the Battle of the Somme.

Thanks very much for your letter and parcel. Many of us enjoyed the contents. As a matter of fact it arrived at a most opportune moment – we were in the trenches. That is the reason I was unable to write there and then, but I hope you received the official p.c [postcard]. We had a rather rough time up there but are now resting... Really there is next door to no news. One cannot say everything & – well all that remains is I am quite well and the weather has not been at all good. We see rather more life & more grub now since we have left the "navvies". I don't think anyone was very sorry to leave. By the way I'm afraid I'm putting the cart before the horse. I don't think I told you that we moved and are now with our regiment. Now I'm afraid that is all.

In 1911 the Goff family lived at 63 Chelsham Road, Clapham, where they had seven rooms. Jesse William Goff, then 13 and an only child, lived with his father, William Percy, 43, a Prudential assurance agent from Poole, Dorset, and mother, Grace Mary (née Williams), 38, an assistant mistress at London County Council school.

A. L. GOODING

Alfred Laurence Gooding, killed in action on 7 June 1917.

Rifleman, Royal Irish Rifles, Service no. 42122; formerly King's Royal Rifle Corps.

Alfred Laurence Gooding was born in Lambeth and enlisted in Battersea.

W. J. GOODING

Walter Joseph Gooding, killed in action on 25 February 1917, aged 19.

Private, Welsh Regiment, 19th (Pioneer) Bn., Service no. 31983.
Remembered at Bard Cottage Cemetery, Ypres, Belgium.

Walter Joseph Gooding left a brother, Harry I. Gooding, who lived at Clevedon, Papworth Everard, Cambridge.

H. GRAINGER

Not identified.

J. A. GRAINGER

Not identified.

H. GRANGER

Horace Granger, died on 10 October 1918, aged 30.

Private, London Regiment, 2/22nd Bn. (The Queen's), Service no. 684457; formerly 23rd London Regiment. Remembered at Kantara War Memorial Cemetery, Egypt.

Horace Granger was born in South Lambeth and enlisted at St. John's Hill, Clapham Junction. The 1911 census shows him living with his parents and a sister in six rooms at 20 Rutland Street, South Lambeth. His father, John Granger, 71, was a house decorator from Broadhembury, Devon and his mother, Ann Granger, 66, was from Tunbridge Wells, Kent.

F. J. GRANT

Not identified.

P. T. W. GRANT

Philip Thomas Wilson Grant, killed in action on 15 October 1915, aged 18.

Second Lieutenant, Wiltshire Regiment, 8th Bn., attached 5th Bn. Remembered at Green Hill Cemetery, Turkey.

In 1911 the Grant family lived in 10 rooms at 52 Stockwell Park Road. Philip Thomas Wilson Grant attended St. Olave's Grammar School in Queen Elizabeth Street, Southwark between May 1908 and December 1912 (the school has since moved).

Grant's 41-year-old father, also called Philip Grant, was a butcher originally from Withington, Lancashire; his mother, Isabel, 35, was from Irvinestown, County Fermanagh, Northern Ireland. There was a younger sister, a boarder, and a live-in servant.

F. W. GRAY

Frederick Walter Gray, died on 12 April 1917, aged 34.

Private, Essex Regiment, 2nd Bn., Service no. 35426. Remembered at Athies Communal Cemetery Extension, Pas de Calais, France.

Frederick Walter Gray was born in Lambeth and enlisted in Clapham. His widow, Alice Gertrude Gray, lived at 43 Marylebone High Street, London.

T. W. GRAY

Not identified.

E. J. B. GREEN

Not identified.

G. C. GRIFFITHS

Not identified.

S. W. GRIFFITHS

Sidney Wallace Griffiths, killed in action on 2 July 1918, aged 19.

Private, The Buffs (East Kent Regiment), 6th Bn., Service no. 25351. Remembered at Bouzincourt Ridge Cemetery, Albert, France.

Sidney Wallace Griffiths was born in Lambeth in about 1899, one of six children. In 1911 he lived at 8 Aldebert Terrace, South Lambeth with his father William Griffiths, 53, a blacksmith working for the railway, originally from Morriston, Glamorganshire, and mother Carrie, 46, from Oldswinford, Worcestershire.

A. C. GROUT

Alfred Grout, killed in action on 25 September 1915, aged 20.

Private, Royal Berkshire Regiment, 8th Bn., Service no. 13775.
Remembered at Dud Corner Cemetery, Loos, France and at St. Andrew's
Church, Landor Road, Stockwell.

Alfred Grout was born in Lambeth and lived in Stockwell. In 1901, aged 6,
he and his three siblings lived with their 31-year-old widowed mother at
30 White Hart Street, Kennington. The census names his mother merely as
"C. Grout" and does not state where she was born.

A. B. GUDE

Alfred Bernard Gude, died on 16 June 1915, aged about 19.

Private, London Regiment, 24th Bn. (The Queen's), Service no. 1556.
Remembered at Wandsworth (Streatham) Cemetery, Garratt Lane,
Tooting, south-west London and at Waterloo Station War Memorial,
London SE1.

Alfred Bernard Gude was born in Clapham and enlisted in Kennington. In
1911 the Gude family lived at 26 Willington Road, Stockwell, where they
occupied four rooms. Alfred Bernard Gude, an only child, was a messenger
lad for the London & South Western Railway. His father, Thomas George
Gude, 39, born in Battersea, was an engine driver for the L&SWR. His
mother, Alice Milly, 47, was born in Clapham.

C. P. GUY

Charles Philip Guy, died of wounds on 26 November 1914, aged 31.

Private, The Queen's (Royal West Surrey Regiment), 1st Bn., Service no.
7658. Remembered at Zantvoorde British Cemetery, near Ypres, Belgium.

Charles Philip Guy was born in Gloucester and lived in Clapham. After the
war, his wife, Margaret Hannah Guy, lived at 30 Portland Place South (this
street has now gone and the remnant has been renamed Portland Grove),
near Clapham Road.

H

C. W. HALL

Charles William Hall, killed in action on 14 April 1918, aged about 25.

Private, Royal Sussex Regiment, 11th Bn; also Machine Gun Corps, attached 39th, Service no. G/10772. Remembered at St. Venant-Robescq Road British Cemetery, Robecque, Pas de Calais, France.

In 1911 Charles William Hall, then 18, lived with his widowed mother, Mary Chamberlain Hall, 59, at 13 Priory Road, South Lambeth, where they occupied three rooms. Mary was from Chatteris, Cambridgeshire. Charles, an only child, was born in Lambeth. He worked as a clerk for a bottled beer manufacturer.

W. A. HALL

William A. Hall, killed in action on 9 October 1916, aged 21.

Rifleman, London Regiment, 1/5th Bn. (London Rifle Brigade), Service no. 302230. Remembered at Thiepval Memorial, Somme, France.

In 1911 William A. Hall was a 15-year-old office boy. He lived with his family at 19 Cavendish Grove (now disappeared, this street ran between Hartington Road and Wandsworth Road), where they occupied six rooms. His father, Henry Charles Hall, 44, who was born in Lambeth, worked in the building trade as a painter. His mother, Priscilla Amelia Hall, 46, was born in Pimlico. William was one of nine children.

H. F. HANDEL

Harry Frank Handel, died of illness on 9 March 1915, aged 34.

Gunner, Royal Field Artillery, 20th Reserve Bty., Service no. 16005. Remembered at Lambeth Cemetery, Blackshaw Road, Tooting, south-west London. Stepfather of *George Frederick Billingsley* and *Sydney Walter Billingsley.*

Harry Frank Handel died at his home at 2 Arlington Mansions, 18a Morat Street, Stockwell on 9 March 1915 from pneumonia, disease of the heart valves and heart failure. *Soldiers Died in the Great War 1914–1919* states that he was born in Kennington and enlisted in Holborn.

The 1911 census shows that Handel, then 29, had been married to Ada Harriet Billingsley, 42, for a year. He was then an Army pensioner, having previously served in the Boer War, and was now working as a cook. The family lived in three rooms at 101 Cornwallis Road, Upper Holloway, north London. Harry and Ada had a son, Robert Harry, 11 months (they went on to have a daughter, Ida Helen, in 1915).

The household included Harry's stepsons Sydney Billingsley and George Billingsley, and a stepdaughter, Winifred Kate Billingsley, 9. Harry was the son of Harry Robert Handel, a pipe importer born in Lambeth.

G. HANSFORD

George Hansford, died of wounds on 28 April 1915, aged 25.

Rifleman, London Regiment, 12th Bn. (The Rangers), Service no. 2917. Remembered at St. Sever Cemetery, Rouen, Seine-Maritime, France.

In 1911 George Hansford, 22, was a bell wireman, living at 6 Stamford Buildings, near Meadow Place, South Lambeth with his widowed father Harry Hansford, 51, a brass finisher born in Westminster, and four of his eight siblings. The family occupied three rooms.

W. J. HARMAN

William Joseph Harman, died on 5 December 1917.

Lance Corporal, King's Royal Rifle Corps, 7th Bn., Service no. R/7894. Remembered at Wandsworth (Streatham) Cemetery, Garratt Lane, Tooting, south-west London.

A. P. HAROLD

Arthur Pearce Harold, killed in action on 9 December 1917, aged about 34.

Private, Norfolk Regiment, 12th Bn. (Norfolk Yeomanry), Service no. 320761. Remembered at Jerusalem War Cemetery, Israel and at St. Andrew's Church, Landor Road, Stockwell.

In 1911 Arthur Pearce Harold worked as a newspaper clerk. He lived in three rooms at 13 Prideaux Road, Stockwell with his parents, Edward Charles Harold, 64, a chemist's assistant from Tunbridge Wells, Kent, and Elizabeth Ann Harold, 62, a music teacher from Maidstone, and a sister.

C. M. HARRADINE

Charles Morley Harradine, died of wounds on 19 July 1918, aged about 19.

Rifleman, King's Royal Rifle Corps, 12th Bn., Service no. 47322. Remembered at Ligby-St. Flochel British Cemetery, Averdoingt, Pas de Calais, France.

In 1911 Charles Harradine was 11 and living with his father, Sidney Harradine, 36, an undertaker's coachman originally from Hensworth, Hertfordshire, mother Mary Harradine, 46, from Tottenham, and a younger sister at 12 Gaskell Street, off Larkhall Rise, Clapham, where they had four rooms.

A. J. HARRIS

Alfred James Harris, killed in action on 17 October 1918, aged 19.

Private, Royal Sussex Regiment, 2nd Bn., Service no. G/18601. Remembered at Vadencourt British Cemetery, Maissemy, Aisne, France.

In 1911 Alfred James Harris was a 12-year-old schoolboy living with his parents and five of his seven siblings at 14 Larkhall Lane, Stockwell, where they occupied seven rooms. His father Frederick James Harris, 51, a brewery stoker and Eliza Mary Harris, 56, did not give birthplaces on the census return. Alfred enlisted in Camberwell.

F. C. HART

Frederick Charles Hart, killed in action on 26 May 1915.

Corporal, London Regiment, 1/23rd Bn., Service no. 54. Remembered at Le Touret Memorial, Pas de Calais, France.

Hart was born in Clapham and enlisted at Clapham Junction.

E. F. HASKELL

Ernest Fowler Haskell, killed in action on 21 March 1918.

Private, Lincolnshire Regiment, 2/5th Bn., Service no. 242087. Remembered at Arras Memorial, Pas de Calais, France.

Ernest Fowler Haskell was born in Lambeth, where he enlisted.

G. J. HATCH

George John Hatch, killed in action on 6 April 1917, aged 20.

Lieutenant, Royal Flying Corps and London Regiment, 17th Bn. (Poplar and Stepney). Remembered at Cabaret-Rouge British Cemetery, Souchez, Pas de Calais, France.

George John Hatch appears on the 1911 census as a 14-year-old schoolboy living with his family at 9 St. John's Road (now St. John's Crescent), Brixton, where they had 11 rooms. George's father, John Cosens Hatch, 48, originally from Stonehouse, Devon, was the manager of a vinegar brewery. His wife Maria Hatch, 49, was from Southwark. They had four children, of whom George was the youngest. A cousin, 33-year-old George Foster, born in Peckham, also lived in the house, as did Violet Winter, a 21-year-old live-in servant from Chelmsford, Essex.

F. C. HAYDEN

Frederick Charles Hayden, died on 22 August 1918, aged 36.

Private, London Regiment, 24th Bn. (The Queen's), Service no. 724529. Remembered at Bray Vale British Cemetery, Bray-sur-Somme, France.

Frederick Charles Hayden, a 35-year-old married travelling salesman living at 2 Stanley Villas, Studley Road, Stockwell, attested on 8 December

1915 and joined the Army Reserve. He was mobilised on 28 August 1916 and posted to France the next day, leaving behind his wife, Emily, 41, and their daughter Ethel, 9. It is unclear from the records whether 14 days' leave, granted on 31 July 1918, enabled him to return to London to see his family or were spent near the front. In any case, he died (whether in action or of wounds – the records state both) shortly afterwards, on 22 August. Few details of his military life are available, but the medical examination on mobilisation records him as 5 feet 5 inches tall, with a 36½ inch chest. He had both upper and lower dentures. His effects consisted only of two military discs.

The 1911 census shows a 29-year-old Frederick, who was born in Thaxted, Essex, working as a warehouseman and living with Emily, their daughter, in-laws and a boarder at 2 Stanley Villas, Studley Road Stockwell.

H. G. HAYES

Henry George Hayes, killed in action on 23 September 1915, aged 21.
Private, Durham Light Infantry, 10th Bn., Service no. 3/26023; formerly 14284, Dragoon Guards. Remembered at Poperinghe New Military Cemetery, Belgium.

Henry George Hayes was a brass finisher's apprentice. In 1911 he lived in three rooms at 27 Wilkie Buildings, Westminster with his parents and four siblings. His father, Charles Edward, 42, born in Westminster, was a cutter in the cap trade. His mother, Florence Eleanor, 39, was from Hackney.

R. C. HAYES

Robert Charles Hayes, killed in action on 30 July 1916, aged 24.
Lance Corporal, Middlesex Regiment, 20th Bn., Service no. G/14909. Remembered at Arras Memorial, Pas de Calais, France.

The 1911 census shows Robert Charles Hayes, then aged 18, working as a clerk in a type foundry. He lived with his parents and younger brother in three rooms at 33 Hargwyne Street, Stockwell. His 41-year-old father, also called Robert Charles, a timekeeper for the London County Council sewerage department, was from Portsmouth, Hampshire. His mother, Emily Kate, 39, was from Wandsworth.

W. A. HAYNES

William Alfred Haynes, killed in action on 30 October 1917.

Lance Corporal, Bedfordshire Regiment, 4th Bn., Service no. 12374. Remembered at Tyne Cot Memorial, Zonnebeke, West-Vlaanderen, Belgium.

A tentative identification. The man whose details appear here was born in and lived in Lambeth, and also enlisted there. I have not been able to find a specific association with Stockwell.

H. T. HEAD

Not identified.

R. C. HEATH

Robert Charles Heath, killed in action on 4 November 1918.

Private, Hertfordshire Regiment, 1/1st Bn., Service no. 42295; formerly South Staffordshire Regiment. Remembered at Ghissignies British Cemetery, Nord, France.

Robert Charles Heath was born in Farnborough, Hampshire and lived in Stockwell. He enlisted in Camberwell.

W. A. HENDERSON

Not identified.

A. HERRIOTT

Andrew Herriott, killed in action on 24 August 1918, aged 21.

Lance Corporal, London Regiment, 12th Bn. (The Rangers), Service no. 470471. Remembered at Bray Hill British Cemetery, Bray-sur-Somme, France and at St. Andrew's Church, Landor Road, Stockwell. Brother of *Archibald Herriott* and *John Herriott*.

In 1911 the Herriott family, three of whose sons are on the Memorial, lived at 27 Gateley Road, Brixton, where they occupied seven rooms. John Herriott, 51, was an electrical engineer from Berwick-upon-Tweed and his wife, Mary, 51, was from Edinburgh. They had eight children, of whom six lived at home, including Archibald, 18, an electrician, and John, 16, a bookseller's assistant, and Andrew, 14, still at school.

A. HERRIOTT

Archibald Herriott, killed in action 26 May 1915, aged 22.

Private, London Regiment, 1/24th Bn. (The Queen's), Service no. 2816. Remembered at Le Touret, Pas de Calais, France and at St. Andrew's Church, Landor Road, Stockwell. Brother of *Andrew Herriott* and *John Herriott.*

J. HERRIOTT

John Herriott, died on 17 February 1919, aged 26.

Lieutenant, Machine Gun Corps, 41st Coy. Remembered at Etaples Military Cemetery, Pas de Calais, France. Brother of *Andrew Herriott* and *Archibald Herriott.* Awarded the *Military Cross.*

John Herriott was awarded the Military Cross for "conspicuous gallantry and good work". The citation reads as follows:

> During a counter-attack on September 29th, 1918, near Menin, the infantry with whom he was co-operating withdrew to a line 400 yards behind him. He covered their withdrawal; then, seeing that he could inflict casualties from where he was, he decided to remain in position. For two hours he was well in front of the infantry and engaged the enemy on two sides. From his position, to which he brought a second gun for the purpose, he was able to cover the infantry advance when the situation was restored.

D. J. T. HIBBERT

David James Thomas Hibbert, killed in action on 3 May 1918, aged 24.

Lance Corporal, Royal Welsh Fusiliers, 1st Bn., Service no. 57427. Remembered at Giavera Memorial, near Montebelluna, Italy.

The 1911 census shows David James Thomas Hibbert, then 16 and the eldest of three sons, working as an errand boy and living with his parents and siblings in two rooms at 126 Dorset Road, Stockwell. His father, David Charles James Hibbert, 45, was a gas fitter, born in Walworth. His mother, Susannah Maria, 41, was born in Southwark. Hibbert enlisted in Hounslow, west London.

W. H. HIGGINS

William Henry Higgins, died on 26 October 1918, aged 22.

Private, London Regiment, 1/25th Bn. (Cyclists), Service no. 741277. Remembered at Kirkee 1914–1918 Memorial, near Poona, India.

William Henry Higgins was the son of Henry and Florence Higgins of 40 Jeffreys Road, Clapham. He lived in Clapham and enlisted in Fulham.

C. R. G. HILL

Charles Richard George Hill, died of wounds on 20 March 1918, aged 37.

Private, London Regiment, 1/13th Bn. (Kensington), Service no. 495791; also Machine Gun Corps, attd. 56th Coy. Remembered at Etaples Military Cemetery, Pas de Calais, France.

Charles Richard George Hill was a compositor (typesetter), born in Camberwell. His wife, Ethel May Hill, 34, was from Brentford, Middlesex. In 1911 the couple lived in five rooms at 17 Clitheroe Road, Stockwell. They had no children. Charles enlisted in Camberwell.

H. J. HILL

Harold Joseph Hill, died from gangrene on 17 May 1917, aged 21.

Lance Corporal, Machine Gun Corps, 53rd Coy., Service no. 43809. Remembered at Mont Huon Military Cemetery, Le Tréport, France.

In the mid-1990s, while rummaging in the 50p box of an Oxfam shop, Peter Munt-Davies found a copy of *The British Army from Within* by E. Charles Vivian, published around 1914. He bought it for the inscription alone.

Written inside the front cover were the letters "H. H". Below, in a different handwriting, was "Harry got his wishes. Harry got one stripe. He got to fire the machine guns." Below that, in the same handwriting was "Harry got his name on the memorial in Stockwell."

Peter felt compelled to find out more.

At that time, the vast resources of the internet were not available, so he went to Stockwell and made a list of all the names that matched the initials "H. H." Then he spent a day in the reading room of the Imperial War Museum not far away in North Lambeth, and after a few hours found his man and solved the riddle.

"He had one stripe so was a Lance Corporal," says Peter. "He fired a machine gun so he had to be in the M.G.C. – the Machine Gun Corps. His name was Harry. Lance Corporal Harold Joseph Hill, born 17 May 1896, died of wounds on 17 May 1917. He is buried in Mont Huon Military Cemetery in Le Tréport, France. I found a reference giving the name of the base hospital where he died, near Le Tréport, and learnt that his mother was present at his death from gangrene. I was in Normandy a few years ago and I went to pay my respects. The hospital was easy to find. It was the one they built of wood and canvas near Le Tréport. At the end of the war they took it down and all they left behind were the graves. When I visited, the cemetery was in a thousand-acre cabbage field miles from anywhere.

"The book had been smoke damaged and then water damaged, so I suspect it had been in a house fire. Harry Hill lived in 32 Herbert Road, Stockwell, which I think was damaged during the Blitz so maybe that was the cause." Herbert Road, now gone, ran almost parallel with Sidney Road, between Stockwell Road and Aytoun Road.

Harry's Service records survived in the National Archives. These records tell us more about Harry the person.

Harold Joseph Hill worked for the Admiralty as a clerk. On 13 November 1915, the day he volunteered at Tufton Street, Westminster, J. S. Barnes, Head of War Registry, wrote a note: "Mr. H. J. Hill has received permission to leave the Admiralty in order to enlist in the army." Later, on 9 December 1915, the Admiralty made a request which sets out all the possibilities for their former clerk: "43809 H. J. Hill. Please notify Admiralty in event of this man's discharge, death etc, or of his being granted a commission or being reported missing or a prisoner of war."

This duly happened, with a note coming back to the Admiralty on 6 June 1917 informing them that Hill had died of wounds on the 17 May 1917.

Harry Hill, 5 feet 5 inches tall and weighing 8½ stone with a chest measurement of 35 inches, was wounded in action on 6 May and admitted to hospital with gunshot wounds to the abdomen, forearm and back the following day. He died of gangrene 10 days later.

In 1911 he was living with his parents and sister at 153 Trentham Street, Southfields, south-west London where they occupied five rooms. His father, Joseph Snare Hill, 57, was an ornamental plasterer originally from Westminster, and his mother, Emma Elizabeth Hill, 55, was from Hanwell, Middlesex. Harry had a sister, Henrietta Emma Hill, 18, a compiling clerk, and three half-siblings.

W. J. HILL

Not identified.

C. F. P. HILLIER

Charles F. P. Hillier, killed in action on 27 October 1914, aged 35.

Private, Royal Fusiliers, 4th Bn., Service no. L/7574. Remembered at Le Touret Memorial, Pas de Calais, France.

Charles Hiller, who had previously served in the Boer War, was born in Cork, Ireland in about 1879. His family moved to London and by 1911 was living in three rooms at 9 Hemans Street, off Wandsworth Road. Charles's widowed mother, Ellen Hillier, 62, had seven children, three of whom lived with her.

A. E. HILLS

Not identified.

J. T. HILLS

John Thomas Hills, died of wounds on 30 November 1917, aged 38.

Rifleman, London Regiment, 1/17th Bn. (Poplar and Stepney), Service no. 74105. Remembered at Orival Wood Cemetery, Flesquières, France and at St. Andrew's Church, Landor Road, Stockwell.

John Thomas Hills was a dustman, originally from Chelsfield, Kent. In 1911, aged 31, he lived with his wife Emma, who was from Crockenhill, Kent, in three rooms at 31 Hargwyne Street, Stockwell. They had one child, Dorothy, aged 6.

Hills joined up in 1916, and later that year embarked for France. While on the Western Front he fought in the Battle of the Somme and in an engagement at St. Eloi. He died in fighting at Arras in November 1917.

A. C. HILLYER

Albert Charles Hillyer, killed in action on 6 August 1917.

Rifleman, Royal Irish Rifles, 15th Bn., Service no. 44401; formerly London Regiment. Remembered at Wieltje Farm Cemetery, near Ypres, Belgium.

A tentative identification as a connection between the man whose details are given above and Stockwell is yet to become apparent.

F. HILTON

Frederick Hilton, died on 10 September 1918, aged 21.

Rifleman, Rifle Brigade, 1st Bn., Service no. 5723. Remembered at Abbeville Communal Cemetery Extension, France. Brother of *William Hilton.*

William and Frederick Hilton were sons of Sarah Annie Hilton of 1 Trigon Road, Oval.

W. G. HILTON

William George Hilton, died of wounds on 5 October 1915, aged 21.

Private, East Surrey Regiment, 7th Bn., Service no. 688. Remembered at Chocques Military Cemetery, Pas de Calais, France. Brother of *Frederick Hilton.*

A. HINE

Alfred Hine, died of wounds on 7 September 1917, aged 22.

Driver, Royal Field Artillery, "A" Bty., 28th Bde., Service no 925397. Remembered at Nunhead (All Saints) Cemetery, Linden Grove, south-east London. Possibly the brother of *William Frederick Hine.*

Alfred Hine, born in Bethnal Green, east London in 1895, was one of six children of licensed victuallers Thomas George and Frances Hine, of 24 Union Street, Clapham. In 1911 the family lived in nine rooms at 36 Grove Road, Upper Holloway, north London but in 1901 had lived in Wilcox Road, South Lambeth.

W. F. HINE

William Frederick Hine

Private, London Regiment, 24th Bn., Service no. 5696. Possibly the brother of *Alfred Hine.*

This is a tentative identification, as no W. F. Hine with links to Stockwell or south London exists in either the Commonwealth War Graves Commission database or in *Soldiers Died in the Great War 1914–1919*

W. F. Hine may have been the brother of Alfred Hine. There is a Pension record in the National Archives for a William Hine of 4 Park Place, Hercules Road, Lambeth, a "liftman" who was aged 22 and 10 months in

1916. He was 5 feet 6½ inches tall, with a 40-inch chest and had a tattoo of a "ballet girl" on his right forearm.

Hine's next of kin was his sister Mrs. Reading of 23 Fairford Grove, Lower Kennington. One wonders, if the identification is correct, why he did not give his parents, Thomas and Frances Hine at Union Road, as next of kin.

Hine was at home until 2 August 1916 when he was sent with the British Expeditionary Force to France. There, on 18 September 1916, he shot in the right hand. This proved to be a "Blighty wound" – that is, it necessitated immediate repatriation. He was invalided out of the Army, awarded a weekly pension of 22s. and exempted from further medical examination.

It has not been possible to ascertain when or how this William Hine died. However, the civil records show that a man named William Hine died in Fulham, west London in 1920, aged approximately 25.

A. HOARE

Ernest Austin Hoare, killed in action on 21 December 1915, aged 18.

Corporal, Royal Engineers, 186th Special Coy., Service no. 106556.
Remembered at Cambrin Churchyard Extension, Pas de Calais, France.

At the time he signed up on 7 August 1915, Ernest Austin Hoare declared that he was 20 years old, born in Sidcup, Kent and living with his family at 12 Lansdowne Road, Stockwell. He described himself as a chemist. He appears to have lied about his age, as records show that he was born in the latter half of 1897 and was therefore only 18.

Hoare attended St. Olave's School (then located near London Bridge) between 1909 and 1912. After six months at the Albany Engineering Works, he became assistant to Dr. Fyleman, an analytical chemist, of Victoria Street. He was so interested in this work that in September 1913 he decided to take his studies further and joined The Borough Polytechnic Institute. When war broke out, Dr. Fyleman became works chemist at Osram's lamp factory in Wembley, north London and Hoare went with him. In July 1915 he was granted a scholarship at the Imperial College of Science and after gaining a promise that his place would be held over for him on his return, joined the Royal Engineers.

The Service history file for Ernest Hoare includes an interesting document outlining the Army's appeal for chemists: Men between 19 and 45 with training in chemistry were especially sought for service with the Royal Engineers. The physical standards for height and chest measurement were ignored if candidates were otherwise fit, and spectacles were permitted. Successful candidates would immediately be promoted to Corporal. Pay would be 2*s*. 6*d*. per week. Those interested were instructed to go to the recruiting office in Great Scotland Yard.

After a month as a "Pioneer", Hoare was promoted to Corporal. He embarked for France with the British Expeditionary Force on 16 August. After taking part in two major gas attacks in September and October, he was killed at Chambrin on 21 December when he was hit by a trench mortar. The next day he was buried by his colleagues 800 yards from the front line.

The Service record shows that Hoare was just over 6 feet tall, with a 39½ inch chest. He weighed 9¾ stone.

In 1911 Ernest Hoare's family lived at 228 South Lambeth Road. His father, John Hoare, 45, a police constable from Chatham, Kent, and mother, Martha Hoare, 45, from Troston, Norfolk, had five other children. The Hoares later moved to 12 Lansdowne Road, Stockwell.

J. E. HOBBS

Joseph Edward Hobbs, died on 19 September 1917, aged 20.

Gunner, Royal Field Artillery, Reinf. Base Depot., Service no. 970079. Remembered at Salonika (Lembet Road) Military Cemetery, Greece.

In 1911 Joseph Edward Hobbs, listed in the census as Edward Hobbs, was 13 and still at school. He lived with his father, also called Joseph Edward Hobbs, 39, a fitter's mate for an electrical light company, mother Edith Hobbs, 35, and two brothers in three rooms at 62 Hargwyne Street, Stockwell.

B. C. HOFT

Bertie Hoft, died of wounds on 7 May 1916, aged about 19.
Private, Argyll and Sutherland Highlanders, 10th Bn., Service no. 10050.
Remembered at Bailleul Communal Cemetery Extension, Nord, France.

In 1911 Bertie C. Hoft was a 13-year-old schoolboy and part-time newsboy; his brother Hermann L. Hoft, who also fought in the war but survived, was a van guard in a mineral water factory. They were sons of German-born Hermann Hoft, 47, a syrup maker for a mineral water factory (there were several such factories in Vauxhall at this time), and his wife Christiana, 48, who was born in London. The family lived at 27 Brooklands Road, Stockwell. There were four other children.

A. E. HOGG

Alfred Edward Hogg, killed in action on 5 November 1917, aged 29.
Private, Seaforth Highlanders, 1st Bn., Service no. S/12345. Remembered at Basra Memorial, Iraq.

The 1911 census return for Alfred Edward Hogg's family home does not include him. His father Edward Hogg, 55, a mercantile clerk born in Bermondsey, and his wife Jessie Mary, 48, born in Blackfriars, lived with their eight other children in 10 rooms at 56 Sidney Road, Stockwell.

It is possible that Alfred Hogg was working as a footman for Lord Edmund Talbot, M.P., at his home at 1 Buckingham Palace Gardens, London, where the family of four employed nine servants to maintain their 20-roomed house, as there is a man of this name, aged 22 and born in Southwark, on the census return for that address.

A. H. HOLMAN

Alfred Harold Holman, died of wounds on 11 May 1916, aged about 23.
Gunner, Royal Field Artillery, 182nd Bde., Service no. 34678. Remembered at Dud Corner Cemetery, Loos, France. Brother of *John Orlando Holman.*

In 1911 Alfred Harold Holman, an 18-year-old warehouse porter, and his brother John Orlando Holman, 15, a junior clerk, lived in four rooms at 45 Riverhall Street (now disappeared, this street was parallel with Camellia Street), South Lambeth with their mother Sarah Jane McQuillin, 49, her husband Stephen McQuillin, 49, and three of their five brothers. Sarah Jane was a domestic servant from Yeovil, Somerset. Stephen was a fitter's labourer, born in Walworth. Alfred Holman enlisted in Chelsea.

J. O. HOLMAN

John Orlando Holman, killed in action on 3 June 1917, aged about 21.
Rifleman, King's Royal Rifle Corps, 17th Bn., Service no. R/35467.
Remembered at Vlamertinghe Military Cemetery, Ypres, Belgium. Brother of *Alfred Harold Holman.*

A. E. HOMEWOOD

Arthur Ernest Homewood, killed in action on 4 November 1918, aged 20.
Private, Northamptonshire Regiment, "B" Coy. 6th Bn., Service no. 59585.
Remembered at Preux-au-Bois Communal Cemetery, Nord, France.

In 1911 Arthur Ernest Homewood, 13, who was at school and worked part-time as a grocer's errand boy, lived with his two brothers and widowed mother at 18 Radnor Terrace (now disappeared, it was near Wilcox Road), South Lambeth, where the family occupied four rooms. Eliza Ann Homewood, 53, born in Bermondsey, earned her living as a charwoman (cleaner) in private houses.

J. F. HONER

Joseph Frederick Honer, killed in action on 1 July 1916, aged about 18.
Rifleman, London Regiment, 12th Bn. (The Rangers), Service no. 471573.
Remembered at Gommecourt British Cemetery No. 2, Hebuterne,
Pas de Calais, France.

Joseph Frederick Honer was born in 1898, the son of Percy Honer, a postman, and Edith Mary Honer, of 22 Thorne Road, South Lambeth. By 1911 Joseph's father had died and the family – Edith, 33, Joseph Frederick, 13, and Dorothy, 6 – were living with Edith's father Frederick and other family members at 11 Lansdowne Gardens, South Lambeth. Joseph was at school and also working part-time as an errand boy for an oilman.

F. W. HOPKINS

Not identified.

W. T. HORNSBY

William Thomas Hornsby, died on 16 June 1917.

Corporal, London Regiment, 2/1st Bn. (Royal Fusiliers), Service no. 202656. Remembered at Arras Memorial, Pas de Calais, France.

Hornsby was born in Clapham, lived in Lambeth and enlisted in Paddington, west London.

G. C. HORSLEY

Not identified.

S. C. HOWDEN

Samuel Charles Howden, died on 5 April 1918, aged 19.

Private, Royal Sussex Regiment, 7th Bn., Service no. G/23011. Remembered at Bouzincourt Ridge Cemetery, Albert, Somme, France.

In 1911, 12-year-old Samuel Charles Howden lived at 155 Pullens Buildings, Amelia Street, Walworth, south-east London. His 36-year-old father, also called Samuel Charles Howden and originally from Hackney, was a motor cab driver. His mother, Emily, 32, was from Walworth. There were three other children.

W. B. HUDSON

William Berks Hudson, killed in action on 8 October 1916, aged 27.

Rifleman, London Regiment, "A" Coy. 6th Bn. (City of London Rifles), Service no. 4015. Remembered at Warlencourt British Cemetery, Pas de Calais, France.

In 1911 ledger clerk William Berks Hudson, 22, lived with his widowed mother and his aunt at 24 Chantry Road, Brixton. Matilda Hudson, 50, and her unmarried sister, Elizabeth Anne Berks, 47, from Newcastle, Staffordshire, both worked as draper's assistants. William was an only child.

H. E. HUMPHREYS

Henry Edward Humphreys, killed in action on 9 July 1918.

Private, London Regiment, 1/5th Bn. (London Rifle Brigade), Service no. 315288. Remembered at Dainville British Cemetery, Pas de Calais, France.

Henry Edward Humphreys lived in South Lambeth. He enlisted in Camberwell.

W. E. HUMPHREYS

William Edward Humphreys, died on 21 October 1914.

Private, Middlesex Regiment, 1st Bn., Service no. 10514. Remembered at Le Trou Aid Post Cemetery, Fleurbaix, Pas de Calais, France.

H. C. HUNT

Henry Charles Hunt, died on 9 April 1917, aged 25.

Lance Corporal, Middlesex Regiment, 11th Bn., Service no. G/50055. Remembered at Arras Memorial, Pas de Calais, France.

Lift porter Henry Charles Hunt, aged 20 in 1911, was the eldest child of Henry Hunt, 42, a painter's labourer, and Matilda Hunt, 40. The couple had seven children. The family shared four rooms at 148 Wandsworth Road with a boarder. At some point between 1911 and his death in 1917, Henry married Elizabeth Caroline (last name unknown). Their address was 122 Bennerley Road, Battersea. Henry enlisted in Kingston upon Thames.

H. HUNTER

Harry Hunter, died of wounds on 5 November 1917, aged 30.

Second Lieutenant, Royal Flying Corps. Remembered at Wimereux Communal Cemetery, Pas de Calais, France.

Civil Service clerk Harry Hunter, aged 22 in 1911, was one of five children of Robert Hunter, 54, a Lambeth-born organ builder, and Ann Mercy Hunter, from Stockwell. The family lived in nine rooms at 87 Clapham High Street. Robert's sister, Ann Esther Hunter, 56, lived with the family. There was a live-in domestic servant.

F. M. HUNTLEY

Frank Morley Huntley, killed in action on 3 May 1917, aged 39.

Rifleman, London Regiment, 1/9th Bn. (Queen Victoria's Rifles), Service no. 393151. Remembered at Arras Memorial, Pas de Calais, France.

In 1911 Kennington-born bookseller Frank Morley Huntley, then aged 32, lived with his wife, Fanny Beatrice Huntley, and their four children, who were aged between 10 months and eight years, and a boarder, at 10 St. Stephen's Terrace, South Lambeth. Huntley enlisted in Camberwell.

H. G. W. HURT

Harry George Walter Hurt, died on 25 October 1916, aged 24 .

Private, Bedfordshire Regiment, 7th Bn., Service no. 15120. Remembered at Thiepval Memorial, Somme, France.

The 1911 census shows Harry George Walter Hurt, 18, a clerk, living at 22 Langley Lane, Kennington. His father, Frederick G. Hurt, 58, was a white-smith (he worked with "white" or light-coloured metals such as tin and pewter) from St. Pancras. His mother, Martha Hurt, 56, was from Poplar, east London. Their six children lived with him, including a widowed daughter and her two children. Harry Hurt enlisted in Westminster.

J. W. HUSSEY

Joseph Wellman Hussey, died on 24 May 1915, aged about 37.

Serjeant, 9th (Queen's Royal) Lancers, "B" Sqdn., Service no. 4288. Remembered at Hop Store Cemetery, near Ypres, Belgium. Winner of the *Cross of St. George* (Russian).

Joseph Wellman Hussey, born in Thorncombe, Dorset, had previously served in the Boer War. In 1911, he was living alone in one room at 78 Wilcox Road, South Lambeth and working as a railway porter for the London & South Western Railway. In 1912, aged 34, he married 22-year-old Elsie Ann Cameron, who was living at 88 Wilcox Road. Hussey enlisted in Sevenoaks, Kent.

A. Y. HUTCHINSON

Albert Young Hutchinson, killed in action on 24 October 1914, aged 39.

Private, 11th (Prince Albert's Own) Hussars, Service no. 16206.
Remembered at Ypres (Menin Gate) Memorial, Belgium.

In 1911 Albert Young Hutchinson was living in one room at 24 Tasman
Road, Stockwell. He was 36, single, and working as a goods receiving clerk.
He was born at Haggerston, east London.

J. C. HUTCHINSON
Not identified.

J. S. HYMES

John S. Hymes, died of wounds on 29 May 1917.

Rifleman, London Regiment, 1/9th Bn. (Queen Victoria's Rifles), Service
no. 394311. Remembered at Etaples Military Cemetery, Pas de Calais,
France.

This is a tentative identification. In 1911 John Simpson Hymes, 29, lived
at 16 Westgate Road, Dartford. He was a sales manager, born in Liverpool.
His wife, Ruby Clara Hymes, 24, was born in Lambeth, and their son, John
Edward Hymes, 10 months, was born in Clapham.

I

A. E. INGRAM

Arthur Edward Ingram, killed in action on 7 November 1914.

Private, Worcestershire Regiment, 3rd Bn., Service no. 8804. Remembered at Ypres (Menin Gate) Memorial, Belgium.

Arthur Edward Ingram was born in Lambeth and lived in Clapham.

A. IRELAND

Arthur Ireland, killed in action on 22 November 1917.

Rifleman, Royal Irish Rifles, 15th Bn.; formerly London Regiment. Remembered at Thiepval Memorial, Somme, France.

Arthur Ireland was born in Peckham and lived in Brixton. He enlisted in Wandsworth.

J

E. T. H. JACKSON

Edward Thomas Henry Jackson, killed in action on 3 May 1917, aged 34.
Rifleman, Rifle Brigade, 9th Bn., Service no. S/26110. Remembered at Arras Memorial, Pas de Calais, France.

A tentative identification as a specific conection to Stockwell is yet to emerge. Edward Thomas Henry Jackson was the son of Edward and Annie Jackson, of 35 Chertsey Street, Church Lane, Tooting, and husband of Emily Jackson, of 37 Romney Buildings, Millbank, Westminster. He was born in County Mayo, Ireland.

W. H. JACKSON

William Henry Jackson, killed in action on 15 October 1914, aged 28.
Private, Middlesex Regiment, "D" Coy., 4th Bn., Service no. 9011. Remembered at Vieille-Chapelle New Military Cemetery, Lacouture, France.

William Henry Jackson was born in Paddington and lived in Hounslow. His widow, Ethel May Jackson, lived at 3 Seneca Road, Clapham.

S. JAMES

Samuel James, died of wounds as a prisoner of war on 10 August 1918, aged about 19.
Private, The Buffs (East Kent Regiment), 7th Bn., Service no. 14197. Remembered at Tincourt New British Cemetery, Somme, France.

When Samuel James joined the Army he gave his next of kin as his father, also called Samuel. However, the Army form has been amended. The elder Samuel has been deleted and "Miss D. A. James – sister" added. Samuel's 65-year-old father, a bricklayer, had died of a cerebral haemorrhage on 19

October 1918, weeks after his son perished in the war. James, who described himself as a decorator's assistant, had signed up aged 18 at Lambeth on 6 January 1917 and joined the Training Reserve of the Royal Sussex Regiment, transferring to the regular battalion on his 18th birthday, and then joining the East Kents.

Standing only 5 feet 4 inches tall and weighing 7½ stone, with a 37-inch chest, his physical development was judged to be only "fair." There is one recorded misdemeanour on James's record: he was slack while on sentry duty at Colchester on 22 October 1917, for which he was confined to barracks for three days. James went missing at the front on 30 June 1918. Later, it turned out that he had sustained a gunshot wound to his chest, been taken prisoner and died on 10 August 1918 in a field hospital at Péronne.

James, the middle of three children, lived at 37 Burgoyne Road, Stockwell with his parents and sister. His father, Samuel James, 56, was a bricklayer, originally from Ludchurch, Pembroke. His mother, Catherine James, 35, was from Lambeth.

E. J. JARVIS

Edward John Jarvis, killed in action on 19 July 1916.

Gunner, Royal Field Artillery, 46th Bty., Service no. L/43916. Remembered at Thiepval Memorial, Somme, France.

Edward John Jarvis was born in Clapham and enlisted at Camberwell.

J. H. C. JEFFERIES

John Henry Charles Jefferies, killed in action on 28 February 1917.

Lance Corporal, Royal Fusiliers, 2nd Bn., Service no. L/16723; formerly Hussars. Remembered at Thiepval Memorial, Somme, France.

John Henry Charles Jefferies was born in and lived in Clapham. He enlisted at Clifton Street.

A. A. JEFFERY

Arthur Alexander Jeffery, killed in action on 1 July 1916, aged about 27.

Private, East Surrey Regiment, 8th Bn., Service no. 4802. Remembered at Thiepval Memorial, Somme, France.

The 1911 census shows that Arthur Alexander Jeffery, was boarding at 88 Portland Place North, South Lambeth with his brother Albert V. Jeffery.

Arthur, 22, was a commercial clerk; Albert, 23, was a dairy utensil maker. Arthur enlisted in St Paul's churchyard.

Both brothers were born in Lambeth. Arthur Jeffery married at some time between 1911 and his death in 1916. After the war, his widow remarried, becoming Mrs. D. Blacklock, and moved to Toronto, Canada.

E. J. JEFFERY

Not identified.

F. W. JEFFERY

Frederick William Jeffery, killed in action on 21 December 1917, aged 19.

Private, London Regiment, 2/24th Bn. (The Queen's), Service no. 720315. Remembered at Jerusalem War Cemetery, Israel.

Frederick William Jeffery was the son of James and Annie Jeffery, who lived at Mawbey Street, South Lambeth.

L. W. JENN

Leonard William Jenn, died of gunshot wounds to the abdomen on 9 August 1916, aged 19.

Private, London Regiment, 14th Bn. (London Scottish), Service no. 7270. Remembered at Warlincourt Halte British Cemetery, Saulty, France.

Leonard William Jenn stated in his will that his effects – identity disc, letters, photos, pocket book, cigarette case, lighter – should go to his widowed mother, Annie, who at the time of the 1911 census was living at 7 Delverton Road, Newington, near Elephant and Castle. Her husband, Henry Jenn, had been a wholesale fruit salesman from Islington, north London. They had two sons.

Before the war, Jenn was a waiter at the Bonnington Hotel, Southampton Row (his occupation in 1911 was junior clerk for an iron barge builder). He stood only 5 feet 4½ inches tall but he was stocky, his chest measuring 40 inches.

Jenn received a gunshot wound to the abdomen on 9 August 1916 at the Battle of Morlancourt. The orderlies at No. 43 Casualty Clearing Station could not save him. He had served a mere 244 days.

S. E. JETTEN

Stephen Jetten, died on 31 August 1918, aged 28.

Serjeant, Royal Fusiliers, 4th Bn., Service no. L/13259. Remembered at H.A.C. Cemetery, Ecoust-St. Mien, Pas de Calais, France.

In 1911 Stephen Jetten, 22, was a Private with 3rd Battalion of the Royal Fusiliers, at Vacoas, Mauritius. His widowed mother, Mary, from Wych, Hampshire, lived with two other sons (she had eight children) at 78 Paradise Road, Stockwell. The children's father, Charles, had been a railway porter originally from Isington, Hampshire.

E. JONES

Not identified.

H. JONES

Not identified.

R. C. JONES

Not identified.

R. W. JONES

Not identified.

T. P. JONES

Not identified.

W. H. JONES

William Henry Jones, died on 25 April 1918, aged 29.

Petty Officer, Royal Navy, H.M.T.B. *90*. Service no. 229583. Remembered at Portsmouth Naval Memorial and at St. Andrew's Church, Landor Road, Stockwell.

William Henry Jones was the son of Harry Jones; his widow, Ellen Millicent Jones, lived at 2 Garden Row, off Stockwell Road.

A. E. JORDAN

Albert Edward Jordan, killed in action on 19 October 1915, aged 21.

Private, Grenadier Guards, 2nd Bn., Service no. 17330. Remembered at Vermelles British Cemetery, Pas de Calais, France. Brother of *Frank Andrew Jordan*.

In 1911 Albert Edward Jordan, 17, a carman, and Frank Andrew Jordan, 19, a Private in the 6th Rifle Brigade (Army Reserves), lived in three rooms at 4 Nealdon Street, Stockwell with their widowed mother, Mary, 49, and four of their eight siblings.

F. A. JORDAN

Frank Andrew Jordan, killed in action 25 September 1915, aged about 23.

Rifleman, Rifle Brigade, 2nd Bn., Service no. 6/9524. Remembered at Ploegsteert Memorial, Belgium. Brother of *Albert Edward Jordan*.

J. JORDAN

Not identified.

F. JOSLIN

Frederick Ernest Joslin, killed in action on 11 May 1918, aged 24.

Gunner, Royal Field Artillery, "A" Bty. 38th Bde., Service no. L/30147. Remembered at Cinq Rues British Cemetery, Hazebrouck, Nord, France.

In 1911 Frederick Joslin, a 16-year-old shop assistant, was living with his family in four rooms at 51 Stockwell Green. His father, Albert Joslin, aged 43 and from Rotherhithe, south-east London, was a general labourer in a granary. His mother, Agnes Joslin (née Sqirkell), 43, was from Needham, Suffolk. There were five children. Frederick's two brothers, Albert, 20, a carter, and George, 18, a shop assistant, served in the war and survived.

K

F. J. KELLOW

Francis John Kellow, died of wounds on 8 September 1918, aged 22.
Private, The King's (Liverpool Regiment), 1/6th Bn., Service no. 381862; formerly London Rifle Brigade. Remembered at Pernes British Cemetery, Pas de Calais, France.

Francis John Kellow volunteered in November 1915 and was posted to France in January 1918. He fought in the second Battle of the Somme, the Aisne and the Marne, and at the fourth Battle of Ypres, where he died.

In 1911, 14-year-old Francis was living in a three-roomed flat over the family shop at 12 Lingham Street, Stockwell. His father, John George, 43, was a shoemaker from Torquay, Devon; his mother, Emily Kellow, 42, was from Brixton. There were two siblings.

J. S. KELLY

John Strachan Kelly, killed in action on 22 October 1917, aged 31.
Private, Surrey Yeomanry (Queen Mary's Regiment), "A" Sqdn., Service no. 45038. Remembered at Struma Military Cemetery, Greece.

John Strachan Kelly was born in Aberdeen in about 1886. His family moved to London and at age 25, in 1911, he was living with his parents and siblings at 13 Dunbar Road, Forest Gate, east London (they later moved to 6 Benedict Road, Brixton). Kelly's father, Timothy Kelly, 50, was a customs and excise officer, originally from County Roscommon, Ireland. His mother, Agnes Kelly, 49, was from Aberdeen, Scotland. There were six siblings, five of them living at home. At the time of joining up John Kelly worked for the Board of Trade Seamen's Registry as an assistant clerk.

H. J. KEMP

Hugh John Kemp, died of wounds on 22 October 1914, aged 22.
Lance Corporal, 16th (The Queen's) Lancers, "C" Sqdn., Service no.
L/3287. Remembered at St. André Communal Cemetery, Nord, France.
Brother of *Sydney Frank Kemp.*

Hugh John Kemp joined the 3rd London Brigade of the Royal Field Artillery
(Territorial Army) on 16 February 1909. He gave his age as 17 years and
two months and stated that he was a clerk at A. Stedall (the nature of the
business is unknown). He was 5 feet 5½ inches tall and his chest measured
36 inches. Kemp's physical development was deemed "good" (the officer
who completed the form had started to write "poor" but struck it out).

On 10 February 1911 Kemp left the Territorial Army to enlist in the
regular Army. He joined the Lancers of the Line. By now he had grown to
just over 5 feet 6¾ inches and his chest measured 39 inches. At the time of
the 1911 census he is found with his regiment in the barracks at Woolwich
Common, south-east London.

Meanwhile, in the family home at 40 Lansdowne Gardens, Stockwell, his
parents, Frank J. Kemp, 55, a hop factor's clerk, and his wife Ellen Kemp,
52, lived with nine of their 11 children (including Sydney Frank Kemp), a
niece and a nephew.

S. F. KEMP

Sydney Frank Kemp, killed in action on 16 April 1918, aged 34.
Second Lieutenant, Oxfordshire and Buckinghamshire Light Infantry,
Bucks Bn.; previously 11th Hussars of the Line. Remembered at
St. Venant-Robecq Road Cemetery, Robecq, Pas de Calais, France. Brother
of *Hugh John Kemp.* Awarded the *Military Cross.*

Sydney Frank Kemp's Service record shows that he had served in the 7th
Hussars of the Line and had been discharged in 1905, having served his
term. At the time he re-enlisted on 26 August 1914, Sydney Frank Kemp
was working as a prison warder.

Given Kemp's military and service background, it is somewhat surprising
to see a long list of transgressions on Kemp's conduct sheets. His crimes
were all committed while he was serving in the ranks of the 11th Hussars,
that is before he was granted a commission, and included absence from
Reveille, absence from billet, drunkenness, leaving the ranks without

permission, neglecting to obey an order and making improper remarks to a warrant officer and to a commanding officer.

In April 1917, Kemp joined the 3rd Reserve Cavalry Regiment, went on to the Officer Cadet Battalion at Berkhamsted in June, and ended up in the Oxfordshire and Buckinghamshire Light Infantry. Perhaps Kemp found the confidence and motivation he needed. He was certainly appreciated by his regiment after he died. He and his fellow officers were described by Major G. K. Rose in *The Story of the 2/4th Oxfordshire and Buckinghamshire Light Infantry* (1920) as "an infusion of new blood and vigour."

Sydney Kemp, 5 feet 6 inches tall and weighing 8 stone, blue-eyed and fair-haired, married Eva Wisdom at St. Barnabas Church, South Lambeth on 3 February 1916. He was the eldest of 11 children of Frank John and Ellen Kemp of 40 Lansdowne Gardens, Stockwell.

V. KEMP-GILES
Not identified.

R. W. KENNEDY
Not identified.

A. H. KENT
Alfred Henry Kent

A tentative identification. A report in *The South London Press* (5 January 1916), states that this name appeared on a commemorative "war crucifix", now lost, outside St. Anne's Church, South Lambeth Road.

W. KEYS
William Keys, killed in action on 9 May 1915, aged 34.

Lance Serjeant, Seaforth Highlanders, 4th Bn., Service no. 2009.
Remembered at Le Touret Memorial, Pas de Calais, France.

In 1911 William Keys, born in County Westmeath, Ireland, was 29 and working as an assistant schoolmaster at a London County Council school. He lived with his parents and siblings at 5 Grantham Road, Stockwell, where the family occupied seven rooms. His father, also called William Keys, 59, originally from County Antrim, was a miller at a grain-drying works. His mother, Agnes, 55, was from County Down. They had eight children.

W. G. KIGHTLY

William G. Kightly, died on 11 December 1918, aged about 34.

Private 2nd Class, Royal Air Force, 2nd Aircraft Depot, Service no. 127770. Remembered at Terlincthun British Cemetery, Wimille, France.

In 1911 William G. Kightly, 26, was living with his wife, Florence May, 23, and 10-month-old daughter, Lilly Annie, at 2 Clyston Street, off Wandsworth Road, where they had one room. He gave his occupation as bottle washer.

F. R. KING

Frank Radcliffe King, killed in action on 14 September 1916, aged 30.

Second Lieutenant, The King's (Liverpool Regiment), "D" Coy., 14th Bn. Remembered at Doiran Memorial, Greece.

In 1911 Frank Radcliffe King, 25, was working as an insurance clerk with the Law Union and Rock Insurance Company. He lived with his parents and three of his four siblings at 57 Aytoun Road, Stockwell, where the family occupied eight rooms. Frank's father, George Edward King, 57, orginally from Gorleston, Suffolk, was a headteacher working for London County Council (he later became a Justice of the Peace, an Alderman and Guardian for the Borough of Lambeth, and in 1928 Mayor of Lambeth). His mother, Julia Constance King, 54, was from Islington, north London.

On 6 October *The South London Press* reported his death and quoted from a letter from his Commanding Officer, Colonel Lambert, to his father:

> I regret to say your son was killed two days ago fighting gallantly. We had taken a position held by the Germans, and he and the bombers guarded our right flank and did great execution. He will be a great loss to the regiment, as he was so keen, and a most promising officer, but he died a soldier's death. The regiment fought splendidly, and though we had heavy casualties – four other officers in the battalion being killed – we caused great losses to the Germans. My sincere sympathy in your bereavement.

King had been made Bombing Officer of his battalion, but did not want his family to know, as this would have worried them. In 1917 *The South London Press* reported the death of King's mother from pneumonia and "shock resulting from the death in action of her dearly-loved younger son". On the day King was killed, his elder brother, Ernest, was severely wounded.

J. F. KING

John Frederick King, died on 21 March 1918, aged 39.

Private, London Regiment, 2nd Bn. (Royal Fusiliers), Service no. 231178. Remembered at Chauny Communal Cemetery British Extension, Aisne, France.

John Frederick King, a carman, joined the Army twice. First he volunteered for the Army Service Corps (Horse Transport) on 5 January 1915. His medical description paints a picture of someone short and stocky: 5 feet 2¼ inches tall with a 40-inch chest. He had a mole on the back of his neck and scars on the left side of his back and left leg. At the top of his form he has signed a note: "I am willing to allot from date of enlistment 6*d*. [sixpence] per day of my pay to support my wife and family." He had left behind Jenny (née Hawkins), Frederick Ernest, 9, and Agnes Louise, 8.

This period of service lasted a mere three days. On 7 January he was discharged as "not likely to become an efficient soldier." As the war progressed, however, this opinion may have been revised or King may have been subject to the compulsory draft. Whatever happened, he later joined the London Regiment and died near Aisne in March 1918.

W. G. KING

William George King, died in an accident on 10 January 1917,
aged about 40.

Private, Royal Army Medical Corps, 30th Amb. Train, Service no. 51125. Remembered at St. Pierre Cemetery, Amiens, Somme, France.

William George King volunteered in January 1915, and shortly afterwards was posted to France. He worked on the ambulance trains, and was killed in January 1917 when he was run over by one. Ambulance trains were used to transport wounded soldiers to the French coast so that they could return to England, normally through Dover, for treatment and recuperation.

In 1911 King, 33, lived in three rooms at 23 Wilcox Road, South Lambeth. He was a house painter. He and his wife, Margaret Annie, 28, had a one-year-old daughter, Edith Mabel. They shared their home with a boarder.

L

H. T. LACKEY

Henry Thomas Lackey, died of wounds on 21 September 1917.

Private, Duke of Wellington's (West Riding Regiment), 10th Bn., Service no. 235398. Remembered at Lijssenthoek Military Cemetery, Poperinge, West-Vlaanderen, Belgiuim.

Henry Thomas Lackey enlisted at Lambeth in September 1916 and in the following year was sent to the front. He fought at the Battles of the Somme and Ypres, and died after being severely wounded at the Menin Road. Lackey was born in Walworth and lived at 6 Mary's Cottages, Eastcote Street, Stockwell.

H. W. LAIDLER

Henry William Laidler, died on 25 July 1918, aged 38.

Sapper, Royal Engineers, Gen. Base Depot, Service no. 188508. Remembered at Basra War Cemetery, Iraq.

In 1911 Henry William Laidler, then 31 and working as a plumber, lived in three rooms at 42a Lingham Street, Stockwell. His wife Emily worked as a cigarette box maker, and they had a three-year-old daughter, Lilian.

W. A. LAMERTON

William Alfred Lamerton, killed in action on 2 July 1918, aged 35.

Sapper, Royal Engineers, 48th Divisional Signal Coy., Service no. 217128. Remembered at Magnaboschi British Cemetery, Italy.

William Alfred Lamerton, a bricklayer, attested at Lambeth Town Hall on 10 December 1915, just before the national compulsory call-up came into force. Despite being a healthy-sounding 5 feet 8¼ inches tall with a 40-inch chest and weighing 10 stone, his physical development was judged to be only "fair." Lamerton was assigned to the Army Reserve and mobilised in December 1916. He joined the 48th Divisional Signal Company on 6 May 1917 and was killed in action in Italy in July 1918, leaving his wife Louisa a widow caring alone for Doris, their young daughter.

In March 1920, Louisa filed her Army Form W. 5080, in which relatives listed the next of kin of the late soldier. She almost forgot herself by signing as "wife," which she scrubbed out and replaced with "widow." She lived at 6 Emily Mansions, Landor Road, Stockwell.

H. LANGFORD
Not identified.

J. LARCOMBE
James Larcombe, killed in action on 15 September 1916, aged 20.

Rifleman, King's Royal Rifle Corps, 7th Bn., Service no. R/14879.
Remembered at Thiepval Memorial, Somme, France.

James Larcombe, a 19-year-old compositor (typesetter) from Stockwell, one of five children of Robert Larcombe, a tram conductor from Crewkerne, Somerset, joined up on 3 August 1915 at Battersea. He stood 5 feet 3½ inches tall and weighed 8 stone; his chest measured 38½ inches and he wore glasses. There was just one conduct issue in his file. In March 1916 he was punished with three days' confinement to barracks for hesitating to obey an order. Larcombe's Army career ended at the Battle of the Somme, where he was missing in action and then declared dead.

On 2 November 1916, his mother Louisa, clinging to hope, wrote to the Rifles Record Office from her home in Hubert Grove, Stockwell:

> ...my son, Private J. Larcombe... was missing after being in action on 15th Sept. last, there has also being [sic] one of his letters returned marked on the outside wounded on the 21st/9/16 and present location uncertain. Dear Sir, as I am very anxious to know what has become of him, I should be most gratefully obliged if you could [make a] few inquiries about him off some of the lads that was with him on that date or any other possible way and kindly oblige.

There is no record in the file of the Army's reply.

G. C. LASHAM

George Charles Lasham, killed in action on 26 August 1916, aged 28.
Gunner, Royal Garrison Artillery, 9th Siege Bty., Service no. 7912.
Remembered at Péronne Road Cemetery, Maricourt, France.

In 1911 postman George Lasham, 22, lived at 137 Hartington Road, South Lambeth, where his family occupied six rooms. His father, John Lasham, 51, was an engineer's pattern maker, born in Lambeth. His mother, Eliza Lasham, 47, was from Lathbury, Buckinghamshire. Lasham had seven siblings. On 11 January 1916 he married Louisa Alice Garvey. She later gave her address as 7 Elwell Road, Clapham.

A. J. LASKEY

Albert John Laskey, killed in action on 1 July 1916, aged about 22.
Lance Corporal, Border Regiment, 1st Bn., Service no. 22997; formerly East Surrey Regiment. Remembered at Thiepval Memorial, Somme, France.

In 1911 Albert John David Laskey, 17, was employed as an errand boy. He later became a greengrocer's assistant, working for the Lackey family business at 6 Industrial Terrace, Brixton. However, he lost this job as business was slack, according to Thomas Lackey, who provided a testimonial to the Army on Laskey's good conduct. Laskey joined the East Surrey Regiment as a Private on 3 August 1913 at Kingston upon Thames.

Previously, Laskey lived with his family in four rooms at 33 Edithna Street, Stockwell. His father, William David Laskey, 46, originally from Hempnall, Norfolk, was a night porter in a block of flats. His stepmother, Sarah Jane Eliza Laskey, 38, was from Islington, north London. There were three half-siblings and two boarders.

The physical description of Laskey brings to mind a solid, well-built man. He was 5 feet 6½ inches tall, 10 stone, with a 36-inch chest. He had a fresh complexion, with brown eyes and brown hair, a scar inside his right knee and a mole to the right of his abdomen.

There was only one misdemeanour on Laskey's conduct sheet: at Kingston upon Thames he was absent for three hours on 18 June 1915, for which he was punished with five days' confinement to barracks and the loss of five days' pay. Nevertheless, in July he was promoted to Lance Corporal.

Laskey went missing on 1 July 1916, the first day of the Battle of the Somme. His family then had an agonising wait to discover what had happened to him. On 19 September his wife, Florence Lily, wrote from her home at 55 Victor Road, Teddington, "I am asking if you [have heard] anything more of my husband... He was reported missing on July 1st." His stepmother wrote too. "Will you please let me know if you have any definite news of my son," she pleaded on 26 March 1917.

A. R. LAWRENCE

Alfred Robert Lawrence, killed in action on 28 March 1918, aged 27.

Private, London Regiment, 1st Bn. (Royal Fusiliers), Service no. 205241, attd. 1/4th Bn., Remembered at Arras Memorial, Pas de Calais, France.

This is a tentative identification. Alfred R. Lawrence, a 21-year-old sign-writer, lived at 39 Burman Street (now gone, it was off St. George's Road, opposite West Square), Southwark, with his parents, Alfred Lawrence, 45, a private coachman, and Mary Louisa Lawrence, 42, a bookfolder. The family occupied four rooms. Alfred was an only child. His parents later gave their address as 65 Knowle Road, Brixton.

R. W. LEACH

Robert Were Leach, died of wounds on 16 October 1916, aged 25.

Corporal, Wiltshire Regiment, 1st Bn., Service no. 11233. Remembered at Contay British Cemetery, Contay, Somme, France.

In 1911 Robert Were Leach, 19 and working as a clerk with the South West Gas Company, lived at 37 Landor Road, Stockwell, where his family occupied four rooms. His father, George Were Leach, 42, was a railway inspector, born in Uffcombe, Devon. His mother, Julia Mary Leach, 43, was from Yeldham, Essex. Robert had two younger brothers. He enlisted in St. Paul's Churchyard.

J. LEE

John Lee, killed in action on 3 October 1916, aged about 41.

Private, Middlesex Regiment, 19th Bn., Service no. PW/1826.
Remembered at Thiepval Memorial, Somme, France.

John Lee, a chimney sweep aged 40, enlisted at Lambeth on 19 April 1915.
He left behind his wife Edith (née Milne), to whom he allotted a portion of
his pay, and four children aged between seven and one. Another child was
born in 1916. Lee gave his address as 94 Lingham Street, Stockwell.

At 5 feet 7½ inches and 11 stone, with a 43-inch chest, Lee was better
built than many recruits and his physical development was judged to be
"good." He was killed in action at the Somme, having served one year and
168 days. The Army sent on his effects: letters, a purse and some photos.

G. LEVER

George Lever, died on 17 September 1916, aged 19.

Private, The Queen's Own Royal West Surrey Regiment, 11th Bn., Service
no. G/11157. Remembered at Thiepval Memorial, Somme, France.

In 1911 George Lever, whose father was also called George Lever, was
14 and at school. He lived with his family at 70 Hubert Grove, Stockwell,
where they occupied five rooms. George (senior), 56, was a carpenter, originally from Lovant, near Salisbury, Wiltshire. His wife Annie, 52, was from
Clapham. They had six children.

A. LEVY

Not identified.

S. LEVY

Samuel Levy, died on 21 December 1918, aged 24.

Private, Middlesex Regiment, 2nd Bn., Service no. G/57450. Remembered
at St. Sever Cemetery Extension, Rouen, France.

This is a tentative identification. The 1911 census includes Samuel Levy, a
17-year-old student, living at 88 Clapham Road with his father, Solomon
Levy, 54, a tailor and coat maker, born in Russia, mother Eva, 53, also born
in Russia, and six siblings, plus a boarder and a servant.

H. W. LIPPOLD

Henry Walter Lippold, killed in action on 28 September 1918, aged 42.

Rifleman, London Regiment, "D" Coy., 2/16th Bn. (Queen's Westminster Rifles), Service no. 550848. Remembered at Tyne Cot Memorial, Heuvelland, West-Vlaanderen, Belgium.

In 1911 Henry Walter Lippold lived at 28 Grantham Road, Stockwell with his widowed mother, Rosalie Henrietta Lippold (née Uffman), 75, who was born in the Strand, London, and two sisters. The family occupied seven rooms. Henry was a clerk for a stationers. His father, watchmaker Conrad Lippold, was a naturalised British subject from Hanover, Germany.

Lippold enlisted in 1914 at Westminster. His widow, Elizabeth, whom he had married some time after 1911, lived at 107 Nutfield Road, Thornton Heath, Surrey.

C. LISSENDEN

Cecil Lissenden, killed in action on 7 October 1918, aged 20.

Lance Corporal, Machine Gun Corps (Infantry), 200th Coy., Service no. 156714; formerly Royal West Surrey Regiment. Remembered at Laventie Military Cemetery, La Gorgue, Nord, France.

In 1911 Cecil Walter Lissenden, aged 12, lived at 34 Stockwell Park Road, an eight-roomed house, with his widowed father, Cecil Cooper Lissenden, a 44-year-old London-born singing teacher, and his grandparents.

C. P. LLOYD

Claude Percy Lloyd, killed in action on 20 November 1917, aged 24.

Private, Oxford and Bucks Light Infantry, "A" Coy. 10th Bn., Service no. 240489. Remembered at Fifteen Ravine British Cemetery, Villers-Plouich, Nord, France.

In 1911 Claude Percy Lloyd, 17, was working as a printer's reader and living with his widowed mother, dressmaker Annie Elizabeth Lloyd, 44, born in Westminster, and an elder brother in two rooms at 29 Tradescant Road, South Lambeth. His Irish father, Arthur Wellesley Lloyd, was a schoolmaster.

T. LOADER

Thomas Loader, killed in action on 8 August 1915.

Serjeant, Welsh Regiment, 8th Bn., Service no. 2749. Remembered at Helles Memorial, Turkey.

Thomas Loader was born in Kingston upon Thames, Surrey, where he enlisted, and lived in Clapham. He died in the Gallipoli campaign.

W. G. LOVETT

William Lovett, killed in action on 27 October 1915, aged 20.

Private, London Regiment, 1/23rd Bn., Service no. 1719. Remembered at Loos Memorial, France.

William Lovett's mother, Sophia Lovett, lived at 136 Larkhall Lane, Stockwell.

F. J. LOWLES

Frederick James Lowles, died of wounds on 18 September 1918, aged 19.

Private, Northamptonshire Regiment, 6th Bn., Service no. 49765. Remembered at Doingt Communal Cemetery Extension, Somme, France and at St. Andrew's Church, Landor Road, Stockwell.

Frederick James Lowles enlisted in August 1917 at Camberwell, and embarked for France the following year. He was wounded twice, at Arras and at Villers Bretonneux. He later rejoined his unit, and was severely wounded at Péronne. He died in hospital from his injuries.

In 1911 Frederick James Lowles, then aged 11, lived in three rooms at 4 Edithna Street, Stockwell. His father George William Lowles, 46, was a paper-hanger, born in Tower Hill, east London. His mother, Elizabeth Lowles, 44, was born in Lambeth. Frederick had three siblings.

J. G. LOWTHER

John George Lowther, killed in action on 7 June 1917, aged 30.

Serjeant, The Queen's Own Royal West Surrey Regiment, 11th Bn., Service no. G/10804. Remembered at Ypres (Menin Gate) Memorial, Belgium.

John George Lowther was born in Newcastle-upon-Tyne, and enlisted at Lambeth. His widow, Cecilia, lived at Speenham Road, Brixton.

H. LUBEL

Hyman Lubel, killed in action on 30 May 1918.

Private, Prince of Wales's (North Staffordshire Regiment), 8th Bn., Service no. 50395; formerly Royal Army Ordnance Corps. Remembered at Soissons Memorial, Aisne, France.

Hyman Lubel was born in Mile End, east London, lived in Brixton and enlisted at Whitehall. He is remembered in the *British Jewry Book of Honour 1914–1918.*

A. G. LUCKHURST

Arthur George Luckhurst, killed in action on 23 August 1918, aged 19.

Private, The Queen's Own Royal West Surrey Regiment, 6th Bn., Service no. 70071. Remembered at Méaulte Military Cemetery, Somme, France.

Arthur George Luckhurst lived in Clapham and enlisted at Kingston upon Thames. His mother lived at 31 Union Street, Clapham.

C. E. LUFF

Charles Edmund Luff, killed in action on 10 March 1915.

Corporal, London Regiment, 1/3rd Bn. (Royal Fusiliers), Service no. 1130. Remembered at Le Touret Memorial, Pas de Calais, France.

Charles Edmund Luff was born in the West End of London, enlisted at Edward Street, Paddington, west London and lived in Stockwell.

M

O. J. L. MacKENZIE

Osmond J. L. MacKenzie, killed in action on 15 September 1916, aged 19.
Rifleman, London Regiment, 1/6th Bn. (City of London Rifles), Service
no. 1662. Remembered at Thiepval Memorial, Somme, France. Brother of
Roderick Emile Leadbetter MacKenzie.

The 1911 census shows Osmond and Roderick MacKenzie, aged 13 and
12, living with their family in five rooms at 10 Atherfold Road, Stockwell.
Their father, James Leadbetter MacKenzie, 41, originally from Edinburgh,
was a journalist. Their mother, Kate MacKenzie, 41, was from Inverness.
The boys had seven siblings.

R. E. L. MacKENZIE

*Roderick Emile Leadbetter MacKenzie, killed in action on 2 September
1917, aged 19.*
Rifleman, Royal Irish Rifles, 14th Bn., Service no. 14/42565; formerly
King's Royal Rifle Corps. Remembered at Hermies British Cemetery,
Pas de Calais, France. Brother of *Osmond J. L. MacKenzie.*

J. MANDALE

Joseph Temple Mandale, died on 20 November 1915, aged about 34.
Lance Corporal, The Buffs (East Kent Regiment), 8th Bn., Service no. 1728.
Remembered at Douai Communal Cemetery, Nord, France.

In 1911, Joseph Temple Mandale, 30 and born in Brixton, was living at 61
Bessborough Place, Pimlico. He worked in the wine trade, was married to
Gertrude Eleanor, 20, from Westminster, and had a baby so new he had not
yet been named. Mandale enlisted at Camberwell.

A. S. MANNING

Arthur Stanley Manning, killed in action on 23 December 1915,
aged about 25.

Wheeler, Royal Horse Artillery and Royal Field Artillery, Service no.
60740. Remembered at Kut War Cemetery, north of Baghdad, Iraq.

Arthur Stanley Manning was a career soldier. He enlisted in the Royal Horse
and Royal Field Artillery on 9 December 1909 at 88 New Kent Road, having
previously worked as a printer's engineer and served an apprenticeship.
Manning was then 19 years old, 5 feet 7½ inches tall and 9¾ stone. His
chest measured 36 inches; his eyes were blue and his hair was brown.

Manning's work as a battery wheeler was solid. At the time he renewed
his commitment to the Army on 11 December 1914, he had gained two good
conduct badges and his military character was described as "very good."

He was killed in action on 25 December 1915 at Kut-al-Amarah in the
Persian Gulf. He had served a total of six years and 15 days. His sister,
Mrs. May Adelaide Parsons, who lived at 9 Meadow Road, South Lambeth
received a registered letter from the Records office at Dover enclosing
a communication from the Viceroy of India. Unfortunately, a copy of the
Viceroy's letter is not included in Manning's Service file.

On 1 March 1916 the War Office requested a copy of Manning's Record
of Service "showing the Indian period" and later Lieutenant E. F. Durand, on
behalf of the adjutant General of India, sent a letter of condolence to May.

Manning was one of at least six children of James L. B. Manning, a
machine operator born in Holborn, central London and Mary Manning,
born in Lambeth.

A. MARJERAM

Albert Marjeram, killed in action on 20 December 1917, aged 21.

Private, London Regiment, 2/2nd Bn. (Royal Fusiliers), Service no.
232420. Remembered at Tyne Cot Memorial, Heuvelland,
West-Vlaanderen, Belgium.

In 1911 Albert Marjeram, then 15, worked as a van guard for the London
& South Western Railway. He lived with his parents and two of his seven
siblings in three rooms at 2 Kibworth Street, Dorset Road, off Clapham
Road. His father, William Marjeram, 55, was a night watchman born in
Lambeth. His mother, Ruth Marjeram, 54, was from Manchester.

C. T. MARKHAM

Charles Thomas Markham, killed in action on 6 April 1918, aged about 23.

Private, London Regiment, 2nd Bn. (Royal Fusiliers), Service no. 232431; also Royal Fusiliers, attached 7th Battalion. Remembered at Pozières Memorial, Somme, France.

A tentative identification. The 1911 census includes a Charles Markham, born in Wandsworth and living at 75a Ellerslie Road, Clapham. He was 16 and working as a grocer's assistant. The household included his father, William Markham, 46, a carpenter and joiner from Framingham, Suffolk, and his mother, Mary Ann Markham, 45, from Holborn, central London. Charles had five siblings, three of whom lived at home.

F. MARLOW

Frederick Marlow, killed in action on 9 May 1915, aged about 20.

Private, London Regiment, 1/13th Bn. (Kensington), Service no. 2999. Remembered at Ploegsteert Memorial, Comines-Warneton, Hainaut, Belgium, at St. Andrew's Church, Landor Road, Stockwell, at 1 Victoria Street, London SW1 and at Caxton House, Tothill Street, London SW1.

Before Frederick Marlow enlisted in the Army, he was an abstractor in the Board of Trade's Labour Department. The date of his appointment was 29 May 1912 and his salary was £45.

Marlow is remembered on the war memorial plaque unveiled at 1 Victoria Street, London SW1 on 11 November 2002 (it replaced the Board of Trade Roll of Honour which has been missing for many years). Marlow is also commemorated on the Memorial to the Staff of the Ministry of Labour, hanging in Caxton House, Tothill Street, London SW1.

Frederick Marlow's brother George, a clerk at the Admiralty, also served in the Army (London Regiment, 15th Battalion). He was discharged in late September 1918 as no longer physically fit for war service after suffering a gunshot wound to the left wrist.

In 1911 the Marlow family lived at 15 Stansfield Road, Stockwell, where they occupied six rooms. John Marlow, 53, a joiner from Twickenham, Surrey and Catherine Marlow, 51, from Gypsy Hill, south-east London had five children.

F. A. MARSH

Not identified.

R. J. MARSHALL

Richard James Marshall, killed in action on 24 March 1918, aged 45.

Serjeant, Royal Field Artillery, "B" Bty. 186th Bde., Service no. L/40226. Remembered at Pozières Memorial, Somme, France.

Richard James Marshall was a commercial coachman. The 1911 census shows him, aged 39, living with his wife, Waterloo-born Charlotte Jane, also 39, at 6 Eastcote Street, Stockwell, where they had four rooms. They had two children. Marshall enlisted at Camberwell.

F. C. J. MASON

Frank Clifford John Mason, killed in action on 24 August 1916, aged 16.

Private, Middlesex Regiment, 17th Bn., Service no. PS/2538. Remembered at Euston Road Cemetery, Colincamps, Somme, France.

On 12 July 1915 Frank Clifford John Mason, an only child living with his mother and stepfather, lied about his age in order to enlist. He was born in September 1899 and was two or three months shy of his 16th birthday. He claimed to be a 19-year-old clerk, and this was accepted. A little over a year later he was dead.

Frank's father had also been called Frank Mason and was described in the 1901 census as a "manager specialist," aged 58 and born in Pimlico. The 1891 census lists him as a "chef and manager" and shows that he had a previous family. He was married to Esther, at 54 seven years older than himself, and there was a grandson, one-year-old Thomas F. M. Tickling, so the couple must have had a daughter. They lived at 22 Stansfield Road, Stockwell.

Some time after 1891, Frank senior became a widower; in 1899 he married again. His bride, Maud Mary from Ipswich, was almost half his age. Soon there was a child, the Frank listed on the Memorial. But Frank senior died in 1904, leaving Maud a widow and Frank junior without a father. Less than two years later, in 1906, Maud herself married for the second time, this time to a man closer to herself in age.

Arthur Petherick, shown as 31 on the 1911 census, was a railway clerk born in Dorking, Surrey in 1880. The family, Maud, Arthur and Frank junior, now lived at 22 St. Michael's Road, Stockwell with three boarders.

Mason was puny. The examining officer described his physical development as "slight," and he stood only 5 feet 4½ inches tall with a 34½-inch chest. Possibly he was immature emotionally as well. While training at Northampton in March 1916, he was in trouble for insubordination and for making improper remarks to an N.C.O., for which he was punished with 14 days' detention.

But the war was soon over for Mason. He was posted to France on 21 April 1916 and just over four months later, on 24 August, he was killed in action, having served a total of one year and 44 days. He had not yet reached his 17th birthday.

On 28 August 1918, Frank's effects – photos, identity disc, diary and postcards – were forwarded to his mother and stepfather. The Army asked for acknowlegement of receipt, but Mrs. Petherick's reply questioned the whereabouts of her son's other possessions. "I wish to point out," she said, "that seeing these other items were recoverable from my son's body, there were other things such as watch, cigarette cases, fountain pen etc. which should have come to hand."

Maud herself did not live long after this. The records show that she died in March 1919 in Epsom, Surrey and by March the following year Arthur Petherick, Frank's stepfather, was answering the War Pensions Board's queries. He stated that his stepson had no other relatives.

H. W. MAY

Herbert William May, died of wounds on 22 October 1918, aged 19.

Private, Machine Gun Corps, 2nd Battalion, Service no. 129402; formerly London Regiment. Remembered at Etaples Military Cemetery, Pas de Calais, France.

Herbert William May first joined the London Regiment in April 1915 when he was about 16. He enlisted at St. John's Hill, Wandsworth and was accepted into the 23rd Battalion of the London Regiment (Territorial Force).

May was 5 feet 7 inches tall, just over 9 stone and 35½ inches around the chest. His physical development was judged to be "good." He stated that he was 19.

This was a lie and on Christmas Day 1915, having served nearly seven months, he was discharged "having made a mis-statement as to age."

Later he joined the Machine Gun Corps and died of wounds at Etaples.

The 1911 census shows May, then 12, living in a three-roomed apartment at 51 Riverhall Street (now gone, this street ran parallel with Camellia Street), South Lambeth. His parents, Walter Charles May, 40, a general labourer, and Mary Ann May, 45, were both from Box, Wiltshire. Herbert had two siblings. The family later moved to 76a Thorparch Road, on the other side of Wandsworth Road.

W. MAY
Not identified.

D. MAYBANK
Douglas B. Maybank, killed in action on 29 June 1918, aged 30.

Serjeant, King's Royal Rifle Corps, 20th Bn., Service no. R/24284. Remembered at Sandpits British Cemetery, Fouquereuil, Pas de Calais, France.

Douglas B. Maybank was mobilised at the outbreak of war, and was almost immediately drafted to France. He took part in the Retreat from Mons, the Battles of the Marne, the Aisne, Ypres and the Somme. He died on the Cambrai front in the Advance of 1918.

The 1911 census shows Maybank, aged 23 and working, like his father, as a grainer and marbler (he painted wood grain effect and stained paper or other materials to look like marble), living at 22 Aytoun Road, Stockwell. The household included his father William Maybank, 50, originally from Epsom, Surrey, mother Harriett Maybank, 48, from Ellingham, Norfolk, four siblings and two other relatives. In 1912 Douglas married Florence Alice Clark at St. Andrew's Church, Landor Road. After he died, she gave her address as 29 Tasman Road, Stockwell.

G. H. MAYES
George Henry Mayes, died of shrapnel wounds on 12 June 1915, aged 35.

Private, Royal Marines, R.M. Div. Train, R.N. Div., Service no. Deal/1834 (S). Remembered at Lancashire Landing Cemetery, Turkey.

George Henry Mayes died of a shrapnel wound to his right side in 2nd (R.N.) Field Ambulance. He left a widow, Elizabeth M. Mayes, of 10 Stafford Road, Brixton.

D. McCONLOUGH
Not identified.

G. R. McDOWALL
George Robert McDowall, killed in action on 10 May 1916, aged about 45.
Serjeant, Royal Engineers, 69th Field Coy., Service no. 59064.
Remembered at Bully-Grenay Communal Cemetery, British Extension,
Pas de Calais, France and at St. Andrew's Church, Landor Road, Stockwell.

On 4 October 1900 George Robert McDowall, 27, the son of a labourer,
married Emma Cecil Giffin, 21, at St. Andrew's Church. He was a serving
Serjeant with the 2nd Dragoons. In 1911 Emma was living at 33 Nealdon
Street, Stockwell with her three children.

J. W. McEVOY
James William McEvoy, died of wounds on 28 April 1918, aged 21.
Gunner, Royal Field Artillery, 378th Bty. 169th Bde., Service no. 93025.
Remembered at Mont Huon Military Cemetery, Le Tréport, France.

James William McEvoy's parents, James and Elizabeth McEvoy, lived at 35
Sutherland Street, Pimlico. They are shown on the 1901 census living at
38 Lansdowne Road, South Lambeth with James, then a four-year-old, and
six boarders.

C. J. E. MEACOCK
Claude James Edwin Meacock, killed in action on 26 August 1918,
aged about 20.
Corporal, London Regiment (Royal Fusiliers), 1st Bn., Service no. 200253.
Remembered at Summit Trench Cemetery, Croisilles, Pas de Calais,
France.

In 1911 Claude Meacock lived at 11a Goldsborough Road, near Wandsworth Road, with his parents and five siblings. His father, James Meacock,
39, was a chargeman of cleaners for the London & South Western Railway,
born in Bayswater, west London. His mother, Anna Mary Meacock, 41, was
from Croydon.

H. G. MEAD

Harry George Mead, died of pulmonary tuberculosis on 4 November 1920, aged about 42.

Private, Royal Fusiliers, 37th Battalion, Service no. 37888; transferred to Labour Corps. Remembered at Lambeth Cemetery, Screen Wall, Blackshaw Road, Tooting, south-west London.

In 1919, when the Pension Board assessed Harry George Mead, they found him 100 per cent disabled. His symptoms included shortness of breath, expectoration (spitting up sputum), anaemia and haemoptysis (coughing up blood). His general condition was poor.

Mead had contracted pulmonary tuberculosis, and this was attributed to his war service. He had been posted for duty in July 1916 and had served two years and 217 days in France.

It was clear that Mead, a printer before the war, would be unable to return to work. The Pensions Board awarded him 27*s.* 6*d.* a week for six months, and 40*s.* for 64 weeks thereafter, with 10*s.* for his wife, Ada. There was a note in the file to investigate the status of their adopted son, Robert, then aged 12.

W. S. MEECH

William Samuel Meech, killed in action on 6 February 1916.

Private, Black Watch (Royal Highlanders), 9th Bn., Service no. S/8961. Remembered at Loos Memorial, Pas de Calais, France.

William Samuel Meech was born in Lewisham, south-east London. He volunteered in May 1915 and was killed in action at the Battle of Loos. He lived at 17 Pulross Road, Stockwell.

T. J. MEREDITH

Thomas Joseph Meredith, died on 9 September 1918, aged 23.

Gunner, Royal Field Artillery, "B" Bty. 99th Bde., Service no. 69867. Remembered at Salonika (Lembet Road) Military Cemetery, Greece.

In 1911, 15-year-old Thomas Meredith, an apprentice bookbinder born in Lambeth, lived with his parents and six siblings at 21 Neptune Street, Stockwell (this street, now disappeared, was near Wilcox Road). The family occupied four rooms. Thomas's father, also called Thomas, was 37, born in Lambeth and worked as a printer's labourer. His mother, Annie, 35, was born in Westminster. Thomas and Annie later gave their address as 40 Wilcox Road, South Lambeth.

F. H. MERREDEW

Frederick Henry Merredew, killed in action on 26 May 1915, aged 25.

Serjeant, London Regiment, "C" Coy. 1/24th Bn. (The Queen's), Service no. 377. Remembered at Le Touret Memorial, Pas de Calais, France.

Frederick Henry Merredew, who was born in South Lambeth, was a player piano maker. The 1911 census shows him, aged 21, living with his family at 36 Glenferrie Road, St. Albans, where they occupied six rooms. His father, Arthur James, 47, born in Clerkenwell, was also involved in the player piano trade, working as a wood machinist. Player pianos are self-playing pianos containing a mechanism that operates the piano action, usually via perforated paper. Merredew's mother, Sarah Mary, 46, was from Kensington, west London. He had eight siblings, seven of them living at home.

T. P. MESSENGER

Thomas Percy Messenger, died on 28 May 1918, aged 22.

Lance Corporal, London Regiment, 1/1st Bn. (Royal Fusiliers), Service no. 202245. Remembered at Soissons Memorial, Aisne, France.

In 1911 Thomas Percy Messenger, a 15-year-old grocer's errand boy, lived at 46 Horace Street (now disappeared, this street was near Wilcox Road), South Lambeth, where his family occupied four rooms. His father, John, 56, a wood and coal merchant from Ashton Keynes, Wiltshire, and mother, Elizabeth, 52, from Blackheath, south-east London, had 13 children. Five were listed on the census for this address.

S. C. MILES

Sidney Charles Miles, died of wounds on 30 March 1918.

Private, London Regiment, 23rd Bn., Service no. 701380. Remembered at Péronne Road Cemetery, Maricourt, Somme, France.

Sidney Charles Miles was born in South Lambeth and lived in Battersea. He enlisted at Clapham Junction.

E. J. MILBORROW

Ernest John Milborrow, died on 11 July 1918, aged 28.

Gunner, Royal Field Artillery, 17th Bty. 83rd Bde., Service no. 93005. Remembered at St. Souplet British Cemetery, Nord, France.

In 1911, Ernest John Milborrow, 20, was an unemployed laundry warehouseman, living with his parents and six of his seven siblings in four rooms at 83 Hargwyne Street, Stockwell. His father, Ernest Alfred Milborrow, 43, a silk tie cutter, and his mother, Ellen, 45, were both born in Lambeth.

Ernest Milborrow's Service history file has not survived but those for his brothers William and Arthur Milborrow have. They both joined the Royal Field Artillery, 162nd (Howitzer) Brigade in Camberwell on the same day, 27 March 1916, and were given adjacent Service numbers.

William Milborrow, aged 23 and 5 feet 5¾ inches tall, and working as a butcher when he enlisted, rose through the ranks and was demobbed in 1920 as a Serjeant. His career included two disciplinary issues. He was reprimanded in October 1915 for insubordinate conduct to an officer and again in July 1918 for absence from parade. Milborrow's medical history included having his infected teeth removed and inoculations against typhoid. He caught flu in March 1919, just at the start of the pandemic, but evidently recovered.

Arthur Thomas Milborrow, 5 feet and 3 inches tall, described himself as a bank messenger, and was 19 when he enlisted. He was disciplined in February 1917 for being absent from parade, and in March 1918 for going absent from leave for a day. He was hospitalised for two days with diarrhoea and for eight with a sprained foot ("nothing found," said the doctors). Arthur Milborrow was demobbed as a Driver in 1919.

A. M. MILLER

Arthur Morley Miller, died of wounds on 30 September 1917, aged 27.

Lance Serjeant, King's Royal Rifle Corps, 20th Bn., Service no. C/4039.
Remembered at Lijssenthoek Military Cemetery, Poperinge,
West-Vlaanderen, Belgium.

Arthur Morley Miller joined the King's Royal Rifle Corps at Battersea on
28 June 1915. He gave his address as 27 Courland Grove, Clapham and
described himself as a clerk. The Army assessed him as being 5 feet 5
inches, with a 37-inch chest. He had two moles under his left nipple.

In October 1916 he was wounded and was sent back to England for
treatment. At the London General Hospital in Poplar, east London, a doctor
described the shrapnel wound to his left hand as a flesh wound with the
bones not affected but the tendons exposed. He was discharged after three
months and sent back to the front.

He must have had at least one other period of leave because he
married Kathleen Florence Cherrill in London on 16 February 1917. She
later received his effects: a crucifix, two razors, a French book, letters, a religious book, a cap badge, dentures, diary, a wristwatch and strap, photos, a
fountain pen and a whistle. By the time he died of wounds on 20 September
1917 Miller had risen to Lance Serjeant.

In 1911, aged 20, Miller was working as a builder's clerk and living at
27 Courland Grove, Stockwell where his family – parents, seven siblings
and half-siblings and an aunt – occupied six rooms. His father, Lambeth-
born Arthur William Miller, 53, worked as a carman. His mother, Emma
Eliza Miller, 49, was from Marylebone, central London. Three siblings lived
elsewhere.

C. H. MILLER
Not identified.

G. S. MILLER
Not identified.

J. C. MILLER

John Charles Miller, died of wounds 19 May 1918, aged 21.

Private, Australian Infantry, A.I.F., 21st Bn., Service no. 7267. Remembered at Querrieu British Cemetery, Somme, France.

John Charles Miller, a single man working as a clerk, was living at 300 Queens Street, Melbourne, Australia when he signed up for service on 12 December 1916. Within days he was on the troop ship *Ballarat* heading for Devonport, England, where he arrived in late April 1917.

Miller was pulled up twice – for failing to report for duty when warned and for going absent without leave, for which he was punished with 24 hours' detention. He was also made to forfeit two days' pay (10s.).

By September 1917 he had joined his battalion. He had a period of leave in England between 16 January and 16 February 1918, and on 19 May he suffered a shell wound to his left leg, which shattered. He died of wounds in the 5th Australian Field Ambulance. Miller left all his possessions to his widowed mother, Amy Miller of 296 Clapham Road.

Miller was 5 feet 10 inches and 10½ stone, and his chest measured 41 inches. He had a scar on his right knee. He had blue eyes and brown hair.

J. E. MILLER

Joseph Evan Miller, killed in action on 27 March 1918.

Rifleman, Rifle Brigade, 3rd Bn. Service no. S/36204. Remembered at Pozières Memorial, Somme, France

Joseph Evan Miller was born in Sydenham, south-east London and lived in Stockwell. He enlisted in Lambeth.

W. A. MILLS

William Arthur Alfred Mills, died on 30 May 1918, aged 19.

Private, Devonshire Regiment, 2nd Bn., Service no. 30986. Remembered at Chambrecy British Cemetery, Marne, France.

In 1911 William Arthur Alfred Mills was 12 and living with his parents and sisters at 8 Tradescant Road, South Lambeth, where they occupied four rooms. His father, William Hugh Mills, 49, was a railway porter from Islington, north London. His mother, Laura Mills, 46, was from Bermondsey. William had two siblings. He enlisted in Lambeth.

F. E. MILNES

Frederick Edward Milnes, died on 24 June 1918 , aged 28.

Private, 12th (Prince of Wales's Royal) Lancers, Service no. 917.
Remembered at Berlin South-Western Cemetery, Germany. Brother of
William Alexander Milnes.

The 1911 census shows that Frederick Edward Milnes, 22 and single,
was serving as a Private with the 12th Royal Lancers in Potchefstroom,
Transvaal, South Africa. He was born in Kennington. His parents, Frederick
and Annie Milnes, lived at 3 Albert Mansions, South Lambeth Road.

W. A. MILNES

William Alexander Milnes, died on 4 October 1917, aged 25.

Corporal, Seaforth Highlanders, 2nd Bn., Service no. S/12198.
Remembered at Tyne Cot Memorial, Heuvelland, West-Vlaanderen,
Belgium. Brother of *Frederick Edward Milnes.*

On the night of the 1911 census, 18-year-old William Alexander Milnes
was visiting his friends the Martin family at 8 Smeaton Road, Southfields,
Wandsworth, south-west London. (The Milnes family had lived in Smeaton
Road at the time of the 1901 census.) William was a chemist's assistant. He
was born in Wandsworth and enlisted at Finsbury, north London.

F. S. MINTER

Frank Sidney Minter, killed in action 10 March 1917, aged about 35.

Private, Royal Fusiliers, 22nd Bn., Service no. 60899; formerly East Surrey
Regiment. Remembered at Thiepval Memorial, Somme, France

In 1911 Frank Sidney Minter was a 29-year-old commercial traveller
selling herbs and seeds. He was born in South Lambeth, and was married to
Ada Mary, also 29, from Stockwell. They lived in three rooms at 49 Jeffreys
Road, Stockwell, and had one child, Lilian Ada, five months. Ada Mary's
mother, Mary Goldsmith, 63, a laundress born in the City, lived with them.
Frank enlisted in Clapham and later lived in Tooting, south-west London.

J. MITCHELL
Not identified.

T. H. MIZEN

Thomas Henry Mizen, died on 30 December 1915, aged about 20.

Able Seaman, Royal Navy, H.M.S. *Natal*, Service no. 202018. Remembered at Chatham Naval Memorial, Kent.

The *Natal* was an armoured cruiser, launched on 30 September 1905. She was sunk by an internal explosion in the Cromarty Firth on 30 December 1915 when, shortly after 3.20pm and without warning, a series of violent explosions tore through the ship, which capsized five minutes later.

The most probable explanation was that a fire had broken out, possibly due to faulty cordite, which ignited a magazine. The exact number of casualties is unknown, but estimates range from 390 to 421. Some were killed in the immediate explosions; others drowned as the ship turned over or they succumbed to the freezing water. Most of the bodies recovered from the sea were interred in Rosskeen Churchyard, Invergordon, with a few buried in the Gaelic Chapel graveyard in Cromarty.

Thomas Mizen was born in South Lambeth and registered at St. Anne's and All Saints Church, South Lambeth Road on 1 June 1894 by his parents, Thomas Mizen, a "general dealer", and Elizabeth Ada Mizen. They gave their address as 16 Portland Cottages, Kennington.

At the time of the 1911 census Thomas Mizen, then 43, and Elizabeth A. Mizen, 42, lived with their children at 43 Simpson Street, Stockwell. Thomas senior was then a wood chopper; Thomas junior a carman. There were five other children.

J. V. MOONEY

Jarlath Vincent Mooney, killed in action on 27 March 1917, aged 23.

Private, 8th (King's Royal Irish) Hussars, Service no. H/14352. Remembered at Villers-Faucon Communal Cemetery Extension, Somme, France.

The 1911 census shows Southend-born Jarlath Vincent Mooney, 17, living at 105 Franciscan Road, Tooting, south-west London where his family had three rooms. He was a clerk in "mercantile offices". Mooney's mother, Christiana, 39, was born in Shoreditch, east London. I did not find his father, Jarlath A. Mooney, a travelling debt collector from Ireland, on the 1911 census. Jarlath had an elder sister, Kathleen, a shorthand typist.

S. MORGAN

Sidney Morgan, killed in action on 11 November 1916.

Rifleman, Rifle Brigade, 2nd Bn., Service no. S/15651. Remembered at Caterpillar Valley Cemetery, Longueval, Somme, France.

Sidney Morgan was born in Highgate, north London and lived in Stockwell. He enlisted in Newbury, Berkshire.

J. MORRIS

James Morris, died of wounds on 2 August 1917.

Corporal, Royal Garrison Artillery, 110th Heavy Bty., Service no. 148649; formerly Middlesex Regiment. Remembered at Loos Memorial, France.

James Morris was born in Stockwell and lived in Brixton. He enlisted in London.

H. T. MOSS

Henry Thomas Moss, died on 28 October 1917, aged 46.

Gunner, Royal Garrison Artillery, 46th Anti-Aircraft Bty.; formerly Royal Field Artillery and 3rd Gloucester Regiment. Remembered at Lambeth Cemetery, Blackshaw Road, Tooting, south-west London. Father of *Henry Louis Moss*, whose name is listed side-by-side with his.

Henry Thomas Moss, a house painter, was born at Gosport and enlisted at Lambeth. In 1911, aged 40, he shared nine rooms at 114 Stockwell Road with his wife, Elizabeth Alice, 38, and 11 of his 12 children.

H. L. MOSS

Henry Louis Moss, killed in action at Gallipoli on 10 August 1915, aged about 23.

Private, Duke of Edinburgh's (Wiltshire Regiment), 5th Bn., Service no. 11338. Remembered at Helles Memorial, Turkey. Son of *Henry Thomas Moss*. His name is listed next to his father's.

Henry Louis Moss was born in Walworth and lived in Clapham. He enlisted at St. Paul's Churchyard. In 1911, aged 19 and working as a goldsmith, he lived at 114 Stockwell Road with his parents, Henry Thomas and Elizabeth Alice Moss, and 10 of his 11 siblings.

F. J. MOULDER

Frederick James Moulder, killed while carrying a despatch on 23 August 1918, aged 21.

Private, London Regiment, "C" Coy. 1/14th Bn (London Scottish), Service no. 512364. Remembered at Bucquoy Road Cemetery, Ficheux, Pas de Calais, France.

Frederick James Moulder joined the Army in the early days of the war and worked as a company and battalion runner since the days of the Somme push of 1916.

On 4 October 1918, *The South London Press* carried a short obituary of Moulder, who was killed while carrying a despatch, in which his comrade, Private E. A. McKearon, is quoted: "He was well known throughout the battalion and had earned the esteem and respect of all who knew him."

Moulder appears on the 1911 census as a 14-year-old resident at 41 Ballater Road, Brixton. His father, also called Frederick, 51, was a general labourer working for a builder, and was originally from Basingstoke, Hampshire. His mother, Elizabeth, 50, was born in Stockwell. There were three siblings. The family later moved to 35 Cottage Grove, Stockwell.

A. J. MULLETT

Arthur Joseph Mullett, died of wounds on 1 July 1916, aged about 19.

Pioneer, Royal Engineers, 3rd Battalion Special Brigade, Service no. 130014; formerly London Regiment. Remembered at Bailleul Communal Cemetery Extension, Nord, France. Brother of *George Thomas Mullett.*

In 1911 Arthur Joseph Mullett, then a 14-year-old schoolboy, lived at 12 Ely Place, Stockwell with his parents and two of his four siblings. His parents were from Dorset: Henry Mullett, 51, a horsekeeper for a brewery, was born in North Matravers; Harriett, 52, was from Swanage. The family occupied four rooms. His brother, George Thomas Mullett, who is on the Memorial with Arthur, was serving with the Dorsetshire Regiment. Arthur enlisted in Holborn, central London.

G. T. MULLETT

George Thomas Mullett, killed in action on 21 May 1918, aged about 28.

Serjeant, Dorsetshire Regiment, 1st Bn., Service no. 8760. Remembered at Arras Memorial, France. Brother of *Arthur Joseph Mullett.*

George Thomas Mullett's Army career stretched over eight years. He signed up with the Dorsetshire Regiment in Dorchester on 15 November 1909, ending his civilian role of barman. Perhaps some of his old habits stayed with him – in 1911 he was severely reprimanded for allowing a man to smoke cigarettes on parade.

Evidently, Mullett learned from his mistake – there are no other misdemeanours on his conduct record. Rather, the files detail his steady rise through the ranks. He was promoted to Corporal in October 1913 and to Serjeant in September the following year.

Mullett married Lucy Emma Cane at St. Michael's Church, Stockwell on 16 April 1916. Lucy had a six-year-old son, Lewis George Cane, whom Mullett lists on his Army form as "illegitimate".

On 1 July 1916, Mullett's brother Arthur Joseph Mullett was killed. George Thomas survived until May 1918. A note in the file says that on 31 May 1918 he was wounded. Two weeks later this was amended to "wounded and missing" and then in late August to "to be regarded for official purposes as having died."

On enlistment Mullett was described as 5 feet 7⅞ inches tall; he weighed a little under 10 stone and had a 36-inch chest. He had hazel eyes and brown hair. There was a scar on his right cheek.

H. MULLETT

Hubert Mullett, died on 10 August 1917, aged about 25.

Private, The Queen's Own Royal West Surrey Regiment, 11th Bn., Service no. 11626. Remembered at Godewaersvelde British Cemetery, Nord, France.

Hubert Mullett, 19, a clerk for an engineering company, lived with his family in eight rooms at 101 Stockwell Park Road. His father, James Edwin Mullett, 60, was an architect from Camberwell. His mother, Alice, 51, was from Marylebone. Hubert had six siblings.

A. G. MURPHY

Alfred George Murphy, died on 29 March 1918, aged 19.

Private, Machine Gun Corps (Infantry), 203rd Coy., Service no. 126952; formerly Bedfordshire Regiment. Remembered at St. Sever Cemetery Extension, Rouen, Seine-Maritime, France.

Alfred George Murphy enlisted in February 1917, and was later transferred to the Machine Gun Corps. He was sent to the front the following year.

In 1911 Murphy, aged 12, lived with his parents, Walter Robert John Murphy, a 39-year-old butcher originally from Westminster, and Alice Mary Murphy, 37, also from Westminster, and six siblings in five rooms at 6 Priory Grove, Stockwell.

J. C. MURRAY

Not identified.

W. L. MURRAY

William Lawrence Murray, killed in action on 25 September 1915, aged 21.

Rifleman, London Regiment, 6th Bn. (City of London Rifles), Service no. 2251. Remembered at Maroc British Cemetery, Grenay, Pas de Calais, France.

In 1911 William Lawrence Murray was a junior clerk working for the Amalgamated Press and living with his mother Elizabeth Alice Murray, 44, born in Holborn, central London, in a three-roomed apartment at 15 Rhodesia Road, Stockwell.

N

H. L. F. B. NADAUD

Henry Louis Frederick Bonnetaut Nadaud,
killed in action on 21 March 1918,
aged 39.

Major, London Regiment, 1/24th Bn. (The Queen's). Remembered at Fins New British Cemetery, Sorel-Le-Grand, Somme, France and at Westminster Cathedral, London SW1.

In 1911 Henry Nadaud, then aged 32 and working as a bank clerk for the London Joint Stock Company, lived at 100 Lansdowne Road, Stockwell with his parents, Louis Nadaud, 59, a retired civil servant, born in Soho, central London, and Marie Nadaud, 53, born in France; his brother Charles Nadaud, 28, an electrical engineer; an aunt, Theresa Nadaud, 57; and a live-in domestic servant.

A veteran of the London Regiment, having served in the Cadet Corps of the City of London Cadet Corps attached to the Kings Royal Rifle Corps, Nadaud was shot in the left arm on 25 May 1915 at Givenchy. Three days later he was on the *Patrick* headed for "Mrs. Lindsay's Hospital" – and home. By mid-August he was not yet fit enough to return to the front, and his service record does not tell us exactly when he made it back to France.

Nadaud was promoted to Major on 1 June 1916. A little under two years later, he was killed in action at Metz during heavy German bombardment and "many gas shells". He died alongside three others and was buried the next day in the civilian cemetery at Equancourt (his body was later moved to Fins). He had served for more than 10 years.

A note in the regimental history of the Lambeth and Southwark Volunteers, says that Nadaud was awarded the Territorial Decoration and that his name is recorded on the war memorial inside the Catholic Westminster Cathedral in Victoria, central London.

F. NAISH

Frank Naish, killed in action 18 September 1918, aged about 24.

Private, Wiltshire Regiment, 1st Bn., Service no. 37514; formerly Royal Berkshire Yeomanry. Remembered at Targelle Ravine British Cemetery, Villers-Guislain, Nord, France.

This is a tentative identification. In 1911, there was a Frank Naish, a 17-year-old clerk, living at 3 Belgrave Terrace, Brixton, where his family had eight rooms. He was one of five children of Francis Naish, 46, who worked in a carriers department and was born in Castle Cary, Somerset, and Clara Naish, 45, from Jersey. Two boarders lived with the family.

W. H. NETHERCOTT

Walter Henry Nethercott, killed in action on 10 October 1917, aged about 26.

Company Quartermaster Serjeant, Rifle Brigade, 3th Bn., Service no. Z/2766. Remembered at Tyne Cot Memorial, Heuvelland, West-Vlaanderen, Belgium.

Walter Henry Nethercott, 23, a clerk, enlisted on 12 September 1914. He was described as having a healthy complexion with brown eyes and auburn hair. He had a mole on the tip of his left shoulder. He stood 5 feet 7½ inches tall, weighed just over 9½ stone and his chest measured 35½ inches.

The Army recognised Nethercott's talents early. He rose through the ranks, was promoted to Serjeant in the field in July 1916 and was made Company Quartermaster Serjeant three months later.

In March 1915 Nethercott married Marjorie Ballance of 15 Walberswick Street, South Lambeth. She gave birth to a daughter, Margarette Phyllis, a year later. Nethercott's parents were deceased and he had no siblings.

In February 1918, four months after Nethercott was killed, the Army sent Marjorie his effects: a fountain pen, a disc and chain, a diary, Kitchener's message, a copy of *A Rifleman Should Know*, a lock of hair. However, a Mr. John Mayo, received Nethercott's medals, sent to him at 93 Larkhall Rise. The file does not tell us why this was done, and when Marjorie, then still living at Walberswick Street, wrote to request that they be sent to her, the Army replied that they had already been sent to Mr. Mayo. Marjorie was given a weekly pension of 22*s.* 6*d.* for herself and Margarette.

In 1901 10-year-old Walter Nethercott was living with his widowed grandmother, Mary A. Nethercott, 60, at 31 Wheatsheaf Lane, off South Lambeth Road. Mary was born in Godstone, Surrey, Walter in Battersea. There are no other members of the household listed. I have not traced Walter Nethercott in the 1911 census.

A. W. NEWCOMBE

Alfred William Newcombe, killed in action on 27 June 1917, aged about 24.

Private, Bedfordshire Regiment, 8th Bn., Service no. 33465. Remembered at Philosophe British Cemetery, Mazingarbe, Pas de Calais, France.

In 1911 Alfred Newcombe, 17, worked as a grocer's assistant and lived at 89 Priory Grove, South Lambeth where his family occupied four rooms. His father, William Newcombe, 42, was a labourer from Wembworthy, North Devon; his mother, Betsy Newcombe, 43, was from Peterborough, Cambridgeshire. Newcombe was born in Marylebone, central London and enlisted at Bedford.

A. J. NEWMAN

Not identified.

J. H. NEWMAN

James Henry Newman, killed in action on 17 September 1916, aged about 18.

Private, London Regiment, 1/24th Bn. (The Queen's), Service no. 3409. Remembered at Thiepval Memorial, Somme, France.

In 1911 James H. Newman was a 13-year-old schoolboy. He lived with his parents and six of his 11 siblings in four rooms at 39 Horace Street, South Lambeth (now gone, this street was near Wilcox Road). His father, James Newman, 51, was a railway guard from Sturminster Newton, Dorset. His mother, Mary Jane Newman, 51, was from Holt, near Wimbourne in Dorset.

C. NEWTON

Not identified.

R. NICHOLSON
Not identified.

A. NIGHTINGALE
Not identified.

H. A. NIXON
Harry Albert Nixon, killed in action on 1 July 1916, aged about 27.
Private, Middlesex Regiment, 2nd Bn., Service no. L/12127. Remembered at Thiepval Memorial, Somme, France.

Harry Albert Nixon, a career soldier, enlisted in 1906. He was drafted to the Western Front shortly after the outbreak of war.

Nixon's Army Service records are extensive, as you might expect with such a long period of service (over eight years). He joined the Middlesex Regiment at Winchester, the city of his birth, on 24 February 1908, aged 19 and five months, leaving behind his civilian life as a van guard.

In 1908 Nixon's general condition was good. He stood taller than average at 5 feet 6½ inches and weighed just over 9½ stone. His chest measured 37½ inches. With a fresh complexion, grey eyes and fair hair, he must have been among the more healthy of recruits. However, Nixon was possibly something of a difficult character. He remained a Private throughout his long Army career and it could have been that his poor conduct record accounted for his lack of advancement.

In January 1910 he was pulled up for inattention on the range. At Dum Dum (West Bengal) he was absent from parade. He was punished for using improper language towards an N.C.O. At Malta he was punished for "improper conduct – walking arm in arm with other soldiers" and "using obscene language." In September 1913 in Aden (in Yemen) he was punished for "using improper language towards a N.C.O." and soon after shipped out to the 2nd Battalion. In Valletta, Malta he was disciplined for "interfering with the military police."

Nixon became infected with syphilis in August 1911 in Darjeeling. He sought treatment two weeks later and by 1912 the Army doctors at Dum Dum were treating him regularly. His appointments were weekly, although he is often marked as "absent," presumably because he was on operations. Nixon was dosed with mercury and iodides – although neither treatment would have been very effective. Better medications had been developed by the German Nobel prize-winning physician Paul Erlich in 1906 but these were not yet widely available.

When the Great War started, Nixon was sent to France. He fought at Ypres, Loos, and Albert and was killed in action on 1 July 1916, the first day of the Battle of the Somme. He was listed as "missing," but his next of kin were not notified until 15 August. Eventually, he was classed as killed in action.

After his death, Nixon's effects were sent to his younger sister, Mrs. Alice Maude Weaver, who lived at 42 Margate Road, Brixton. "I recive [sic] the photos quite safe," she wrote in reply, "thanking you very much for sending them." Later, in 1919, when sent Harry's medals, she wrote: "Recive [sic] with thanks. Thank you very much for sending me the 1914 Star, I am very proud of my Poor Brother." On Army form W. 5080, in which relatives gave the names and addresses of family of the deceased, only two siblings were declared: Daisy Dorithey [sic] and Fredrick. In reality there were or had been at least 11 siblings.

In 1911 Harry's family lived at 31 Priory Grove, South Lambeth, where they occupied four rooms. The household consisted of his parents, Frederick C. Nixon, 55, a general labourer born in Stepney, and Alice Nixon, 49, born in Dorset. The couple had 12 children, six of whom lived at home.

H. NORRIS

Not identified.

A. NUNN

Not identified.

A. E. NUNN

Alfred Edward Nunn, died on 10 May 1918, aged 19.

Private, The Queen's Own Royal West Surrey Regiment, "A" Coy., 7th Bn., Service no. 63634. Remembered at St. Sever Cemetery Extension, Rouen, Seine-Maritime, France.

In 1911 Alfred Edward Nunn, then 12, lived in five rooms at 38 Landor Road, Stockwell, with his parents, Alfred Nunn, 49, a "motorman" for London County Council transport, who was originally from Suffolk, and Emily Nunn, 43, from Croydon. Alfred was one of two children.

H. C. NUTHALL

Herbert Charles Nuthall, killed in action on 25 April 1915, aged 31.

Private, Royal Warwickshire Regiment, 1st Bn., Service no. 7498.
Remembered at Seaforth Cemetery, Cheddar Villa, Belgium.

Herbert Charles Nuthall was born in Camberwell and lived in Brixton. He was the son of Henry and Jane Nuthall. His widow, Gertrude Beatrice Nuthall, lived at 12 Lingham Street, Stockwell.

O

L. W. OAKES

Leonard William Oakes, killed in action on 27 September 1917, aged 18.

Corporal, The Queen's Own Royal West Surrey Regiment, 1st Bn., Service no. G/37014. Remembered at Tyne Cot Cemetery, Zonnebeke, West-Vlaanderen, Belgium.

In 1911 Leonard William Oakes, 12, lived at 64 Paradise Road, Clapham with his widowed father, John Thomas Oakes, 56, a platelayer for the railway, originally from Burton-on-Trent, Staffordshire, four of his five siblings and a boarder. Oakes was born in Croydon, Surrey and enlisted there.

E. F. OEHRING

Ernest Frederick Oehring, killed in action on 11 January 1918, aged 21.

Private, Machine Gun Corps (Infantry), 142nd Coy., Service no. 71553. Remembered at Thiepval Memorial, Somme, France.

In 1911 14-year-old Ernest Frederick Oehring was working as an engraver's errand boy. He lived at 85 Ferndale Road, Clapham, where his family had seven rooms. His father, Frederick A. Oehring, 44, was a bookbinder's finisher, born in Lambeth; his mother, Alice, 38, was also from Lambeth. Ernest had a younger sister. Frederick A. Oehring's father, also called Frederick A. Oehring, was a tailor born in Leipzig, Germany but was by 1891 a naturalised British subject. Ernest enlisted at Camberwell.

G. ORMOND

George Ormond, killed in action on 30 September 1918, aged 22.

Private, Royal Fusiliers, 11th Bn., Service no. G/37729. Remembered at Unicorn Cemetery, Vend'huil, France and at Waterloo Station War Memorial, London SE1

George Ormond, a van shifter for the London & South Western Railway, was born in Lambeth and lived in Clapham. He enlisted in London. His mother, Harriet Ormond, who lived at 56 Larkhall Lane, Stockwell, was born in Fordington, Dorset. Ormond's father, William Ormond, a railway porter, was from Tolpuddle, Dorset.

G. F. OSBORNE

George Frederick Osborne, died of wounds on 10 July 1918, aged 23.

Rifleman, Rifle Brigade (Prince Consort's Own), Service no. 48694; formerly Royal Engineers (Postal Section); posted to London Regiment (Post Office Rifles). Remembered at Pernois British Cemetery, Halloy-les-Pernois, Somme, France.

George Frederick Osborne was born in Lambeth and lived in Clapham. He enlisted in central London. His mother, Lydia Osborne, lived at 110 Dorset Road, Clapham Road.

P

C. W. PACE

Charles William Pace, killed in action on 15 September 1916,
aged about 26.
Private, London Regiment, 1/24th Bn. (The Queen's), Service no. 722461.
Remembered at Thiepval Memorial, Somme, France.

Charles William Pace was 26, working an an outdoor porter and living at 55 Dawlish Street, off Wilcox Road when he signed up at Camberwell on 4 March 1916. Pace gave his mother Sarah as next of kin, but this was later amended to his new wife, Florence (née Meredith), of 21 Seaham Street, Nine Elms whom he married at St. Barnabas Church, South Lambeth on 23 July 1916.

The file includes a letter from 19 October 1916 written on his mother's behalf. Over a month after her son had died, she pleaded with the Army: "I have received no letter or tidings from him for some time now... If he has been wounded or fallen sick and has been removed to hospital would you please endeavour to trace him through your Records." Clearly for his mother the most likely possibility – that he was dead – was too dreadful to set down in a letter. Pace's record states merely "missing after action." He had served 280 days.

He stood 5 feet 1 inch tall, with a 36-inch chest.

The 1911 census describes Charles William Pace, then 21, as a tea packer from Walworth. He and his elder brother James Stephen, 24, a window cleaner, also born in Walworth, lived with their widowed mother, Sarah Ann Pace, 56, who was from Bermondsey, at 14 Gladstone Street, Stockwell, where they had two rooms. Six other siblings lived elsewhere.

J. PACKER

John Packer, killed in action on 26 March 1918, aged 28.

Private, Royal Fusiliers, 4th Bn., Service no. G/17678. Remembered at Arras Memorial, Pas de Calais, France.

In 1911 John Packer, 21, worked as a carman and shared five rooms at 4 Currie Street, near Nine Elms Lane, Battersea, with his widowed father, Joseph, 59, a grocer from Chelsea, and two siblings. Joseph and his deceased wife, Mary Ann, had five other children. On Christmas Day 1914, John Packer married Lily Cecilia Baker at St. Anne's Church, South Lambeth.

E. E. PAGE

Ernest Edward Page, killed in action on 7 June 1917.

Rifleman, London Regiment, 1/21st Bn. (First Surrey Rifles), Service no. 653413. Remembered at Ypres (Menin Gate) Memorial, Belgium.

Born in Whetstone, Middlesex, lived in Lambeth, enlisted in Camberwell.

C. J. PAINTER

Charles John Painter, killed in action on 15 May 1917.

Serjeant, London Regiment, 2/4th Bn. (Royal Fusiliers), Service no. 281508. Remembered at Arras Memorial, Pas de Calais, France.

Charles John Painter lived in Stockwell and enlisted in Hoxton, east London.

E. J. PALMER

Not identified.

H. PARDUE

Henry Thomas Payn Pardue, killed in action on 10 May 1917, aged 33.

Serjeant, London Regiment, 1/12th Bn, (The Rangers), Service no. 473280; formerly 16th London Regiment. Remembered at Arras Memorial, Pas de Calais, France.

In 1911, Henry Thomas Payne Pardue, 27, was living with his aunt Annie Warren, 39, his sister Gladys, a dancer, and Annie's four children at 85 Shakespeare Road, Stoke Newington, north London. His siblings were scattered across the country. Meanwhile, Pardue's father, Charles John, 63, a widower, had remarried and started another family. He had at least 14 children from his two marriages.

C. F. PARKER

Charles Frederick Parker, killed in action 21 March 1918, aged 34.

Private, Machine Gun Corps (Infantry), 34th Coy., Service no. 142427. Remembered at Arras Memorial, Pas de Calais, France.

Charles Frederick Parker (pictured with his wife and two children) was born on 23 November 1884 at 95 Dunnetts Road, St. Pauls, Deptford, south-east London. He was one of 10 children of William James Parker, an engineer originally from Liverpool, and Elizabeth Emma Rutt from Southwark.

In 1905 Charles, aged 20, and Daisy Laura Hales, 21, married at Christ Church, Blackfriars and by 1911 they were living in two rooms in Block Q of the Blackfriars Peabody Estate with their daughter, Elsie Daisy, then aged two (a son, William, was born later). Charles was employed as an assistant stationary engineerman for the London Hydraulic Company.

Charles Frederick Parker enlisted in the Royal Field Artillery in Brixton

in 1916 and was later transferred to the 34th Company Machine Gun Corp (Infantry). In February 1917, Charles was recovering at the Soldiers' Rest, St. Mary Street, Cardiff. He had trench foot, a condition caused by continuous immersion in water. At the front, the water table was often only a few feet below the surface which meant that the men lived almost permanently in wet conditions.

Operation Michael, the major German counteroffensive known as the "Kaiser's Battle," was launched along a 50-mile front at dawn on 21 March 1918, following a massive preliminary bombardment. The Germans broke through the British lines and the 34th Machine Gun Corps was almost completely surrounded. Parker was killed.

A. PARSONS

Not identified.

A. E. PARSONS

Albert Edward Parsons, killed in action 7 June 1917, aged about 36.

Rifleman, London Regiment, 1/21st Bn. (First Surrey Rifles), Service no. 653411. Remembered at Ypres (Menin Gate) Memorial, Belgium.

In 1911 Lambeth-born Albert Edward Parsons, 30, a drapery ware-houseman, lived in five rooms at 40 Bellefields Road, Stockwell with his wife, Jessie Emily, 29, from Southwark, two young sons and a boarder.

A. A. G. PASKINS

Albert A. G. Paskins

Driver/Gunner, Royal Air Force, Service no. 69796. Albert Paskins served in France from 24 July 1915. Date of death is unknown.

J. W. PATRICK

John Walter Patrick, killed in action on 4 September 1916, aged 23.

Private, Royal Fusiliers, 12th Bn., Service no. 18989. Remembered at Thiepval Memorial, Somme, France.

In 1911 John Walter Patrick, 17, a carman, lived with his parents and five of his six siblings in four rooms at 11 Union Street, Clapham. His father, William Patrick, 56, was a general labourer, originally from Farnham, Surrey; his mother, Mary Jane, 54, was from Newington, south-east London.

F. C. PAYNE

Fred Cecil Payne, killed in action on 13 June 1917, aged about 39.

Private, Manchester Regiment, 18th Bn., Service no. 42266. Remembered at Perth Cemetery (China Wall), Ypres, Belgium.

Fred Cecil Payne was born in Westminster and lived in Stockwell. He enlisted in London.

F. J. PAYNE

Frederick John Payne, killed in action on 4 July 1916, aged about 27.

Private, Dorsetshire Regiment, 6th Bn., Service no. 11440. Remembered at Thiepval Memorial, Somme, France.

In 1911 Lambeth-born Frederick John Payne, 22, was working as a general labourer living at 6 Horace Street (now disappeared, this street was near Wilcox Road), South Lambeth where his family had four rooms. His father, Samuel Payne, 54, was a general labourer from Stogumber, Somerset; his mother, Sarah Ann Payne, 50, was born in Surat, India. Frederick had five siblings, three of whom lived at home.

E. R. G. PEACOCK

Edwin Robert Gilbert Peacock, died of wounds on 3 September 1918, aged about 27.

Serjeant, Machine Gun Corps, 17th Bn., Service no. 3261; formerly Royal Fusiliers. Remembered at Varennes Military Cemetery, Somme, France.

In 1911 stonemason Edwin Robert Gilbert Peacock, 20, boarded with Charles Smith, aged 50 and also a stonemason, and his family at 24 Lingham Street, Stockwell. In 1901 Edwin, one of four sons, lived in Prittlewell, Essex, where his father was a council dust inspector. His mother, Ellen, then 49, later moved to 38 Gaskill Street, Clapham.

P. W. PEARCE

Percy William Pearce, died of wounds on 17 July 1916, aged 20.

Lance Corporal, The Queen's Own Royal West Surrey Regiment, 11th Bn., Service no. 1432. Remembered at Boulogne Eastern Cemetery, France.

Percy William Pearce, aged 14 in 1911 and working in a wheelwright's shop, lived with his parents, six siblings and a boarder in five rooms at 28 Tradescant Road, South Lambeth. He was one of eight children of George S. Pearce, 46, a railway police constable from Godalming, Surrey, and his wife Marian, 46, from South Lambeth.

G. PEARCEY

George Pearcey, died on 19 January 1919, aged 34.

Private, London Regiment, 1st Bn. (Royal Fusiliers), Service no. 202274. Remembered at Lambeth Cemetery, Screen Wall, Blackshaw Road, Tooting, south-west London.

George Pearcey, one of six children, enlisted at Handel Street, near Coram's Fields, London WC1. His widowed mother, Ada Pearcey, a charwoman (cleaner), lived at 104 Stockwell Road.

W. R. G. PEARSON

William Reginald Guy Pearson, died in a flying accident on 20 June 1918, aged 21.

Captain, Royal Air Force, No. 4 Training Depot Station. Remembered at Eastham (St. Mary) Churchyard, Cheshire. Mentioned in despatches.

William Reginald Guy Pearson (pictured, standing, with his family), known as Guy, was a Captain in the R.A.F. He was one of five children of surgeon and physician Dr. Reginald Spencer Pearson and Minnie Savile Pearson, of Clapham Road, London.

In 1911 the family lived in 10 rooms at 14 Lake Street, Leighton Buzzard, Bedfordshire, with two mother's helps. Guy's younger sister Kathleen Mary (second from left) later became the children's author Mary Norton, perhaps best known for writing *The Borrowers*.

Guy Pearson was educated at Ashdown Park and Berkhamsted. He had ambitions to join the clergy. At the outbreak of war, however, he enlisted in the Empire Battalion, Royal Fusiliers, and later received a commission in the Army Service Corps. Pearson went to France in January 1915, joining the Royal Flying Corps soon afterwards in the role of

artillery observer. Returning to England, he completed his training as a Scout pilot, and served in France for nearly a year in a fighting squadron. In over 50 encounters with the enemy he brought down 11 enemy aircraft, and was mentioned in despatches.

Writing from Belgium on 10 November 1917 to his friend Arthur Rose, Pearson, seemingly mature for his 21 years, said: "I agree with you that those who speak of this as 'the last war' have failed to realise that so long as there are men who possess this will [to conquer]... there will be factions inevitable. And further, if this ambition is in the heart of a race, it will most assuredly unite that race in an obsession to subdue other nations, and there will be war."

Pearson became a Flight Commander and was promoted to Captain. He died at the aerodrome at Hooton Hall, Cheshire when the plane he was flying with Lieutenant William Smith MacFarlane from Edinburgh clipped another flown by 20-year-old American airman Vincent Jerome Flynn. Pearson had been training the men in flying and they had been practising air attacks. All three men died in the accident and were buried in the churchyard at Eastham, although Flynn's body was later repatriated to New Jersey. Following the death of their son, Pearson's parents received over 150 letters of condolence, including one sent by the Keeper of the Privy Purse on behalf of the King and Queen.

After the war, Pearson's father played a major part in raising money for the Stockwell Memorial Committee, but was unable to attend its unveiling in May 1922. "Dr. Pearson felt that he could not bear the strain which the ordeal of unveiling and dedicating this memorial would impose upon him," observed *The Brixton Free Press* in a report on the dedication ceremony.

C. A. PELLING
Not identified.

H. T. PELLING
Horace Thomas Pelling, died in an accidental explosion on 26 November 1914, aged 18.

Private, Royal Marine Light Infantry, H.M.S. *Bulwark*. Service no. CH1/8111. Remembered at Chatham Naval Memorial, Kent.

Horace Pelling was born on 9 December 1895 in Clapham. He enlisted on 3 July 1913, embarked on H.M.S. *Bulwark* on 22 October 1914, and died on

26 November 1914, killed by an internal explosion when the ship was off the Kent coast at Sheerness. The explosion left all of the *Bulwark's* officers dead; only 14 of 750 sailors survived and two of these subsequently died in hospital of their injuries.

Three years previously, in 1911, Horace Thomas Pelling, then 15, was a labourer working in the manufacture of ammonia. His father, Horace John Pelling, 40, was a gas fitter, originally from Steyning, Sussex; his mother, Hanna Elizabeth, 41, was from Walworth. Horace had one sibling. The family lived in two rooms at 3 Garnies Street (now gone, although there is a Garnies Close off Sumner Road), Camberwell.

A. PENN

Arthur Penn, killed in action on 19 March 1917, aged 23.

Serjeant, Royal Engineers, 74th Field Coy., Service no. 44243. Remembered at Faubourg d'Amiens Cemetery, Arras, Pas de Calais, France.

The entry for Arthur Penn in *De Ruvigny's Roll of Honour 1914–1918*, includes a passage from the letter his commanding officer wrote to his parents after their son had been killed in action at Arras in March 1917.

> I had known your boy ever since he joined the company when it was formed in England, and for the last six months I had seen a great deal of him as he was my office Sergeant. I had grown to like him very much, and respected him for his manly and sterling good qualities. He was, I know, a general favourite with the other sergeants and greatly liked by the men under him. We buried him here in the Military Cemetery, and all the officers off duty and a large number of N.C.O.s and men attended his funeral.

While he was a Corporal, Penn had shown great presence of mind. During a bombing class at Noeux, he had thrown a burning bomb clear and prevented serious injury to 130 men.

The 1911 census shows that Penn was one of five children of John Thomas Doody Penn, 53, a General Post Office sorter from Chatham, Kent and Victoria Penn, 55, of Ilton, Somerset. Arthur Penn was working as a chauffeur for Shuttleworth & Co. in Bermondsey, south-east London. He lived with his parents, two siblings and a boarder at 73 Union Road, Clapham.

H. W. PENN

Henry or Harry William Penn, killed in action on 16 June 1917, aged 34.

Private, King's Own (Royal Lancaster Regiment), 8th Bn., Service no. 22577. Remembered at Arras Memorial, Pas de Calais, France and at St. Andrew's Church, Landor Road, Stockwell.

Henry Penn enlisted in the Suffolk Regiment at Lambeth on 11 November 1915, and was later transferred to the Lancasters. His Service file gives an indication of how he looked: he was 5 feet tall with a 36½-inch chest, and he had a squint in his left eye.

In June 1916 he was wounded in the face and right arm, and about a year later, he was killed in action. His effects were sent to his mother: photographs, a small bag, four identity discs, a notebook, a letter case, letters, safety razor and blades, a pipe and tobacco pouch, a silver cigarette case, a metal mirror, a regimental book cover, buttons, a farthing, a card and two cap badges.

Henry William Penn lived at 74 Hargwyne Street, Stockwell with his parents, William Penn, 62, a boiler stoker born in Clapham, and Lucy Penn, 57, from Marlow, Buckinghamshire. The family had three rooms. Two siblings lived elsewhere.

H. J. PENNEY

Henry John Penney, died of wounds on 20 October 1916, age 21.

Rifleman, London Regiment, 1/9th Bn. (Queen Victoria's Rifles), Service no. 7074. Remembered at Etaples Military Cemetery, Pas de Calais, France.

In 1911 15-year-old Henry John Penney was a goldsmith's apprentice. He lived at 29 Knowle Road, Brixton, with his parents, Henry Penney, 42, a stonemason from Southwark, and Louisa Mary Penney, 41, from Lambeth, two younger sisters and two boarders. The household occupied four rooms. Henry enlisted in Putney, south-west London.

B. C. PEPLOE

Benjamin Charles Peploe, killed in action on 2 November 1917, aged 25.
Rifleman, London Regiment, 1/11th Bn. (Finsbury Rifles), Service no.
453135; formerly 9th London Regiment. Remembered at Gaza War
Memorial, Israel and at St. Andrew's Church, Landor Road, Stockwell.

Stockwell-born Benjamin Charles Peploe, 19 in 1911, lived at 70 Lingham
Street, where his family had four rooms. His widowed mother, Mildred
Elizabeth Peploe, 54, was a greengrocer from Euston, north London.
Benjamin had four siblings, two of whom lived at home (one with her
husband). The family had lived at Lingham Street, Stockwell for at least
20 years (they were there on the 1901 and 1891 censuses). Benjamin's
deceased father was a fishmonger from Bermondsey, south-east London.

W. G. PERCY

William George Percy, killed in action on 22 May 1916, aged 34.
Lance Corporal, London Regiment, 18th Bn. (London Irish Rifles),
Service no. 3950. Remembered at Cabaret-Rouge British Cemetery,
Souchez, Pas de Calais, France.

In 1911 William George Percy, 29, worked as an optician's assistant. Born
in Kennington, he lived with his wife, Nellie Ethel, 24 and from Leeds, in
five rooms at 52 Hearnville Road, Balham. His parents, meanwhile, lived
at 11 Grantham Road, Stockwell. William Percy, 52, was an optician, and
while Etheldreda Percy, 49, from Portland, Dorset, does not give an occupation in the 1911 census, she was described as an assistant schoolmistress
in the 1901 census.

A. E. PERRY

Arthur Edward Perry, killed in action on 14 July 1916, aged 28.
Private, King's Shropshire Light Infantry, 7th Bn., Service no. 8367.
Remembered at Thiepval Memorial, Somme, France.

In 1911 Arthur Edward Perry's parents and brother were living in four
rooms at 45 Edithna Street, Stockwell. William James Perry, 57, was a coach
painter born in Lambeth; Selina Perry, 62, was from Bothamsall, Notting-
hamshire. They had three children. I have not found Arthur 1911 on the
census, but he is on the 1901 census as an errand boy.

C. E. PHILCOX

Cecil Ernest Philcox, died of wounds received in a training accident on 24 May 1917, aged 21.

Lieutenant, South Staffordshire Regiment, 1st Bn., Remembered at Achiet-le-Grand Communal Cemetery Extension, Pas de Calais, France. Brother of *Percy William Arthur Philcox.* Awarded the *Military Cross*; mentioned in despatches.

Cecil Ernest Philcox was born in 1895. After attending Dulwich College he worked in a timber broker's office in the City (his father, Alfred James Philcox, who died in 1913, was a timber merchant). Philcox enlisted in the ranks of 12th Battalion of the London Regiment (The Rangers). One of his brothers, Percy William Arthur Philcox, was killed in action with the Rangers on 8 May 1915.

Philcox was transferred to the Inns of Court Officers Training Corps at Berkhamsted on 20 April 1915 and in July was given a temporary commission in the 10th (Reserve) Battalion of the South Staffordshire Regiment at Harrogate. He took part in action at High Wood, Mametz, Beaumont-Hamel, Arras, Serre, Martinpuich and Bullecourt.

In November 1916 Philcox was appointed Battalion Bombing Officer. He died on 24 May 1917 at No. 45 Casualty Clearing Station near Bullecourt. Three days earlier, during training, Private T. Hindley threw a defective No. 5 Mills grenade, mortally wounding Philcox, who sustained a factured skull. Lance Corporal Carrington and Hindley himself were also injured. A Field Court of Enquiry, at which three witnesses gave evidence and Hindley made a statement, concluded that no one was to blame for Philcox's death. All described how Philcox had given the order to throw, how Hindley's throw was a good one and made in the regulation manner and how the grenade exploded when only six feet away from the bombing party.

Besides being mentioned in despatches, Philcox was awarded the Military Cross for conspicuous gallantry and devotion to duty.

Cecil and Percy Philcox lived at 255 South Lambeth Road. Their mother, Alice Eliza, was born in Lambeth. There were two other siblings: Alfred Reginald, who in 1911 was working as a timber merchant's clerk like his brother, and Ethel Beatrice.

P. W. A. PHILCOX

Percy William Arthur Philcox, killed in action on 8 May 1915, aged 24.

Rifleman, London Regiment (The Rangers), "C" Coy. 1/12th Bn., Service no. 3252. Remembered at Ypres (Menin Gate) Memorial, Belgium. Brother of *Cecil Ernest Philcox.*

A. B. PHILPOTT

Arthur Bertram Philpott, died on 21 March 1917.

Gunner, Royal Garrison Artillery, 86th Bty., Service no. 33841. Remembered at Baghdad (North Gate) War Cemetery, Iraq.

Arthur Bertram Philpott was born and lived in Clapham, where he enlisted.

T. A. PILGRIM

Thomas Albert Pilgrim, died of pneumonia on 19 May 1918, aged 35.

Company Quartermaster Serjeant, Cheshire Regiment, 86th Bty., Service no. 8761. Remembered at Hartlepool (Stranton) Cemetery, Cleveland.

Thomas Albert Pilgrim's Army career spanned 17 years. During this time he learned about Army discipline, rose through the ranks to be Company Quartermaster Serjeant, grew nearly four inches and acquired medals and tattoos – and a wife. He died of severe pneumonia in West Hartlepool, Cleveland in 1918, despite the best efforts of the medical staff to save him.

In November 1901 Pilgrim, aged nearly 18 and working as a general labourer, enlisted in the Royal Sussex Regiment. He was 17 years and 10 months, 5 feet 5¼ inches tall, blue-eyed with brown hair; he had a scar by his left eye and tattoos on his left arm. At camp in Chichester, he was almost immediately in trouble: irregular conduct (punished with seven days' confinement to barracks); absent from parade (three days); quitting coal fatigue without permission (three days); not complying with an order (five days), and at Jamestown, Ireland, making an improper reply.

More trouble followed. While serving in South Africa he made an improper reply to an N.C.O. for which he was confined to barracks for 14 days. Back in England, at Shorncliffe Camp, Kent he was absent from Reveille. And it was from there, on 4 April 1903 that Pilgrim bought himself out of the regiment for £18.

In November 1907, aged 24, he was back at the recruitment office, enlisting in the Cheshire Regiment. By now he had grown to 5 feet 9 inches, and was a solid 11½ stone, with a 38½-inch chest. He had also acquired some more impressive tattoos: a flower head, a woman, a head, flags and flowers on his left arm; a hand with two cards on his left hand; a snake, a palm tree and "an Indian" on his right arm; a heart on his left knee.

There were only two black marks against him in this period. On 10 March 1909 he bought a pair of boots from a private, "contrary to regulations," for which he was severely reprimanded; on 27 November in Belfast he was found drunk and disorderly for which he was reprimanded again. Generally, however, he had calmed down. Possibly his marriage in 1908 to a 29-year-old widow, Maud Kate Nurse, at Lambeth Register Office had an influence, as he now had responsibilities towards a wife and young stepchild. In this period, Pilgrim acquired some qualifications. In 1908 he earned a third-class certificate of education, rising to second-class in 1910. He qualified as an assistant instructor in signalling in 1911.

Life was changing for Pilgrim. He started to gain promotions, making Serjeant in 1913, and on 9 July 1914, shortly after he suffered a bout of bronchopneumonia that had put him in hospital in Londonderry, he signed up for extended service. His military character was now judged to be excellent, his superior officers describing him as "very hard working and efficient", "reliable", and "trustworthy."

Soon he was off to France to fight the Germans, but he served only three months there (between August and November 1914). Most of Pilgrim's war was served on the Home Front. He was appointed acting Company Serjeant in June 1915 and promoted six weeks later. But then Pilgrim was brought down by a severe case of pneumonia while at West Hartlepool.

The doctor treating him at the No. 8 Durham Voluntary Aid Detachment Hospital, where he was admitted on 14 May 1918, described him as "practically moribund" (that is, approaching death). The medical staff fed him carefully with fluids every half hour, administered strychnine (as a stimulant rather than a poison) and surrounded him with hot water bottles, but he succumbed five days later. He was 35 and had served for over 10 years. Maud Kate received a pension of 24s. 2d. for herself and her child.

Although Pilgrim does not appear on the 1911 census for Lambeth or Wandsworth, his mother, Susannah Silk, 56, and sister, Daisy May Pilgrim, 22, are found at 3 Stockwell Grove, where they had two rooms. In 1901, before he signed up with the Royal Sussex Regiment, the 17-year-old Pilgrim was living with his mother, stepfather Tom Silk, who was a 39-year-old scaffolder from Battersea, and three siblings at that address.

G. H. PORTER

George Hand Porter, killed in action on 12 September 1918, aged about 26.
Serjeant, Royal Garrison Artillery, 126th Heavy Bty., Service no. 290873.
Remembered at Quéant Communal Cemetery British Extension, Pas de
Calais, France.

Porter's three-year Army career in the 126th (Camberwell) Heavy Battery
of the Royal Garrison Artillery was a series of appointments and promotions. On 29 May 1915, before he had even left England, he was appointed
acting Bombardier and within two weeks he was promoted to Bombardier; in less than a month he was made a Corporal. On 29 April 1916 he
proceeded to France.

There, on 15 August 1916, he reverted to Gunner at his own request, but
by November he was again acting Bombardier. Less than two months later
he was a paid Bombardier. By September 1917 he had reverted to acting
Bombardier, immediately becoming a paid Corporal, but by March 1918 he
was an acting Serjeant, and then confirmed in this rank. In April 1918 he
was wounded, but managed to remain on duty. Five months later he was
killed in action.

Porter signed up at Camberwell on 12 May 1915. He was 24. The attes-
tation form shows that he opted to allot sixpence a day from his pay to his
wife – which was just as well because his wife Daisy (née Kennett) was
pregnant with their first and only child. It is likely that Porter was able to
see his baby, Iris Georgina, who was born in November 1915, as he did not
leave England until April the following year.

Blue-eyed with brown hair and a fresh complexion, Porter was 5 feet 8¼
inches tall and weighed nearly 10 stone. His chest measurement was 37
inches, and his physical development was judged "fair."

George and Daisy Porter lived at 66 Kellett Road, Brixton, Daisy and Iris
later moving to 61 Hinton Road, Herne Hill. From that address she sent a
pained note to the Army: "Dear Sir," she wrote on 2 January 1919, "Could
you inform me the reason why my late husband George Hand Porter No.
290873. 126 Heavy Battery R.G.A.'s effects have not been sent to me as it is
nearly four months since he was killed."

These effects, when they reached her, were numerous and included:
two wallets, photos, calendar, metal mirror, watch, pen, guard and chain,
collapsible cup, pocket knife, scissors, gold ring, rosary, cap badge, belt,
match box cover, whistle, safety razor and case, cap badge, belt, tobacco
pouch, cigarette case, celluloid whistle, letters, spectacles, magnifying glass

and three lenses, five compasses, watch protector, razor strap, newspaper cuttings, fob watch, chevrons and brass crown.

In civilian life George Hand Porter had been a copperplate engraver. The job is highly skilled and the process demands sureness of touch combined with a light, delicate artistry. The objects returned to his widow speak of a careful, organised man used to close work.

Before he married in 1914, George Hand Porter lived with his widowed mother and three siblings at 111 Loughborough Road, Brixton. His mother, Martha Porter, 55, was from Walworth, south-east London. The 1901 census shows that George's father, listed simply as J. Porter, was a printer.

A. G. POTTER

Arthur George Potter, died on 13 April 1918, aged 39.

Private, Coldstream Guards, 3rd Bn., Service no. 12028. Remembered at Ploegsteert Memorial, Comines-Warneton, Hainaut, Belgium.

In 1911 31-year-old Arthur George Potter was working as a messenger for the Board of Education. He lived in three rooms at 86 Southville, Wandsworth Road, with his wife Louisa Ann, 39. They were both born in Lambeth.

A decade previously he lived with his parents, John Potter, a 53-year-old railway inspector born in Croydon, and Mary A. Potter, 54, originally from Sellack, Herefordshire, and two brothers at 19 Rosetta Street (now disappeared, this street was near Kenchester Close), South Lambeth. Arthur enlisted at Clifton Street.

E. A. POTTS

Ernest Alexander Potts, died of wounds on 15 October 1918, aged 26.

Second Lieutenant, Royal Fusiliers, 24th Bn. attached 10th Bn. Remembered at St. Sever Cemetery Extension, Rouen, Seine-Maritime, France. Awarded the *Military Cross*.

Policeman's son Ernest Alexander Potts, a former railwayman, volunteered for the Coldstream Guards in September 1914 and was sent to the Western Front later that year. He fought at the Battles of Ypres, Arras, Le Bassée and Givenchy. He was awarded the Military Cross for conspicuous gallantry and devotion to duty in the field during heavy fighting at the Somme in 1918.

Potts enlisted on 3 September 1914, rose to the rank of Lance Serjeant and in early 1918 was discharged to join the Royal Fusiliers on a temporary commission. Severely wounded on 8 October, he died a week later.

At 6 feet 3 inches tall, and weighing just over 11 stone, with a 36½-inch chest, Potts was slender rather than sturdy. He was pale, with blue eyes and brown hair. He suffered from eczema and he was hospitalised for this several times. In early 1917, he was admitted to the Bethnal Green Military Hospital in east London, and treated with a staphylococcal vaccine.

The 1911 census shows that Potts was one of four children of Edward Alexander Potts, 56, born in Gateshead, County Durham, a police pensioner working as a watchman at the Bon Marché department store in Brixton, and Emma Potts, 55, of Kennington. Ernest, then 18, was a railway employee. The family occupied six rooms at 9 Mordaunt Street, Stockwell.

C. E. R. POWELL

Charles Edward R. Powell, killed in action on 18 March 1917, aged 23.

Private, London Regiment, "C" Coy. 2nd Bn. (Royal Fusiliers), Service no. 6966/233236. Remembered at Beaurains Road Cemetery, Beaurains, Pas de Calais, France.

In 1911 Charles Edward R. Powell, 17, was a clerk to a stonemason. He lived with his family at 73 Grosvenor Road, Westminster, where they had three rooms. Powell's father, Charles Edward Powell, 45, was an Army pensioner from the West End of London. His mother, Amy Powell, 38, was from Winchester. Charles and two of his siblings were born on the island of St. Helena, a Crown Colony in the South Atlantic. He lived in Lambeth and enlisted in Westminster.

S. J. PRESCOTT

James S. Prescott, died on 28 March 1918, aged about 31.

Serjeant, Royal Scots Fusiliers, 1st Bn., Service no. 8638. Remembered at Arras Memorial, Pas de Calais, France.

In 1911 James S. Prescott, aged 24, was serving with the 2nd Battalion of the Royal Scots Fusiliers at Harrismith, Orange Free State, South Africa. His parents and sister lived in two rooms at 38 South Island Place, Stockwell. William G. Prescott, 63, from Dover, Kent, was a pensioner of Lambeth Borough Council; Mary Jane Prescott, 67, was from Taunton, Somerset. They had five children. James S. Prescott appears on the 1901 census as a commercial clerk. This remains a tentative identification as the carver of the War Memorial panels appears to have reversed Prescott's initials.

H. J. PRESTON

Henry John Preston, killed in action on 26 May 1915, aged 24.

Lance Corporal, London Regiment, 1/24th Bn. (The Queen's), Service no. 2462. Remembered at Le Touret Memorial, Pas de Calais, France.

In 1911 Henry John Preston, a 16-year-old dyer, was living at 5 Berkeley Street (near Lambeth High Street) with his half-brother, Frederick Dibb, 23, a wine merchant's employee, widowed mother Ellen Preston, 53, a cleaner in an infirmary and two siblings. The family occupied four rooms. Four siblings lived elsewhere. Ellen later lived at 33 Stockwell Road.

T. PROTHEROE

Thomas Protheroe, died of wounds on 26 March 1918, aged 38.

Private, East Lancashire Regiment, 2/5th Battalion, Service no. 39017; formerly Royal Field Artillery. Remembered at Etaples Military Cemetery, Pas de Calais, France and at St. Andrew's Church, Landor Road, Stockwell.

In 1911, Thomas Protheroe, 29, newly married to Florence, 28, lived at 40 Honeybrook Road, Clapham Park, where they had four rooms. Thomas worked as a process engraver in the newspaper industry. They had no children. Both were from Newington, south-east London. Florence later moved to 108 Grantham Road, Stockwell.

F. T. G. PULSFORD

Frederick Thomas George Pulsford, killed in action on 21 April 1915, aged 17.

Rifleman, London Regiment, 1/12th Bn. (The Rangers), Service no. 2338. Remembered at Ypres (Menin Gate) Memorial, Belgium.

Frederick Thomas George Pulsford volunteered, aged 16, on 8 September 1914, and went to France the following March. He survived about six weeks. In a letter to Pulsford's parents, Second Lieutenant H. H. Bentley described how their son had died: Pulsford and his friend Elvin were in a dugout at Zonnebeke helping a badly wounded comrade. All three were killed in a hail of shrapnel when a German shell fell into the dugout and exploded.

"The Rangers lost two fine soldiers in the painless heroic deaths of your son and his friend Elvin," wrote Bentley. "It gives me great pain to have to break this sad yet heroic news to you, because he was always a great friend of mine and one who always did the utmost of his duty." Pulsford was buried at the back of the trenches.

Pulsford's father, Frederick Luke Pulsford, was a heraldic engraver, born in Brixton; his mother, Blanche Bertha Pulsford (née Hawke), was from Saltash, Cornwall. The family, including a younger sister and grandmother, lived at 10 Tradescant Road, South Lambeth where they occupied five rooms. They had lived at this address since at least 1901.

A. E. PURSLOW

Albert Edward Purslow, died of wounds on 18 November 1916, aged 21.

Corporal, The Queen's Own Royal West Surrey Regiment, 7th Bn., Service no. 170. Remembered at Stump Road Cemetery, Grandcourt, Somme, France. Brother of *William Charles Purslow.*

In 1911 William Purslow, 21, and Albert Purslow, 15, were shop assistants, William for a hosier and Albert for an oilman. The brothers lived in four rooms at 15 Burnley Road, Stockwell with their parents Charles Purslow, 50, from Lydford in Devon, a musician, and Alice, 46, from Plymouth, and one of their two other siblings. Albert was born in Stonehouse, Devon and enlisted at Kingston upon Thames.

W. C. PURSLOW

William Charles Purslow, died of wounds on 29 May 1916, aged 26.
Corporal, Rifle Brigade, "B" Coy. 3rd Bn., Service no. S/12717.
Remembered at Bailleul Communal Cemetery Extension, Nord, France.
Brother of *Albert Edward Purlsow.*

William Charles Purlsow died on 29 May 1916 after the amputation of his right arm. Eight days earlier he had sustained a gunshot wound. He had served just under a year, with only about three months in total at the front. According to his Service records, Purslow suffered from otitis media (inflamation of the middle ear) in March and he was treated on an ambulance train. There are few other details, apart from a list of his effects (identity disc, Testament, diary, photos, cap badges, gold ring, letter). He was 25 when he joined up in London on 8 June 1915, and had a fresh complexion, blue eyes and brown hair.

Purslow left a widow, Eleanor Annie Purslow (née Hutchinson), whom he married in late 1915 (the banns were read at St. Michael's Church, Stockwell). Eleanor later remarried, becoming Mrs. Hillyer.

E. A. PYLE

Ernest Albert Pyle, killed in action on 19 March 1918, aged 31.
Private, Royal Fusiliers, 23rd Bn., Service no. G/81351; formerly
Middlesex Regiment. Remembered at Thiepval Memorial, Somme, France.

Ernest Albert Pyle was born in Tottenham, north London, the son of Richard Pyle, a house painter from Islington, and Sarah Jane Pyle, from Bristol. He enlisted in Lambeth in 1915 and served with the Expeditionary Force in France and Flanders. He was killed in action on 19 March 1918.

In 1911, Pyle was working as a house painter on the Holland Estate. He and his wife, Ellen, 25, who was also from Tottenham, had a two-year-old son, Ernest Richard. The family lived in four rooms at 59a Morat Street, Stockwell.

R

F. J. RAISHBROOK

Frederick James Raishbrook, died of wounds on 2 December 1917, aged 20.
Gunner, Royal Field Artillery, Z/29 Trench Mortar Bty., Service no.
955161. Remembered at Tincourt New British Cemetery, Somme, France.

In 1911 Frederick Raishbrook, aged 14 and working as a messenger boy
in a newspaper office, lived at 46 Landor Road, Stockwell with his parents,
siblings and two boarders. The household had five rooms. Frederick's
father, William Raishbrook, 40, a coal porter, was from Clapham, as was
his mother, Louisa, 37. Frederick had three siblings and there were two
boarders including Robert Schleicher, 24, an Austrian pastry cook.

B. C. RANCE

*Bernard Christopher Rance, died on
26 March 1917, aged about 22.*
Gunner, Royal Field Artillery,
27th Bde., Service no. L/11692.
Remembered at Aubigny Communal
Cemetery Extension, France. Brother
of *Charles F. Rance.*

Spring 1915 must have been a trying
time for William and Sarah Rance, with
four of their sons, Bernard, Charles,
James and Richard, volunteering for
service. Two years later, in March and
June 1917, the youngest two, Bernard
and Charles, were killed. Bernard
Christopher Rance volunteered in
March 1915 and was sent to the front

the following December. He fought at Ypres, the Somme, Ancre and Arras.

In 1911 the family was living at 16 Bolney Street, South Lambeth (they later moved to 155 Hartington Road). The household consisted of William Rance, 53, a furniture porter, born in Westminster; his wife Sarah, 53, also born in Westminster; two daughters and three sons, Albert, Bernard and Charlie. Four other children lived elsewhere.

C. F. RANCE

Charles F. Rance, killed in action on 7 June 1917, aged about 19.

Rifleman, London Regiment, 1/6th Bn. (City of London Rifles), Service no. 321283. Remembered at Ypres (Menin Gate) Memorial, Belgium. Brother of *Bernard Christopher Rance.*

Charles F. Rance volunteered in April 1915 and in the following September was drafted to France where he fought in the Somme and at Arras. *The National Roll of the Great War 1914–1918* says that he died at Vimy Ridge on 7 June 1917. According to the Commonwealth War Graves Commission, Rance is remembered at Ypres, Belgium, over 70 miles from Vimy Ridge.

C. H. RANDELL

Charles Henry Randell, killed in action on 25 September 1915, aged about 26.

Private, South Lancashire Regiment, 2nd Bn., Service no. 9114. Remembered at Ypres (Menin Gate) Memorial, Belgium.

I have not found Charles Henry Randell on the 1911 census, but his two sisters, a nephew and a boarder were living with his mother, Lilian Randell, in four rooms at 15 Sterndale Road, Battersea.

H. W. RAY

Henry Ray, died on 26 September 1917, aged 19.

Private, Lancashire Fusiliers, 10th Bn., Service no. 42425. Remembered at Boulogne Eastern Cemetery, France.

There are two candidates for H. W. Ray. The man whose details are given above was Lambeth-born Henry Ray, the son of Daniel David Ray and Catherine Ray, of 9 St. Andrew's Place, Windmill Street, New Cut, Lambeth. He enlisted in Camberwell. The 1911 census shows Henry Ray as a 13-year-old schoolboy living with his family at 17 Mary's Buildings, Tanswell Street, north Lambeth, where the family of nine had four rooms. His father, Daniel, who was from Southwark, earned a living as a costermonger, selling fruit and vegetables from a barrow. His mother Catherine, 39, was from Ireland. The couple had eight children, of whom seven lived at home.

There is also an H. Ray (first name unknown), a Private (Service no. L/15708) in the Middlesex Regiment. He was born in Battersea and died on 26 March 1918.

W. C. RAY

William Charles Ray, killed in action on 23 October 1918, aged 23.

Private, East Surrey Regiment, 8th Bn., Service no. 39290. Remembered at Forest Communal Cemetery, Nord, France.

William Charles Ray lived in Stockwell and enlisted at Hounslow. His widow, Annie Florence Ray, lived at 44 Treganna Street, Brixton Hill.

J. H. RENTON

John James Renton, killed in action on 9 May 1915, aged 23

Private, East Surrey Regiment, 2nd Bn., Service no. 6074. Remembered at Ypres (Menin Gate) Memorial, Belgium.

The Memorial may be in error over Renton's initials. There is no J.H. Renton in the Commonwealth War Graves Commission database but there is a John James Renton who lived at 12 Stockwell Cottages, the son of J. H. Renton. In 1911 John James Renton, 19, a coal porter born in Brixton, lived at 1 Stockwell Cottages, Stockwell Green. John James Renton's father, John Henry, 47, was a nightwatchman for Lambeth Borough Council. He was born in Walworth, Southwark. John James's mother, Kathrine, 44, was a washer, born in Lambeth. The couple had six children, of whom four lived at home.

E. REYNOLDS

Ernest Reynolds, killed in action on 20 January 1918, aged about 20.

Sapper, Corps of Royal Engineers, 104th Field Coy., Service no. 143376. Remembered at Templeux-le-Guérard British Cemetery, Somme, France.

In 1911 Ernest Reynolds, 13, lived at 20 Tradescant Road, South Lambeth. His father, George Reynolds, 49, was a joiner and carpenter originally from Lowestoft, Suffolk. His mother, Jeanie, 45, was from Dufftown, Banffshire, Scotland. Ernest had three siblings. He enlisted at Croydon.

C. RHODES

Not identified.

F. RHODES

Francis Rhodes, died on 2 September 1916, aged 23.

Serjeant, Royal Army Medical Corps, Service no. 37889. Remembered at Basra War Cemetery, Iraq.

Francis Rhodes left a widow, Grace Lilian Rhodes, of 80 Crimsworth Road, South Lambeth.

E. V. RIDGE

Everard Vaughan Ridge, killed in action on 9 April 1917, aged 21.

Lieutenant, Machine Gun Corps (Infantry), 153rd Coy. Remembered at Arras Memorial, Pas de Calais, France.

Solicitor's son Everard Vaughan Ridge, a clerk at the Prudential Assurance Company, enlisted in the Territorial Force on 13 April 1913. He was 17. Ridge was in England from August 1914, serving as Gunner in the 7th County of London Battery Royal Garrison Artillery, until the following September when he was discharged to a commission in the 13th Reserve Battalion Worcestershire Regiment. He later transferred to the Machine Gun Corps, and was killed in action on 9 April 1917. At 5 feet 6 inches tall with a 35-inch chest, Ridge's physical development was described as "good." His family, twice-widowed Edward H. Ridge, 52, originally from Manchester, and five siblings plus a housekeeper, lived at 55 Chelsham Road, Clapham.

R. P. RIDLEY

Reginald Parnham Ridley, killed in action on 23 September 1916, aged 23.

Rifleman, London Regiment, 16th Bn. (Queen's Westminster Rifles), Service no. 589. Remembered at Delville Wood Cemetery, Longueval, Somme, France.

Reginald Parnham Ridley, aged 18 in 1911, was an electrical engineer. He was the eldest of three sons of Eliza Mary Ann Ridley, 47, a dressmaker. The family lived in nine rooms at 420 Clapham Road. Ridley's father, Frederick W. Ridley, was a grain merchant, but does not appear on the census return for this address. Ridley enlisted at Westminster.

W. A. RIDOUT

Walter Albert Ridout, died on 16 June 1916, aged 30.

Private, Canadian Corps Cyclist Battalion, Service no. 119029.
Remembered at Nunhead (All Saints) Cemetery, Linden Grove,
south-east London.

Streatham-born shoemaker Walter Albert Ridout volunteered early in the
war. On 12 November 1914, aged 28, he presented himself to the attesting
officer at Brighton and was signed up to the Royal Sussex Regiment, 8th
Reserve Cyclists Battalion. His form states that he had lived outside the
U.K., in Vancouver, Canada, for more than three years.

Ridout stood 5 feet 5 inches tall, with a dark complexion, dark hair and
grey eyes. His chest measured 36 inches.

By 17 February 1915 he was appointed acting Lance Corporal; he was
promoted to acting Corporal on 11 March. By 20 April he had reverted to
Private. However, on 25 June he was discharged from the Royal Sussex
Regiment to join the Canadian Expeditionary Force at Southwold, Suffolk.

The 1911 census shows Walter Ridout was one of five children of Walter
Y. Ridout, a 60-year-old bootmaker and repairer from Dorset, and Alice
Ridout, 49, who was "assisting in the business." Alice was born in the City
of London. The family – Walter, his parents and two of his four siblings –
lived at 14 Robsart Street, where they occupied five rooms and where they
had been since at least 1901.

N. V. RIVA

Norman Victor Riva, killed in action on 31 March 1915, aged 18.

Private, London Regiment, 2nd Bn. (Royal Fusiliers), Service no. 1891.
Remembered at Ferme Buterne Military Cemetery, Houplines, Nord,
France.

In 1911 Norman Riva, 14, was a dental assistant. He shared five rooms at
46 Priory Grove, South Lambeth, with his parents and five siblings. Riva's
father, Edward Riva, 42, a warehouseman, was from Camberwell; his
mother, Susannah, 41, was born in Westminster.

G. RIXTON

George Rixton, killed in action on 16 September 1916, aged 32.

Sapper, Royal Engineers, 2/1st Lowland Field Coy., Service no. 3483.
Remembered at Thiepval Memorial, Somme, France.

In 1911 George Rixton, then aged 26, was boarding with the Reed family at 1a Elwell Road, Clapham and working as a brewer's cooper (he made or mended beer barrels). Rixton was born in Weymouth, Dorset, where his family still lived. The 1901 census shows that his father, Robert Rixton, then aged 43, was a brewer's cellarman from Muckleford, Dorset.

R. H. ROBERTS

Robert Harry Roberts, died on 7 August 1918, aged about 19.

Private, Royal Sussex Regiment, 1/4th Bn., Service no. G/22229.
Remembered at St. Sever Cemetery Extension, Rouen, Seine-Maritime, France and at St. Andrew's Church, Landor Road, Stockwell.

This is a tentative identification. There is only one Robert Harry Roberts registered as living in Lambeth in 1911. He was a 12-year-old schoolboy living at 21 Cottage Grove, Stockwell with his parents and two sisters. Roberts's father, Lambeth-born Robert Alfred Roberts, 43, was a cloth-worker; his mother, Emma Eliza, 38, was from Islington, north London. Three boarders shared their six-room accommodation.

A. RODGERS
Not identified.

J. ROGERS
Not identified.

J. C. ROGERS
Not identified.

S. H. ROGERS
Not identified.

A. ROSKILLY

Alfred Roskilly, killed in action or died of wounds as a prisoner of war on 3 May 1917, aged 26.

Second Lieutenant, The Queen's Own Royal West Surrey Regiment, 7th Bn. Remembered at Arras Memorial, Pas de Calais, France.

After Alfred Roskilly died, there was some confusion in the War Office as to whether he was killed in action on 3 May 1917 or died just over a month later as a prisoner of war. The authorities had received information via the Red Cross, that an "A. Rostkeilly" of the Royal West Surrey Regiment was held by the Germans. However, no real conclusion emerges from the files, except that, in the absence of firm evidence, the Army accepted the earlier date as Roskilly's date of death. The date was important as it affected the payments owing to the deceased and inherited by his widow.

Roskilly, an assistant clerk in the Post Office Savings Bank at Blythe Road, West Kensington joined the 2nd (Cadet) Battalion of the London Regiment (Civil Service), moving to the 15th Battalion, and on 9 July 1915 transferring to the London Field Ambulance. He served one year and 225 days before being granted a temporary commission in the Royal West Surreys in March 1917. After that, he survived less than 10 weeks.

Arthur Roskilly was the eldest of four children of compositor (typesetter) Alfred Joseph Roskilly, from Dalston, east London, and Clara Roskilly, from Southampton. His military character was described as "very good." He stood 5 feet 7½ inches, weighed 9¾ stone and had a 39-inch chest.

In 1911 the Roskilly family lived at 32 Clitheroe Road, Stockwell, where they occupied six rooms. Arthur married Ruth Lambert at St. Anne's and All Saints Church, South Lambeth Road on 2 April 1914.

T. E. ROSS

Thomas Edward Ross, died on 29 September 1918, aged 24.

Able Seaman, Royal Naval Volunteer Reserve, Hood Battalion R.N. Div., Service no. R/6733. Remembered at Anneux British Cemetery, Nord, France.

Thomas Edward Ross joined the Army Reserve on 24 June 1916. He was drafted for the British Expeditionary Force on 3 September 1918, joined the Hood Battalion five days later, and was killed on 29 September. He left a widow, Emily Ross, who lived at 56 South Island Place, Stockwell.

A. F. V. ROUTLEDGE

Arthur Frederick Victor Routledge, killed in action on 14 April 1917, aged 28.

Private, Leicestershire Regiment, 9th Bn., Service no. G/14788. Remembered at St. Leger British Cemetery, Pas de Calais, France.

I have not been able to find Arthur Routledge (known as Vic) on the 1911 census. However, he is on the 1901 census as a 12-year-old living with his parents, Arthur Chapelhorn Routledge, 40, an upholsterer, and his wife, Selina, 34, and four siblings at 116 Junction Road, Islington, north London. After a period in Bournemouth, Arthur and Selina relocated to 13 Tregothnan Road, Stockwell.

Arthur's nephew, Norman Arthur Routledge, gave me some additional information about the fiancée Arthur left behind. Official data such as the censuses and the Army Service and Pension files do not generally include mention of bereaved friends, girlfriends or fiancées of the war dead, so this little vignette is especially valued:

"Vic's fiancée Maud had the very handsome bronze commemorative plaque for Vic which the authorities sent to all the families of dead soldiers," writes Norman. "She did not marry for a great many years and worked as a cook in Huntingdon. In old age she married three times – no doubt the cookery had something to do with that!"

Maud was unusual in that she married at all. The death of nearly a million United Kingdom servicemen in the war condemned many women to lifelong spinsterhood.

T. W. RUDGE

Thomas William Rudge, killed in action on 18 November 1916, aged about 28.

Private, Queen's Own Royal West Kent Regiment, 7th Bn., Service no. S/6582. Remembered at St. Andrew's Church, Landor Road, Stockwell.

Thomas William Rudge, who enlisted in Maidstone, Kent, is not included in the Commonwealth War Graves Commission database and for this reason his place of burial or official remembrance is not recorded. However, his details are in *Soldiers Died in the Great War 1914–1919*.

In 1911 brewer's labourer Thomas William Rudge, 23, lived at 8 Eastcote Street, Stockwell, where his family had four rooms. His widowed father, Daniel Rudge, 59, from Dedham, Essex, was a pipe joiner for the Metropolitan Water Board. Thomas had three siblings.

F. W. E. RUSSELL

Frank William Edmund Russell, killed in action on 16 August 1917, aged 26.

Rifleman, London Regiment, "D" Coy. 1/5th Bn. (London Rifle Brigade), Service no. 302875. Remembered at Ypres (Menin Gate) Memorial, Belgium.

The 1911 census shows that commercial clerk Frank William Edmund Russell, then 20, was the youngest child of Farnham-born Francis Russell, 49, and Catherine Russell, 49, born in Camberwell. Francis Russell owned a coffee shop at 89 London Road, Southwark, where the family occupied five rooms.

On 2 August 1915, at the Church of St. Saviour with St. Thomas in Southwark, Frank married Katherine Louisa Kies, the daughter of a German baker, who lived at 34 Newcomen Street, Southwark. She later gave her address as 33 St. Martin's Road, Stockwell.

H. RUSSELL

Not identified.

S

G. F. W. SACH

George Frederick William Sach, killed in action on 21 September 1918, aged 21.

Rifleman, London Regiment, 12th Bn. (The Rangers), Service no. 470989. Remembered at Villers Hill British Cemetery, Villers-Guislain, Nord, France and at St. Andrew's Church, Landor Road, Stockwell.

George Frederick William Sach, the son of an Ealing milkman, volunteered aged about 18 in February 1915. He was sent to France in 1917 and fought on the Somme, at Ypres, Arras, Albert, St. Quentin, St. Eloi and Lille. He also served in the Retreat of 1918 but was killed in the Allied Advance, the offensive that led to the demoralisation and retreat of the German armies and, ultimately, to the end of the war.

In 1911 George Sach lived at 28 Edithna Street, Stockwell with his parents George Sach, 39, from Ealing, and Emily Elizabeth Sach (née Betts), 45, from Litcham, Norfolk, his younger brother and four other relatives.

A. G. V. SALES

Albert George Victor Sales, killed in action on 26 September 1917, aged 33.

Private, Leicestershire Regiment, "A" Coy. 2/5th Bn., Service no. 242156. Remembered at Tyne Cot Memorial, Heuvelland, West-Vlaanderen, Belgium.

On 18 April 1918 the Army declared that Albert Sales was "regarded for official purposes as having died on or around 26/9/17." After only three months at the front, Sales had been killed during the chaos of battle and his body was now untraceable.

Sales, a sheet metal worker, presented himself at the recruiting office on 24 February 1916. He gave his address as 82 Larkhall Lane, Stockwell. He was measured: 5 feet 6¼ inches, just over 10 stone and with a 38-inch chest and the Army noted a squint in his right eye. Like many other conscripts, he went into the Army Reserve, waiting his turn to be mobilised. In February 1917, he was trained and sent to France. However, Sales had repeated trouble with a septic foot. He was injured on 28 April, but did not receive treatment until 9 May. Then in late June he was sent to the front, and went missing.

I have not located Sales in the 1911 census, but his mother, Theresa Sales, a 56-year-old railway waiting room attendant from Doncaster, was living at 172 Stewart's Road, off Wandsworth Road with her youngest child, 15-year-old Archibald Oliver Sales, and a married daughter, Elizabeth Gertrude Riley, 29, and her two children.

H. SAUNDERS

Henry or Harry Saunders, died on 7 July 1916, aged 20.

Private, Royal Fusiliers, 9th Bn., Service no. 9254. Remembered at Thiepval Memorial, Somme, France.

This identification is tentative, as I have not managed to connect the Henry Saunders detailed here with Stockwell, although in 1911 he was living in Lambeth. Harry Saunders, then aged 15 and working as a van boy, lived with his parents, Henry Saunders, 48, a blacksmith from St. Mary's Redcliffe, Bristol, and Georgina, 50, from Islington, north London, at 6 Howley Place, Waterloo, where they occupied four rooms. Harry was born in Shoreditch, east London.

S. H. SCOTT

Sidney Herbert Scott, killed in action on 7 October 1916, aged 23.

Private, London Regiment, "A" Coy. 1/7th Bn. (City of London), Service no. 352378. Remembered at Thiepval Memorial, Somme, France.

Sidney Herbert Scott volunteered in July 1915. He was sent overseas in the following year and served in the Somme. He was reported missing on 7 October 1916, and was later presumed to have been killed in action.

In 1911, 16-year-old Sidney was working as a shop assistant for a newsagent. He lived at 24 Edithna Street, Stockwell with his parents, Herbert F. Scott, 47, an electrician from Park End, Gloucester, and Emma E. Scott, 44, who was born in Clerkenwell, four of his five siblings and a cousin.

A. V. SCUTT

Victor Albert Scutt, killed in action on 21 March 1918.

Lance Corporal, The Buffs (East Kent Regiment), 1st Bn., Service no. G/15812. Remembered at Arras Memorial, France.

A tentative identification as the Commonwealth War Graves Commission database and *Soldiers Died in the Great War 1914–1919* record Scutt as Victor Albert rather than Albert Victor. He was born in and lived in Lambeth, and enlisted there.

C. F. SEYMOUR

Not identified.

A. SHARMAN

Arthur Sharman, died of wounds on 31 July 1915, aged 21.

Rifleman, King's Royal Rifle Corps, 8th Bn., Service no. A/187. Remembered at Lijssenthoek Military Cemetery, Poperinge, West-Vlaanderen, Belgium. Brother of *Harry Sharman.*

In 1911, aged 17, Arthur Sharman was working as a labourer; his brother Harry was 11 and at school. They were two of seven children of Edward Sharman, 62, a stone worker from Diss, Norfolk, and Elizabeth Sharman, 50, from King's Lynn, Norfolk. Arthur, Harry, their parents and a sister lived in two rooms at 17 Richmond Place, Stockwell.

The names of Arthur Sharman and his brother Harry were added, out of sequence, to the last panel on the Memorial, presumably after the 1922 unveiling. Edgar Stanley Sharman is also on the Memorial – it is not known if or how he is related to these two brothers.

E. S. SHARMAN

Edgar Stanley Sharman, killed in action on 31 May 1917, aged 25.

Rifleman, Rifle Brigade, 16th Bn., Service no. S/30908. Remembered at Vlamertinghe Military Cemetery, Belgium.

Edgar Stanley Sharman, aged 19 in 1911, was a ship's steward. He lived at 5 Tradescant Road, South Lambeth, with his widowed father, Charles William Sharman, 50, a commercial traveller (he sold hairdressing sundries), originally from Battersea, and two siblings.

H. SHARMAN

Harry Sharman, died on 8 November 1918, aged 18.

Rifleman, King's Royal Rifle Corps, 51st Bn., Service no. TR/13/62040. Remembered at Lambeth Cemetery, Blackshaw Road, Tooting, south-west London. Brother of *Arthur Sharman.*

W. J. SHARP

William James Sharp, killed in action on 22 August 1918, aged 31.

Rifleman, London Regiment, 21st Bn. (First Surrey Rifles), Service no. 656082. Remembered at Norfolk Cemetery, Bécordel-Bécourt, Somme, France.

In 1911, 24-year-old Clapham-born William Sharp was a tram driver. He lived with his widowed father, Joseph Sharp, 65, an unemployed coachman from Pimlico, in two rooms at 1 Northall Street (near Lingham Street), Stockwell. On 14 October 1917 he married Grace Elizabeth Wickes at St. Barnabas Church, South Lambeth. She later lived at 16 Paradise Road, Stockwell.

F. D. SHEA

Frederick David Shea, died of wounds on 19 January 1918, aged 28.

Lance Corporal, The Queen's Own Royal West Surrey Regiment, 11th Bn., Service no. G/11619. Remembered at Giavera British Cemetery, Arcade, Italy. Brother of *George Shea.*

In 1911 Frederick David Shea, 22, was a clerk in a grocery warehouse. He lived in four rooms at 425 Forest Road, Walthamstow, east London, which he shared with his mother, Frances Shea, 49, a widow from Clapham, and two siblings. Ten years previously, when Frederick Shea was a 12-year-old schoolboy, he and his younger brother George lived with their grand-mother, Amelia Couturier, 67, a Clapham-born bookseller, at 209 Clapham Road, along with his uncle, Francis L. Couturier, a bookseller's assistant.

G. SHEA

George Shea, killed in action on 6 September 1916, aged about 19.

Rifleman, London Regiment, 1/5th Bn. (London Rifle Brigade), Service no. 304330; formerly 7th Middlesex Regiment. Remembered at Thiepval Memorial, Somme, France. Brother of *Frederick David Shea*.

George Shea was born in Walthamstow, east London. He enlisted in Hornsey, north London.

A. R. SHEARING

Arthur R. Shearing, killed in action on 1 November 1914.

Private, Highland Light Infantry, 2nd Bn., Service no. 9050. Remembered at Ypres (Menin Gate) Memorial, Belgium

Arthur R. Shearing was born in Clapham and enlisted in London. He served in France for three months before he was killed.

A. H. SHOPLAND

Albert Henry Shopland, died of wounds on 16 August 1917, aged 24.

Lance Sergeant, Canadian Infantry (Quebec Regiment), 24th Bn., Service no. 701250. Remembered at Vimy Memorial, France.

Albert Henry Shopland joined the war effort on 17 March 1916, when he attested at Winnipeg, Canada. He was 23 and worked as a farmer in Yarbo, Saskatchewan.

Shopland was born in Cheltenham, Gloucestershire and as a child had lived at 41a Goldsborough Road, near Wandsworth Road. It is possible that he left England before 1911, as he does not appear on the 1911 census return for the Shopland family at Goldsborough Road (where the family had lived since at least 1901).

Shopland stood 5 feet 11 inches tall, and had a fair complexion with blue eyes and dark brown hair. He stated that he had previously served with the Royal West Surrey Territorials.

Shopland's father, William Robert, 49, was a coach body maker from Bridgwater, Somerset; his mother, Jane, 45, was from Windsor, Berkshire. Three of Shopland's four siblings lived with them.

H. F. SIMPSON

Harold Frederick Simpson, died of wounds on 3 June 1918, aged 22.

Private, Royal Fusiliers, 2nd Bn., Service no. 5190. Remembered at Ebblinghem Military Cemetery, Nord, France.

In 1911 Battersea-born Harold Frederick Simpson, 15, lived at 52 Belle-fields Road, Stockwell, where his family occupied five rooms. He was the eldest of three children of Frederick Simpson, 44, a solicitor's clerk from the City of London, and Clara Jane Simpson, 44, born in St. Marylebone, central London.

L. H. SIMS

Louis Henry Sims, killed in action on 21 August 1917, aged about 30.

Rifleman, King's Royal Rifle Corps, 9th Bn., Service no. R/25464. Remembered at Tyne Cot Memorial, Heuvelland, West-Vlaanderen, Belgium.

Louis Henry Sims was an only child. In 1911, aged 24, he was working as a printer's labourer. He and his parents, Henry William Sims, 51, a copper and steel plate printer born in Lambeth, and Henrietta Sims, 50, from Richmond, Surrey, lived at 31 Ely Place, Stockwell in six rooms, which they shared with three boarders.

E. T. SKUDDER

Ernest Thomas Skudder, died of wounds received in bombing training on 18 February 1918, aged 20.

Rifleman, London Regiment, 21st Bn. (First Surrey Rifles), Service no. 651614. Remembered at Rocquigny-Equancourt Road British Cemetery, Manancourt, Somme, France.

On 18 February 1918, at Cambrai, France, Ernest Thomas Skudder, a 20-year-old Rifleman in the 21st London Regiment, was with his platoon at the front. They were taking part in an exercise to test a new type of grenade, the No. 84, Mark II. Unfortunately, during testing, Skudder remained standing after the order was given to get down, and he died of multiple and severe wounds, to the neck, left shoulder, arm. "Hand spattered," noted an officer in the records.

As was usual in such cases, the Army held a Court of Enquiry in the Field. The notes from this have been lost so we do not know the conclusions it came to. However, superior officers felt that after the Enquiry questions remained. "Was a qualified officer in charge of the 'throwing,' in accordance with instructions contained in Para I, Chapter IX, SS 182 - Part II, please?" they asked. What happened, exactly, to Rifleman A. Silverton, who was apparently caught up in the explosion, and where did he get his much less severe injuries? Were they self-inflicted?

The party had been testing the throwing of grenades with an instructor and an assistant. The thrower stood up with the instructor and aimed over the top of the trench at the rifle butts, which were about 100 yards away. However, 15 yards to the right of this group stood Skudder with the rest of his party behind him. He was not in the line of fire, but, according to one witness, Rifleman W. Richardson, he was the only one not to obey the order to get down. Lance Corporal Gray, whom the officers suspected had failed in his duties, claimed he did not notice anyone not lying down, because he had got into the trench and was facing in the opposite direction.

The bomb landed in the trench near Skudder. The conclusion of the Enquiry includes the line: "If Skudder had obeyed the order given by Sgt. W. Ellis he would not have been wounded. He went forward with the intention of throwing the bomb clear of the trench." This seems to imply that the bomb landed in the wrong place and Skudder tried to pick it up and throw it out of harm's way. In the event, the enquiry team found no wilful negligence. They blamed Gray but decided to take no action as there was no intention to harm Skudder. As for Silverton, there was not enough evidence to decide how he was injured.

Skudder's death, after serving two years and 259 days, bereaved his parents, Emma Elizabeth and Alfred Thomas, and sister Edith Emma. Six months later, in July, Emma died of flu and pleuropneumonia. She was 58.

The Army sent on Skudder's effects to his family: an identity disc, letters, a small pocket notebook, a cigarette case, a Christmas card, a "wounded stripe" (he had received a gunshot wound to his thigh in June 1917), a canvas wallet and a linen bag.

In life, Skudder stood 5 feet 6¼ inches tall. He measured 36½ inches around the chest. His physical development was deemed "good." We know from the *National Roll of the Great War* that he took part in several of the war's most bitter battles, including Hill 60, the Second Battle of Ypres, Loos and Vimy Ridge. During this time he had only one black mark against his name, and that was before he was posted to France – for being absent from Retreat until Tattoo on 21 November 1915, for which he was punished with three hours' pack drill and the loss of two days' pay. He was in England for five months in 1916, during which he was hospitalised for 28 days with "debility following influenza".

The 1911 census shows Skudder, then 13, living in five rooms at 26 Clarence Street, Stockwell with his parents and sister. His father, Alfred Thomas Skudder, 53, was a brewer's drayman from Greenwich; his mother, Elizabeth Emma Skudder, 50, was born in Clapham.

E. A. SLADE

Not identified.

P. H. SLOOTS

Percy Hendrick Sloots, died on 31 October 1918, age 24.

Lance Corporal, East Surrey Regiment, 12th Bn., Service no. 25582. Remembered at Kezelberg Military Cemetery, Wevelgem, West-Vlaanderen, Belgium.

In 1911 Percy Hendrick Sloots was 15 and working as a telegraph messenger for the General Post Office. He lived in four rooms at 86 Stockwell Road with his father, Dutch-born hairdresser George Sloots, 42, and mother, Jane E. Sloots, 46, from Pimlico, and two younger brothers. A boarder, Hugh Vollbrecht, a hairdresser's assistant from Norwich, lived with the family.

On 5 March 1918 Sloots married Lillian Ellen Elizabeth Mann at St. Andrew's Church, Landor Road. She lived at 84 Hargwyne Street, Stockwell and her father worked as a Post Office sorter.

J. C. SMALE

Joseph Charles Smale, died of wounds on 22 January 1916, age 24.

Private, The Queen's Own Royal West Kent Regiment, "C" Coy., 8th Bn., Service no. G/2820. Remembered at Boulogne Eastern Cemetery, France. Brother of *William Herbert Smale.*

In 1911 Joseph Charles Smale, 19, was a laundry foreman; his brother William Herbert Smale, 25, was a soap-maker. They lived with their mother, Martha, 48, stepfather George Tucker, 50, and siblings at 3 Kenchester Street (near Wilcox Road), South Lambeth. George Tucker worked in a laundry and had been married to Martha for six years. They had a six-year-old son. Three of Martha's other children lived in the household.

W. H. SMALE

William Herbert Smale, died on 29 July 1916, aged 30.

Private, East Surrey Regiment, "C" Coy., 1st Bn., Service no. 6810.
Remembered at Thiepval Memorial, Somme, France. Brother of *Joseph Charles Smale.*

C. E. SMALL

Charles Edward Small, killed in action on 31 October 1917, aged 21.

Driver, Royal Field Artillery, "A" Bty. 302nd Bde., Service no. 960469.
Remembered at Jerusalem Memorial, Israel and at St. Andrew's Church, Landor Road, Stockwell.

Charles Edward Small presented himself at the Fulham recruiting office early in the war – on 16 September 1914. We do not know what kind of occupation he left behind as this was not noted in his Service records.

Small was 19 in 1914 and a good 5 feet 7½ inches tall. His vision and physical development was noted as "very good."

On 24 April 1918, his mother Laura wrote to the War Office to enquire about the "watch and silver mizpah ring" which should have been among her son's effects. Mizpah rings, popular at the time, were given when close relatives or lovers were about to be separated.

In 1911, Small, his widowed mother – a dressmaker – and three siblings, lived at 61 Mordaunt Street, Stockwell where they had been since at least 1901. Small's father had been a coach painter from Reigate, Surrey.

E. C. SMART

Edwin Charles Smart, killed in action on 3 September 1917, aged 35.

Rifleman, Monmouthshire Regiment, 1st Bn., Service no. 263068.
Remembered at Loos Memorial, Pas de Calais, France.

On 7 November 1917 Elizabeth Ann Smart, widow of Edwin Charles Smart, wrote to the War Office from her home at 12 Thorpach Road, near Wandsworth Road: "Will you please let me have my marriage and other certificates which I have forwarded to you on 20th of Sept.," she said. "...I am sorry to trouble you only I have a [illegible] means a [illegible] £5 to me and of which I would be glad, being left with four young children." Elizabeth was struggling to manage on the money she had coming in. Edwin's death left her to care alone for the children: Eliza Louise, 6, Alice Maisie, not yet 5, and Edwin Alexander, 3, all born before the couple married at Lambeth Register Office on 5 December 1914, plus Emlyn Thomas Campbell, 13, her son by a previous relationship.

Smart enlisted on 11 December 1915 when he was 34. He was described as 5 feet 8 inches and 10 stone. His chest measured 39 inches and his physical development was "good."

A. G. SMITH
Not identified.

A. F. SMITH
Not identified.

F. D. SMITH
Not identified.

S. G. SMITH
Sydney George Smith, killed in action on 26 September 1917, aged 37.
Company Serjeant Major, London Regiment, 12th Bn. (The Rangers), Service no 470355. Remembered at Tyne Cot Cemetery, Zonnebeke, West-Vlaanderen, Belgium and at St. Andrew's Church, Landor Road, Stockwell.

Only three pages of Sydney George Smith's service record survive. They cover his five-year period of service with the Territorials, from 26 May 1909 to 25 May 1914, when he left the London Regiment (The Rangers) as a Lance Corporal. They state that Smith was 29 when he joined; he was married and living at 13 Effort Road, Highbury, north London; he was a clerk with Ellis & Co.; he was 5 feet 10 inches tall, with a chest of 36½ inches. Smith had married Mabel Annie Mason on 6 September 1902 at St. Andrew's Church, Stockwell. He was employed as a solicitor's clerk.

W. E. SMITH
Not identified.

F. W. SNELLING

A report in *The South London Press* (5 January 1916), states that the name "Frederick Snelling" name appeared on a commemorative "war crucifix", now lost, outside St. Anne's Church, South Lambeth Road.

H. M. SNELLING

W. T. SNELLING

William Thomas Snelling, killed in action on 26 October 1917, aged 21.

Able Seaman, Royal Naval Volunteer Reserve, Howe Bn. R.N. Div., Service no. R/2283. Remembered at Tyne Cot Memorial, Heuvelland, West-Vlaanderen, Belgium.

William Thomas Snelling, born in 1894, formerly of the 2/1st Westmorland and Cumberland Yeomanry, enlisted in the Territorial Force on 30 August 1916, transferring to the R.N.V.R. on 16 June 1917. He joined the British Expeditionary Force on 4 July 1917 and Howe Battalion on 1 September. His family lived at 260 South Lambeth Road, Stockwell.

S. H. J. SORE

Sydney Herbert John Sore, killed in action on 22 March 1918, aged 22.

Private, London Regiment, 2/19th Bn. (St. Pancras), Service no. 614318; formerly 9th London Regiment. Remembered at Jerusalem War Cemetery, Israel.

In 1911 Sydney Herbert John Sore, aged 15, was an architect's clerk. His father, Alfred Sore, 48, was a solicitor's clerk, born in south London; his mother, Mary Emma Sore, 40, was from Tuddenham, Suffolk. Sydney had one sibling. The family lived at 8 Larkhall Lane, Clapham, where they occupied seven rooms. Sore was born in Clapham and enlisted at Oxford Street, London. He served in France, Salonika and Palestine.

R. C. SOUTHON

Reginald Charles Southon, killed in action on 23 October 1916, aged about 19.

Private, Essex Regiment, 2nd Bn., Service no. 13008. Remembered at Thiepval Memorial, Somme, France.

In 1911 Reginald Charles Southon, aged 14, was an errand boy living at 27 Rossiter Road, Balham, where his family shared five rooms. He was born in Hampstead, north-west London, one of two children of John Charles Southon, 46, a gas meter maker from Clerkenwell. John Southon had been married for a year to Reginald's stepmother, Olivia Estall, 48, from Peterborough. Reginald Southon enlisted in Westminster.

F. J. SPENCER

Not identified.

A. F. SPICE

Not identified.

I. SPOONER

Isaac Spooner, killed in action on 1 September 1918, aged 24.

Private, Duke of Wellington's (West Riding Regiment), 9th Bn., Service no. 25552; formerly Royal Army Service Corps. Remembered at Vis-en-Artois Memorial, Pas de Calais, France.

In 1911 ironmonger's assistant Isaac Spooner, 17, lived at 39 Brooklands Road, Stockwell, where his family had six rooms. His father, James Spooner, 55, from Newham, Hampshire, was a train engine driver for London & South Western Railway; his mother, Matilda Spooner, 55, was from Brixton. Three of Spooner's six siblings lived at home. Spooner enlisted in Battersea.

F. SPRAGG

Frank Spragg, killed in action on 28 March 1918.

Lance Corporal, London Regiment, 1/16th Bn. (Queen's Westminster Rifles), Service no. 551013. Remembered at Arras Memorial, Pas de Calais, France.

Frank Spragg lived in Clapham. He enlisted in Westminster.

A. E. STAINER

Alfred Ernest Stainer, died of wounds on 13 August 1916, aged 20.

Private, East Surrey Regiment, 9th Bn., Service no. 17371. Remembered at Carnoy Military Cemetery, Somme, France.

Alfred Ernest Stainer was born in Walworth and lived in Clapham. His parents gave their address as 1 Paradise Road, Stockwell.

J. A. STAMMERS

John Alfred Stammers, killed in action on 4 November 1918, aged about 23.

Driver, Royal Field Artillery, "B" Bty. 155th Bde., Service no. 41606. Remembered at Vis-en-Artois Memorial, Pas de Calais, France.

Few details of John Alfred Stammers's Army career survive. We know he joined the 186th Howitzer Brigade of the Royal Field Artillery on 6 September 1915 at Deptford as a Driver. He was described as 20 years and 306 days old, 5 feet 5½ inches tall, with a 37-inch chest. His general physical development was "good" but he had a varicose vein in his right leg.

The 1911 census shows John Alfred Stammers was a 16-year-old junior clerk. He was the only child of commercial clerk John William Stammers, 43, from Islington, north London and Phoebe Nellie Stammers, 42, from Shore-ditch, east London. The family lived in four rooms at 64c Hackford Road, Stockwell.

W. S. STANDLEY

Walter Samuel Standley, killed in action on 1 October 1916, aged 35.

Private, London Regiment, 1/20th Bn. (Blackheath and Woolwich), Service no. 5330. Remembered at Thiepval Memorial, Somme, France.

Walter Standley was a railway porter. In 1911, aged 28, he lived with his parents and two of his four siblings at 2 Church Terrace, Union Grove, Clapham, where they had seven rooms. His father, Samuel, 55, a wheelwright, and mother, Ellen, 52, were both from Hethersett, Norfolk.

C. J. STANLEY

Charles James Stanley, died on 14 September 1916, aged about 24.

Driver, Royal Field Artillery, 2/47th Div. Ammunition Col., Service no. 2862. Remembered at Dantzig Alley British Cemetery, Mametz, Somme, France.

In 1911 Charles James Stanley lived in four rooms at 23 Clarence Street, Studley Road, Stockwell with his widowed mother, Henrietta Stanley, 46, who was born in Lambeth, and four of his seven siblings. He was 19 and worked as a carter.

W. G. P. STANTON

William George Percy Stanton, killed in action on 30 October 1917, aged 29.

Gunner, Royal Field Artillery, "A" Bty. 290th Bde., Service no. 926496. Remembered at St. Julien Dressing Station Cemetery, Langemark-Poelkapelle, West-Vlaanderen, Belgium.

William George Percy Stanton was born in Bethnal Green, east London. His parents gave their address as 37 Lansdowne Road, South Lambeth.

G. E. STARKEY

George Ernest Starkey, killed in action on 22 March 1918, aged 19.

Private, Durham Light Infantry, 15th Bn., Service no. 78033; formerly Royal Army Service Corps (Motor Transport). Remembered at Pozières Memorial, Somme, France.

George Ernest Starkey had two Army careers, both short. On 12 May 1915 he joined the 21st Battalion of the London Regiment at the Flodden Road recruiting office in Camberwell. He was described as dark complexioned, with brown eyes and dark brown hair. He stood 5 feet 6½ inches, with a 36½ inch chest, and weighed just over 7½ stone. There was a scar on the small of his back and four scars on the fingers of his left hand. He had flat feet. Despite this, his physical development was judged "good."

He said he was a porter, and he said he was of age. Only 167 days passed before he was discovered and discharged. "This man would have continued a good soldier if he had been of the required age," was written in his record. Starkey was 16.

Starkey was back on 17 March 1917, at Grove Park recruiting office. This time he joined the Army Service Corps as a Driver. Although he had grown no taller, he was now broader: 11 stone, with a 39-inch chest. He was fairly swiftly sent to join the 88th Training Reserve, and from there he joined the Durham Light Infantry.

Starkey committed only two misdemeanours: at Seaham Harbour, County Durham on 6 December 1917 he was punished with seven days' confinement to barracks for "inatttention in afternoon parade." In January the following year, and also at Seaham, he was docked three days' pay for "overstaying his pass from 6pm and remaining absent until 10pm" when under orders for embarkation. On 9 January, after nearly a year in England, he sailed for France. He allotted part of his pay to his mother.

There are over 600 names from the Durham Light Infantry on the Pozières Memorial, which relates to the period between March and April 1918 when the Allied Fifth Army was driven back by the Germans across the former Somme battlefields.

Starkey's parents appear to have been separated. The 1911 census shows that he lived in an eight-roomed house at 85 St James's Road, Brixton, with his mother, Letitia A. Starkey, 37, a furniture dealer, originally from The Borough, Southwark, and four siblings. Letitia described herself as both married and the head of the household. There is no mention on the census of George's father (who was also called George). However, he is given as next of kin on George's Army Service file.

H. G. STEED

Henry George Steed, killed in action on 23 March 1918, aged 32.

Private, London Regiment, "B" Coy., 1/23rd Bn., Service no. 702340.
Remembered at Arras Memorial, Pas de Calais, France.

Details of Henry George Steed's Army service are scant. We do, however, know that he was a country boy. He was born in the village of Chadlington, in Oxfordshire, where he and his brother Albert, sons of a carter, were under-carters. We do not know when he came to London, but once there, he found employment as a gardener. He married Hannah Elizabeth and had three children. She later gave her address as 86 Acre Lane, Brixton.

On 10 December 1915 Steed enlisted in the London Regiment at Camberwell. He was described as 5 feet 9 inches tall, with a 40-inch chest. On 23 March 1918 he was wounded in action and went missing. "Death presumed," says the record.

J. W. STEVENSON

John William Stevenson, killed in action on 18 September 1916, aged about 23.

Lance Corporal, King's Royal Rifle Corps, 12th Bn., Service no. R/15974. Remembered at Thiepval Memorial, Somme, France.

A tentative identification. The J. W. Stevenson detailed above was born in Chelsea and lived in Vauxhall. The 1911 census includes a John Stevenson, aged 18, an assistant in a butcher's shop, who was born in Chelsea. He was one of seven children of John Ernest Stevenson, 41, himself a butcher's shop assistant, from Pimlico, and Annie Stevenson, 36, from Westminster. The family lived in seven rooms at 27 Thorne Road, South Lambeth.

H. STILLWELL

Horace Stillwell, killed in action on 28 September 1915, aged about 25.

Private, The Buffs (East Kent Regiment), 2nd Bn., Service no. G/6781. Remembered at Loos Memorial, France.

The file for Horace Stillwell is very damaged and only a few details are decipherable. He joined at Lambeth on 5 September 1914, weighing a little over 8½ stone. He was 5 feet 5 inches tall, unmarried and born in Bethnal Green, east London in 1890. One of his descendants, Glynis Park, writes, "Horace was the youngest of eight children of Thomas Stillwell. His father's first wife, Eliza Charlotte, died of tuberculosis in 1873 aged just 36. In 1911 the family were living at 93 Old South Lambeth Road. Thomas, aged 76, was a beer retailer; his wife Emma was 63. Edwin Ernest, aged 23, and Horace, 21, were both assistant retailers in the business."

H. M. STOCKTON

Herbert Malcolm Stockton, killed in action on 11 April 1917, aged about 21.

Gunner, Royal Field Artillery, "B" Bty. Service no. 49206. Remembered at Feuchy Chapel British Cemetery, Wancourt, Pas de Calais, France. Brother of *Harold Percival Stockton.*

Three Stockton brothers, Alfred, Herbert and Harold, signed up for service. All three joined the Royal Field Artillery, Herbert and Harold as Gunners. Alfred and Harold, who were in the 63rd Brigade, have adjacent Service numbers. Harold died in August 1915, Herbert in April 1917. Alfred survived.

Herbert Malcolm Stockton volunteered in February 1915 aged about 20, and later that same year was drafted to France. He fought at several battles, including that at Armentières.

In 1911 the brothers were living in four rooms at 39 Electric Avenue, Brixton (they later moved to Rumsey Road, Stockwell). Harold P. Stockton, 24, was a butcher's shop assistant, born in Finchley, north London. Alfred Leonard Stockton, 18, was a gas engineer. Herbert Malcolm Stockton, 16, was an apprentice brass finisher. Their parents, Arthur Stockton, 57, a stationer from Islington, north London and Clara F. Stockton, 54, from Thornley, Northamptonshire, had three other children.

H. P. STOCKTON

Harold Percival Stockton, died of wounds on 2 August 1915, aged 28.
Gunner, Royal Field Artillery, "B" Bty. 63rd Bde. Service no. 8332.
Remembered at Bailleul Communal Cemetery Extension, Nord, France.
Brother of *Herbert Malcolm Stockton*.

Harold Percival Stockton volunteered in February 1915, and later that year was drafted to France, where he was a gunner in the Armentières sector. In August 1915 he was severely wounded in action, died of his injuries and was buried at Bailleul. He was born in Finchley, north London.

W. H. STONE

Walter Henry Stone, died of wounds on 2 May 1917, aged 19.
Rifleman, King's Royal Rifle Corps, 8th Bn., Service no. R/34903;
formerly Rifle Brigade and 20th Training Reserve Battalion. Remembered at Bucquoy Road Cemetery, Ficheux, Pas de Calais, France and at St. Andrew's Church, Landor Road, Stockwell.

In 1911 Lambeth-born Walter Henry Stone, aged 13, lived at 13 Hargwyne Street, Stockwell, with his parents, Henry Stone, 40, a carter from Stocking Pelham, Hertfordshire, and Elizabeth Alice Stone, 44, from Tylers Causeway, Hertfordshire. Walter had two younger siblings.

J. STRAND

Joseph Strand, died of wounds on 18 August 1917, aged about 33.

Corporal, King's Royal Rifle Corps, 9th Bn., Service no. 6/9792.
Remembered at Mendinghem Military Cemetery, Poperinge,
West-Vlaanderen, Belgium.

Barman Joseph Strand, 28, was unemployed in 1911. He lived with his widowed mother, Elizabeth Sarah, 58, brother, Herbert Stanley, 25, and a boarder in two rooms at 57 Hartington Road, South Lambeth. Three siblings lived elsewhere. Henry Strand, Joseph's father, was a painter.

G. S. STRANGE

George Steven Strange, killed in action on 11 May 1917.

Private, Royal Fusiliers, 2nd Bn., Service no. 39606. Remembered at
Wancourt British Cemetery, Pas de Calais, France.

George Steven Strange was born in Stockwell and enlisted at Lambeth.

G. W. SULLIVIN

George William Sullivan, died of wounds on 29 June 1917.

Rifleman, King's Royal Rifle Corps, 20th Bn., Service no. R/32443.
Remembered at Mont Huon Military Cemetery, Le Tréport,
Seine-Maritime, France.

A tentative identification. "Sullivin" on the Memorial may be a spelling error for Sullivan. According to *Soldiers Died in the Great War 1914–1919*, George William Sullivan was born in Lambeth and lived in Stockwell.

H. T. SUTTON

Hubert Tindal Sutton, died on 21 November 1914, aged 30.

Private, Royal Inniskilling Fusiliers, 2nd Bn., Service no. 9005.
Remembered at Ploegsteert Memorial, Comines-Warneton, Hainaut,
Belgium.

I have not found Hubert Tindal Sutton in the 1911 census, but his parents, Stanley, 49, a clerk and former pawn-broker from Tenterden, Kent, and Mary, 47, from London, are found at Tendring, Essex. The family had a live-in servant. After the war, they lived at 5 Gauden Road, Clapham.

T

H. TANNER
Not identified.

J. TANNER
Not identified.

O. A. TAYLOR
Oscar Albert Taylor, killed in action on 27 September 1917,
aged about 28.

Rifleman, London Regiment, 2/9th Bn. (Queen Victoria's Rifles), Service
no. 397794. Remembered at Tyne Cot Memorial, Heuvelland,
West-Vlaanderen, Belgium.

In 1911, Lambeth-born 22-year-old clerk Oscar Albert Taylor lived at 41
Landor Road, Stockwell, with his parents, three siblings, a grandfather and
a boarder. His father, Albert William Taylor, 52, was a joiner from Hockering,
Norfolk, and his mother, Rose Taylor, 47, was from Hackney, east London.
Albert's father, 79-year-old William Taylor, a widowed retired gamekeeper
from Hockering, lived with the family. The household had six rooms, and
the family had lived at that address since at least 1901.

T. TAYLOR
Not identified.

L. H. TEAKLE

Leonard Hastings Teakle, killed in action on 2 May 1915, aged 25.

Lance Corporal, London Regiment, "D" Coy. 1/5th Bn. (London Rifle Brigade), Service no. 157. Remembered at Ypres (Menin Gate) Memorial, Belgium and at St. Andrew's Church, Landor Road, Stockwell.

Leonard Hastings Teakle, 21 in 1911, was a bank clerk. He lived in six rooms with his widowed mother, 47-year-old Elizabeth Teakle, from Hackney, east London and three siblings at 26 Finchley Road, Walworth, south-east London. Teakle's deceased father, Hastings Charles Teakle, was a wheelwright from Avening, Gloucestershire.

J. C. TERRETT

Joseph Charles Terrett, killed in action on 26 May 1915, aged 40.

Private, London Regiment, "C" Coy. 1/23rd Bn., Service no. 2746. Remembered at Le Touret Memorial, Pas de Calais, France.

When Joseph Charles Terrett, a school attendance officer, joined the Army on 8 September 1914 at St. John's Hill, Clapham Junction he left behind a wife, Mary Ann, and three sons: 14-year-old Joseph, 10-year-old Reginald, and Geoffrey, who was two.

The Service file for Joseph Terrett does not contain much personal information. We know that he was 39 and had previously served in the 4th Battalion of the East Surrey Regiment, and that he joined his service battalion on 12 November 1914. A torn scrap of paper in the file lists some of his effects including photo, knife and torch.

The authorities wanted to send Terrett's medals to his widow, Mary Ann Terrett, but had difficulty ascertaining her whereabouts. Efforts to find her through her solicitors, Balderston, Warren and Pothecary of Bedford Row, W.C.1, drew a blank; they were not even sure who Terrett was. In 1920 Mrs. Lawrence, Mrs. Terrett's neighbour at Knowle Road (the street has gone but Knowle Close, off Wynne Road, remains), put the authorities right: in June Mrs. Terrett and her children had sailed for a new life in Canada.

T. THORNE
Not identified.

F. W. THURGOOD
Francis William Thurgood, killed in action on 25 September 1915, aged about 20.

Private, The Buffs (East Kent Regiment), 8th Bn., Service no. G/1529.
Remembered at Loos Memorial, Pas de Calais, France.

Mobilised at the outbreak of war, Francis William Thurgood proceeded immediately to France, and fought in the Retreat from Mons, and in the Battles of the Marne and Aisne. He also took part in the fighting at Ypres and was killed in action at Loos in September 1915.

In 1911 Francis William Thurgood was a 16-year-old "doctor's page" living in five rooms at 11 Arlesford Road, Stockwell with his parents, William Francis Thurgood, 42, a night inspector for trams employed by London County Council, and Ellen Thurgood, 40, and six siblings.

W. C. TIDNAM
William Charles Tidnam, died on 9 July 1917, aged 30.

Able Seaman, Royal Navy, H.M.S. *Vanguard*, Service no. 227258.
Remembered at Chatham Naval Memorial, Kent.

Just before midnight on 9 July, 1917, while positioned off Scapa Flow, north-east Scotland, the battleship H.M.S. *Vanguard*, a veteran of the Battle of Jutland, blew up suddenly, taking over 800 of her crew down with her. Although German saboteurs were suspected, the cause was probably a explosion of cordite in one of the two magazines which served the amidships turrets. Ernest "Mick" Moroney, an Able Seaman who witnessed the explosion while on watch duty aboard another ship, described how a nearby trawler was smothered with blood and body parts. Only one body was recovered. There were two survivors. Another Stockwell man, William Albert Crowther, a Stoker, also died in the incident (see page 60).

In 1911, on the night of the census, William Charles Tidnam, 23, the son of a coachman, was staying at the Union Jack Club in Waterloo Road, Lambeth. He was listed as a Navy Able Seaman from Harleston, Norfolk. On 11 December 1916, Tidnam married Kathleen Mary Roberts at St. Michael's Church, Stockwell.

A. G. TILLING

Albert George Tilling, killed in action on 8 June 1917, aged 22.

Gunner, Royal Field Artillery, "A" Bty. 93rd Bde. Service no. 83361. Remembered at Rue-Petillon Military Cemetery, Fleurbaix, Pas de Calais, France.

This is a tentative identification. *The National Roll of the Great War* includes an entry for Albert George Tilling, who volunteered in 1915 in Camberwell, was sent to France later that year, saw action on the Somme and at Ypres, and died fighting at Armentières in 1917.

According to the 1911 census, Tilling lived in six rooms at 82 Wilcox Road, South Lambeth with his parents, John Tilling, 50, and Annie Tilling, 49, four siblings and two boarders. He was a horse-keeper working for the London & South Western Railway, as was his father.

There is, in addition, a Service record for an Albert Tilling born in Lambeth in 1895. This Albert Tilling was an electrician's mate. Two days before his 20th birthday, on 20 August 1914, he signed up with the Dragoons of the Line (2nd Reserve Cavalry Regiment) at Clifton Street. He was tall and thin (5 feet 10 inches and only 9 stone, with a chest of 34½ inches) and his complexion was noted as "sallow" (yellowish). He was accepted as fit for service. After 65 days the Army noticed its mistake – this man's physical development and pulse rate were "poor". What's more, he was suffering from tuberculosis. He was duly discharged on 23 October.

It is unclear whether he enlisted again the following year (meaning that these two biographies relate to the same man), or whether there were two men in Lambeth named Albert Tilling, one of whom is remembered on the Memorial.

F. TOMLIN

Frederick Tomlin, died of wounds on 24 March 1918, aged 38.

Corporal, Machine Gun Corps (Infantry), 108th Coy., Service no. 42235; formerly London Regiment. Remembered at Noyon New British Cemetery, Oise, France.

Frederick Tomlin, a married salesman originally from Tring, Hertfordshire, lived at 98 Dalyell Road, Brixton, and enlisted in May 1916. Tomlin's physical development was described as "good" by the examining officer: he was 5 feet 4 inches tall, had a 36-inch chest and weighed 10 stone. He sustained a gunshot wound to his back on 23 March 1918 and died of his wounds.

A. J. TOOLEY

Albert John Tooley, killed in action on 23 January 1916, aged 23.

Private, London Regiment, 20th Bn. (County of London), Service no. 1797. Remembered at Maroc British Cemetery, Grenay, Pas de Calais, France and at St. Andrew's Church, Landor Road, Stockwell.

In 1911 Albert John Tooley, an only child aged 18, was a student teacher. He lived in a three-roomed apartment at 14 Kimberley Road, Stockwell with his parents, John Tooley, 56, a railway guard from Stockwell, and Bessie Tooley, 56, from St. Columb, Cornwall. He was born in Stockwell.

C. J. TOTHAM

Charles John Totham, killed in action on 2 June 1918, aged 18.

Private, The Queen's Own Royal West Kent Regiment, Service no. G/20867; then London Regiment, posted to 1/20th Bn. Remembered at Dernancourt Communal Cemetery Extension, Somme, France.

I have not found Charles Totham on the 1911 census, but his parents and two siblings are registered at 32 Eastcote Street, Stockwell, where they had two rooms. Arthur John Totham, 33, was a contractor's carman from Coggeshall, Essex; Emma Alice Totham, 33, was from Castle Combe, Wiltshire.

When joining the King's Royal Rifle Corps at Battersea on 10 March 1915, Charles Totham gave his age to the attesting officer as 18 years and 272 days and his occupation as carman. He was posted to Winchester on 12 March and then to Sheerness on 19 March, but was discharged on 19 June 1915 "having made a mis-statement as to age on enlistment." He returned to his family at 24 Lingham Street, Stockwell. Totham must have re-enlisted at a later date.

Totham, only 15 or 16, was a slight lad, standing only 5 feet 3 inches tall, and weighing just over 8½ stone, with a 35-inch chest.

D. TOWNSEND

Not identified.

G. C. TOZE

George Charles Toze, died on 24 May 1915, aged 27.

Serjeant, King's Own (Royal Lancaster Regiment), 1st Bn., Service no. 9451. Remembered at Ypres (Menin Gate) Memorial, Belgium.

In 1911, three years before the outbreak of war, George Charles Toze, aged 21, was registered on the census as a Lance Corporal in the King's Own (Royal Lancaster Regiment), at the Clarence Barracks, at Spithead Forts, Portsmouth, Hampshire. He was born in Kennington.

Meanwhile, at 11 Stockwell Green, his widowed mother, Nellie Toze, 43, a housekeeper from Bampton, Devon, shared her two-roomed home with two other sons and a boarder.

H. P. TOZER

Harold Percy Tozer, died in a flying accident on 16 December 1916, aged 25.

Second Lieutenant, Royal Flying Corps/Durham Light Infantry, 9th Bn. Remembered at East Harnham (All Saints) Churchyard, Wiltshire.

In 1911 Harold Percy Tozer, aged 19, a clerk for a timber merchant, lived with his parents and sister at 31 Lansdowne Gardens, Stockwell. His father, Henry James Tozer, 43, was a solicitor's clerk from Shadwell, east London; his mother, Agnes Emma Tozer, 43, was from Ipswich, Suffolk. Lilian Elizabeth Tozer, Harold's sister, was 16 and working as a clerk for a philatelist (stamp dealer). Both Harold and Lilian were born in South Lambeth. A cook, his wife and young son lodged with the family.

Tozer enlisted in the 4th Battalion of the Cameron Highlanders on 11 September 1914 and served for 347 days as a Private. His enlistment papers describe him as 5 feet 9 inches tall, with a 40-inch chest. He was sent to France on 19 February 1915 and suffered a gunshot wound to the elbow, after which he was invalided back to Fairfield Hospital, Broadstairs.

Later that year he was granted a temporary commission: Second Lieutenant in the Durham Light Infantry. Tozer's service from then until the flying accident that killed him in 1918 is not known. Lieutenant R. R. Gaskell of No. 14 Reserve Squadron, Royal Flying Corps (formerly Royal Engineers) was also killed in the incident.

J. TRACE

James Trace, killed in action on 1 July 1916, aged about 21.

Rifleman, London Regiment, 1/16th Bn. (Queen's Westminster Rifles), Service no. 8867. Remembered at Thiepval Memorial, Somme, France.

In 1911 James Trace was an office boy for a firm of solicitors. He shared four rooms at 70b Hackford Road, Stockwell with his parents and siblings. His father, unemployed cab driver John Trace, 59, was from Torbryan, Devon; his mother, Lucy Trace, 51, was from Leicestershire. Three other children lived at home and there were seven other siblings living elsewhere. Trace enlisted in Westminster.

C. A. J. TREACHER

Cecil Archibald Jacques Treacher, died on 9 May 1918, aged 25.

Private 2nd Class, Royal Air Force, Service no. 33191. Remembered at Lambeth Cemetery, Blackshaw Road, Tooting.

In 1911 Stockwell-born apprentice electrical wireman Cecil Archibald Jacques Treacher, 17, lived with his parents, Joseph Jacques Treacher, 48, an electrical wireman from Clerkenwell, north London, and Sarah Ann Treacher, 50, from Bermondsey, south-east London, and an older brother. Their accommodation at 14 Stansfield Road, Brixton had five rooms, and the family had been there since at least 1901.

S. H. TREMELLING

Stanley Humphrey Tremelling, killed in action on 26 May 1915, aged about 22.

Private, London Regiment, 1/24th Bn. (The Queen's), Service no. 3000. Remembered at Le Touret Memorial, Pas de Calais, France.

Stanley Humphrey Tremelling, aged 18 in 1911, was a machine ruler working for a general printing firm. He lived with his 55-year-old widowed mother, Lucy Tremelling (née Blundell), from Poplar, and 30-year-old stepsister Hilda Tremelling (his deceased father's daughter), who was working as a dressmaker. The family lived in eight rooms at 1 Milkwood Road in Brixton. Tremelling's father had been a patten maker (he made clogs or protective wooden soles to fit under shoes). Tremelling enlisted in Kennington.

B. TRIANCE

Bertram Triance, died on 19 November 1916, aged 28.

Sapper, Royal Engineers, 219th Field Coy., Service no. 164288.
Remembered at Mailly Wood Cemetery, Mailly-Maillet, Somme, France.

At the time of the 1911 census, Bertram Triance, aged 22, worked as a publisher's clerk and lived at 32 Army Street, Clapham with his wife Elizabeth Daisy Triance, 22, and baby daughter, Kathleen Margaret, six weeks. Bertram was born in Kilburn, north-west London, Elizabeth in Walworth, and Kathleen in Clapham. Ten years earlier, Bertram lived at 55 Lower Marsh, Waterloo, with his parents, William H. Triance , 50, a coffee house keeper from Middleton, Norfolk, and Isabella Triance, 45, from Hampstead, north-west London. Bertram was one of at least five children.

J. TRIMMER

James Trimmer, killed in action on 18 August 1916, aged 26.

Serjeant, The Loyal North Lancashire Regiment, 1st Bn., Service no. 9374.
Remembered at Delville Wood Cemetery, Longueval, Somme, France.

The 1911 census shows James Trimmer as a private in the 1st Battalion of the North Lancashire Regiment. He was stationed at the Bhurtpore Barracks, in South Tidworth, Hampshire. His parents, Harry Trimmer, 53, a locomotive engine driver from Holybourne, Hampshire, and Sophia Elizabeth Trimmer, 56, from Marylebone, London were living in four rooms at 94 Wilcox Road, South Lambeth, where they had been since at least 1901. James was one of three children.

R. W. TRUSSLER

Died on 27 April 1916.

Aviation Boatswain's Mate, Royal Navy, H.M.S. *Russell.*

R. W. Trussler, who lived at 29 Crimsworth Road, off Wandsworth Road and who joined the Navy in 1913, was with the *Russell* in the Mediterranean from August 1914. The *Russell* joined the Channel Fleet in November 1914 and after bombarding the coast of Belgium was sent to join the Dardanelles Squadron in the Dardanelles Campaign off the Gallipoli Peninsula.

The battleship stayed at Mudros, a small Greek port on the Mediterranean island of Lemnos, as support for H.M.S. *Hibernia* and she took part in the evacuation of Cape Helles from 7 to 9 January 1916. After the end of the Campaign, the *Russell* stayed on in the eastern Mediterranean.

The ship was steaming off Malta early on the morning of 27 April 1916 when she struck two mines laid by the German submarine U-73. A fire broke out and the order to abandon ship was given. Then there was an explosion and the ship started listing dangerously. She sank slowly, allowing most of her crew to escape, but 27 officers and 98 ratings, including R. W. Trussler, were lost.

A. G. TUFFREY

Arthur George Tuffrey

A tentative identification. I have found no military information on A. G. Tuffrey. However, in the 1911 census there was an Arthur George Tuffrey, a 29-year-old bank messenger born in London, living at 49 Thorne Road, Stockwell, with his wife, Madeline Ruth Tuffrey, 25, from Dunton, Norfolk, and their one-year-old son, Alec Arthur John Tuffrey, born in Lambeth.

W. E. TURPIN

William Evan Turpin, killed in action on 31 May 1918, aged 32.

Gunner, Royal Garrison Artillery, 172nd Siege Bty., Service no. 140311.
Remembered at Montecchio Precalcino Communal Cemetery Extension, near Vicenza, Italy.

William Evan Turpin joined in January 1917 at Clapham, and in the following May was sent to France, where he took part in the fighting at Bullecourt and Messines. Later he was transferred to Italy, where he was killed in action.

The 1911 census shows Turpin, a 25-year-old grocer's assistant, living in three rooms at 15 Elwell Road, Clapham, with his wife, Emma Turpin, 25, from Wolverhampton, and their young son, William Joseph Turpin, 11 months, born in Clapham. William Turpin's parents, Jesse Turpin, a 48-year-old bricklayer's labourer from Little London, Essex, and Mary A. Turpin, 48, from Aberaeron, Cardiganshire, were living at 62 Paradise Road, Stockwell.

U

H. G. UNDERWOOD

Herbert George Underwood, killed in action on 10 August 1917, aged about 34.

Rifleman, King's Royal Rifle Corps, 10th Bn., Service no. A/200471. Remembered at Ypres (Menin Gate) Memorial, Belgium.

In 1911, Herbert George Underwood, a motor cab washer, was 28 and living in four rooms at 4 Dorset Road, Stockwell with his widowed mother, Anne Underwood, 69, from Northamptonshire, and two of his five siblings plus a cousin. Underwood enlisted at Lambeth.

A. E. UPTON

Albert Edward Upton, killed in action on 21 March 1918, aged about 23.

Private, London Regiment, 7th Bn. (City of London), Service no. L/17507; formerly Middlesex Regiment. Remembered at Chauny Communal Cemetery British Extension, Aisne, France.

Albert Edward Upton, aged 16 in 1911, was described by his father Edward Upton on the 1911 census as "youth – not settled." For emphasis, Edward wrote the word "unsettled" again and added, confusingly, "butcher".

Albert lived at 7 Dawlish Street, South Lambeth with his parents, Edward Upton, 54, a goods guard for the London & South Western Railway, who was born in Stockwell, and Mary Ann Upton, 54, from Beaulieu, Hampshire. Albert Edward Upton was one of two children.

F. C. V. UPTON

Frederick Charles Vincent Upton, died on 11 November 1918 (Armistice Day), aged 18.

Air Mechanic 2nd Class, Royal Air Force, 116th Sqdn., Service no. 189301. Remembered at Aylesbury Cemetery, Buckinghamshire.

Frederick Charles Vincent Upton appears as Frederick William Upton on the 1911 census, an 11-year-old schoolboy born in Farnham, Surrey, and the only son of Frederick William Upton, 39, a coffee shop keeper from Betsham, Kent, and Annie Upton, 37, from Farnham, Surrey (she is described as "assisting in the business" on the census). The couple had three daughters. The family lived in five rooms at 2 Portland Place South (now disappeared although the remnant survives as Portland Grove), near Clapham Road.

As Upton is buried in Aylesbury Cemetery, it is probable that he was repatriated after being wounded or suffering from illness, and did not die in the field on the last day of the war.

G. E. VERNEY

George Edward Verney, killed in action on 26 September 1917, aged 33.
Private, Royal Sussex Regiment, 13th Bn., Service no. G/13935.
Remembered at Tyne Cot Memorial, Heuvelland, West-Vlaanderen, Belgium.

Brixton-born George Edward Verney was a baker. Aged 26, he was living with his parents, George Verney, 53, a cab driver from Winslow, Buckinghamshire, and Annie Verney, 60, from Riverhead, Kent, and a younger sibling at 20 Gilbey Road, Tooting, south-west London where the family had five rooms. Three other siblings lived elsewhere. The Verneys later moved to 53 Dalberg Road, Brixton.

A. H. VICKERS

Albert Henry Vickers, killed in action on 28 January 1917, aged 20.
Private, Royal Inniskilling Fusiliers, 2nd Bn., Service no. 10022.
Remembered at Sucrerie Military Cemetery, Colincamps, Somme, France.

Albert Henry Vickers, aged 15 in 1911, was one of 10 children of Thomas George Vickers, 52, a stoker at Lambeth Workhouse, from Poplar, east London, and Sarah Vickers, 51, from Stockwell. Thomas and Sarah lived at 26 Moat Place, a four-roomed tenement, with three of their children. The family had lived at that address since at least 1901. In 1911, Albert was an apprentice bootmaker living with the Goward family at 39 Elm Road, New Malden, Surrey.

T. VINCENT

Thomas Vincent, killed in action on 22 October 1914, aged 19.

Lance Corporal, Bedfordshire Regiment, 1st Bn., Service no. 10262.
Remembered at Le Touret Memorial, Pas de Calais, France.

Thomas Vincent, aged 15 in 1911, was a messenger for the telegraph office of the General Post Office. He lived with his parents and two brothers at 15 Springfield Place (now disappeared, it was in the area near Lansdowne Way and Wandsworth Road), Stockwell. His father, also called Thomas Vincent, 70, worked as a messenger for Lambeth Borough Council and was originally from Islington, north London. His mother, Maria Vincent, 48, was from Hanwell, west London. Thomas had two younger brothers. He enlisted at Hertford.

W. C. VINEY

William Charles Viney, died on 21 February 1918, aged 31.

Gunner, Royal Garrison Artillery, No 1 Depot, Service no. 179460.
Remembered at Lambeth Cemetery, Screen Wall, Blackshaw Road, Tooting, south-west London.

In March 1918 *The South London Press* reported on William Charles Viney's funeral. It explained that Viney had for a long while been exempt from military service because of the "importance of his duties" (he worked for sugar manufacturer James Pascall Ltd) and because he was considered unfit for duty. However, he was re-examined, passed as fit, joined the Royal Garrison Artillery at Camberwell and went to train in Derby. However, three weeks later he had a seizure and never regained consciousness. He was buried with full military honours at Lambeth Cemetery.

Viney's widow, Florence Emily (née Sheaff) and three children, lived at Portland Place South, near Clapham Road. William, then 25, and Florence, 27, had married at All Saints Church, Newington (near Elephant and Castle), on 27 August 1911. William was described on the parish register as a stock-keeper of confectionery, and his father, William Viney, as a general labourer. The 1911 census, conducted a few months earlier, shows William Viney boarding at 7 Freemantle Street, Newington (the address he gives on his marriage record), where he lived with engine fitter Alfred Webster and his family.

C. W. WADMORE

William Childs Wadmore, killed in action on 9 January 1917, aged about 21.

Rifleman, King's Royal Rifle Corps, 10th Bn., Service no. R/31892.
Remembered at Sailly-Saillisel British Cemetery, Somme, France.

I believe there is an error on the Memorial. I can find no trace of a C. W. Wadmore, but there is evidence that a W. C. Wadmore lived in Stockwell at the appropriate time. In addition, *Soldiers Died in the Great War 1914–1919* includes a William Childs Wadmore, born in Stockwell.

The 1911 census tells us that William Childs Wadmore, then 15, was the eldest son of William Wadmore, 43, a carman from Clapham and Eliza Wadmore, 40, from Stockwell. He was employed in what his father called merely "work". William (senior) may have struggled to complete the census return. The names of his children are badly spelt ("harrey" for Harry, for example), and he included one daughter ("douther") who was not at home but at "reformerty school".

Charles Booth, the social observer who walked the streets of London between 1886 and 1903, remarked on the "indescribable filth and squalor" of Bromsgrove Road, which he said was "[by] far the worst place in the division." This was where the Wadmore family lived about 10 years after Booth toured the area – all 10 of them in three rooms at No. 17.

Both William Childs Wadmore and his father, William Wadmore, enlisted. The National Roll of the Great War states that William Childs Wadmore volunteered in September 1915 and was sent to France in December of the same year. He was killed in action at Loos two months later. This conflicts with the Commonwealth War Graves information that he was buried 55 miles away at Sailly-Saillisel.

No Service records have survived for William Childs but Pension records exist for his father, who enlisted in April 1915 and survived. On his Army Pension papers, William Wadmore (senior) described himself as a coal porter and stated that he was a widower – his wife Eliza had died at some point after the 1911 census – with five dependant children. Two of them, Annie and Charles, were "domiciled in Reformatory school".

Wadmore (senior) served in the Army Service Corps in France, but was transferred to the Reserve after he became ill with rheumatism (he also suffered from two episodes of scabies) and was discharged, aged 50, on 19 October 1917. His military character was described as "sober and trustworthy." In 1915 he had told the recruiting officer that he was 44, so it is possible that he lied about his age in order to increase his chances of being accepted. The Pensions Board awarded him a £16 10s. gratuity and a small pension.

J. F. WAKE

John Frederick Wake, died of wounds on 18 May 1918, aged about 19.

Private, Royal Fusiliers, 10th Bn., Service no. 75115; formerly 42273, 99th Training Reserve Battalion. Remembered at St. Sever Cemetery Extension, Rouen, Seine-Maritime, France.

In 1911 John Frederick Wake was a 12-year-old schoolboy. He lived with his family at 25 Bognor Street, Battersea (this street has now disappeared but was once in a tight knot of streets off Thessaly Road). Wake's father, James Stowe Wake, 43, was a painter's labourer originally from Westminster; his mother, Elizabeth Wake, 39, was born in Lambeth. There were five other children.

G. W. WAKELIN

George W. Wakelin, killed in action on 27 July 1916, aged 29.

Private, The Queen's Own Royal West Surrey Regiment, 10th Bn., Service no. G/11762. Remembered at London Rifle Brigade Cemetery, Comines-Warneton, Hainaut, Belgium.

In 1911 estate agent's clerk George W. Wakelin, 24, lived at 40 Sidney Road, Stockwell, with his parents, George Fordham Wakelin, 70, a rent collector born in the West End of London, and Alice Ann Wakelin, 51, from Leckhampton, Gloucestershire, and two younger siblings. The family occupied seven rooms.

A. A. WALLIS

Arthur Ambrose Wallis, killed in action on 8 September 1916, aged 18.

Private, Welsh Regiment, 2nd Bn., Service no. 30098. Remembered at Thiepval Memorial, Somme, France.

In 1911 Arthur Ambrose Wallis was a 13-year-old schoolboy living in three rooms at 29 Fountain Street, off Wandsworth Road, with his parents and seven siblings. His father, Herbert Wallis, 38, was a railway porter from Tunbridge Wells, Kent; his mother, Louisa Wallis, 34, was from Westminster. Wallis enlisted in Camberwell.

W. P. WALLIS

Walter Percy Wallis, died on 3 February 1919, aged 19.

Private, Machine Gun Corps (Infantry), 200th Bn., Service no. 153407. Remembered at Lapugnoy Military Cemetery, Pas de Calais, France.

In 1911 Walter Percy Wallis, a 12-year-old schoolboy and only child, lived at 11 Glendall Street, Stockwell with his parents, Percy William Wallis, 38, a railway riveter from West Malling, Kent, and Sarah Naomi Wallis, 40, from Rye, Sussex. Walter was born in Ashford, Kent. They shared their four-roomed home with John James Seckert, a single 44-year-old restaurant waiter from Maintz, Germany.

F. WARD

Not identified.

G. WARD

Not identified.

W. G. WARE

William George Ware, killed in action on 27 March 1915.

Private, London Regiment, 2nd Bn. (Royal Fusiliers), Service no. 1187. Remembered at Ferme Buterne Military Cemetery, Houplines, Nord, France and at St. Andrew's Church, Landor Road, Stockwell.

The 1911 census shows that William George Ware, 16, was employed as a junior clerk at the Army & Navy Stores in Victoria. He lived at 16

Dalyell Road, Stockwell, with his parents, William Henry Ware, 45, a foreman for a timber merchant, born in Battersea, and Edith Annie Ware, 39, from Chelsea, and an elder sister. The family had eight rooms. Ware enlisted in Westminster.

F. W. WARMAN
Not identified.

A. S. WATERMAN
Arthur Spurgeon Waterman, killed in action on 18 July 1916, aged about 23.
Private, Royal Fusiliers, 12th Bn., Service no. 3295. Remembered at Dranoutre Military Cemetery, Heuvelland, West-Vlaanderen, Belgium.

Arthur Spurgeon Waterman, possibly named after the famous 19th-century evangelist and founder of Stockwell Orphanage Charles Spurgeon, was a house painter. In 1911, aged 19, he lived with his parents and four of his five siblings at 100 Paradise Road, where the family had eight rooms. They had lived at that address since at least 1901. George Phillip Waterman, 56, was a house decorator, born in Clapham; Jane Waterman, 58, was born in Islington, north London.

A. H. WATTS
Alfred Herbert Watts, killed in action on 14 October 1918, aged 20.
Rifleman, Royal Irish Rifles, 15th Bn., Service no. 44390; formerly London Regiment. Remembered at Tyne Cot Memorial, Heuvelland, West-Vlaanderen, Belgium.

In 1911 Alfred Herbert Watts was a 13-year-old schoolboy and part-time milkboy. His father, George Henry Watts, 49, originally from Trowbridge, Wiltshire, was a carman, working for the London & South Western Railway. His mother, Sarah Jane Watts, 46, was from Yarnbrook, Wiltshire. There were two older siblings, a nine-year-old cousin and a boarder in the household, which occupied five rooms at 28 Rosetta Street, South Lambeth (now disappeared, although a Rosetta Close, near Kenchester Close, remains).

G. J. WATTS

George Joseph Watts , killed in action on 23 April 1915, aged 34.
Private, The Queen's Own Royal West Kent Regiment, 1st Bn., Service no. S/1117. Remembered at Ypres (Menin Gate) Memorial, Belgium.

George Joseph Watts's widow, Elizabeth J. Watts, lived at 75 Thorparch Road, Wandsworth Road.

A. E. WAYMARK

Albert Edward Waymark, killed in action on 26 November 1916, aged 37.
Private, Sherwood Foresters (Notts and Derby Regiment), 15th Bn., Service no. 40762. Remembered at Faubourg d'Amiens Cemetery, Arras, Pas de Calais, France.

Details on Albert Edward Waymark are few. We know that he was 5 feet 2¾ inches tall and weighed 9½ stone. He measured 40 inches around the chest. He stated that he was a concrete worker, and was 36 years and 113 days old. He enlisted at Cleethorpes, Lincolnshire on 9 December 1914.

Waymark appears on the 1911 census as a 32-year-old labourer boarding with the Shephard family at Donington-on-Bain, a small village near Louth in Lincolnshire. Waymark had been in Lincolnshire in 1901, when he lived in Wigtoft, Lincolnshire, again boarding. However, the 1891 census shows Waymark living with his parents, William H. Waymark, a valet, and Sarah A. Waymark, at 9 Stamford Buildings, off South Lambeth Road. Sarah later moved to 38 Heyford Avenue, South Lambeth.

H. T. WEATHERLEY

Henry Thomas Weatherley, died on 24 January 1916.
Private, London Regiment, 24th Bn. (The Queen's), Service no. 4712. Remembered at Noeux-les-Mines Communal Cemetery, Pas de Calais, France.

In 1911 Henry Thomas Weatherley was 14 and out of work. He lived with his parents, Alfred Weatherley, 45, a painter from Uxbridge, and Elizabeth Jane Weatherley, 45, from Maldon, Essex, at 158 Larkhall Lane, Stockwell where the family had five rooms. Three siblings lived at home. Henry's uncle Jack John Weatherley, a married baker and father of nine, lived with the family.

A. WEBB

Arthur Webb, died of wounds on 31 August 1918, aged 35.

Serjeant, London Regiment, 21st Bn. (First Surrey Rifles), Service no. 651657. Remembered at St. Sever Cemetery Extension, Rouen, Seine-Maritime, France, and at St. Andrew's Church, Landor Road, Stockwell.

Shortly after draper Arthur Webb presented himself at the Camberwell recruiting office in Flodden Road in June 1915 he started on a rapid trajectory up the ranks. Exactly a month later, he was appointed paid Lance Corporal. By the end of July he was Corporal, by October Lance Serjeant, and before he was posted to France he was Acting Serjeant. By January 1917 he was Serjeant. Webb's conduct was excellent – but not perfect. He was reprimanded for being late for company parade some time in May 1917. It was all over on 31 August 1918, when Webb died of a gunshot wound that had penetrated his spine.

Webb stood 5 feet 4½ inches with a 39-inch chest. He weighed 8¾ stone. He left a collection of effects, all forwarded to his mother, including the usual photos, letters, identity discs, pipe and notebook, but also two pairs of glasses, a watch and chain and a rosary in a tin box.

Webb was an Anglican: his documents state this clearly and he was a member of St. Andrew's Church of England in Landor Road, where he is remembered on the tiled memorial panel. Moreover, before the war, Webb lived in a Church institution. The 1911 census shows him, then aged 27 and working as a commercial clerk, living with his widowed mother, Lambeth-born Mary Jane Webb, 51, three siblings and two boarders (they were young Church of England ministers) at 57 Stockwell Road, a "preventive home" for girls, dedicated to training girls for domestic service. Mary Jane Web later moved to 22 Kendoa Road, Clapham.

A. E. WEBB

Albert Edward Webb, killed in action on 18 April 1918.

Gunner, Royal Field Artillery, "C" Bty. 275th Bde., Service no. 210735. Remembered at Fouquières Churchyard Extension, Pas de Calais, France.

Albert Edward Webb lived in Stockwell. He enlisted at Camberwell.

G. R. WEBB

Not identified.

G. WEDDERBURN

Not identified.

W. WEIGHT

Not identified.

A. G. WELLINGS

Alfred George Wellings, killed in action on 2 August 1917, aged about 23.

Private, Coldstream Guards, 3rd Bn., Service no. 10167. Remembered at Artillery Wood Cemetery, Belgium.

A tentative identification. In 1911 an Alfred George Wellings was working as a page at the Junior Athenaeum Club at 116 Piccadilly, London. He was 17 and born in Vauxhall.

T. H. WELLINGS

Thomas Henry Wellings, died of wounds on 1 October 1918, aged about 19.

Private, The Queen's Own Royal West Kent Regiment, 1st Bn., Service no. 29546. Remembered at Grevillers British Cemetery, Pas de Calais, France.

This is a tentative identification. In the 1911 census the only Thomas Wellings listed for Lambeth was aged 12 and living in two rooms at 35 Camellia Street, South Lambeth with his widowed 43-year-old mother, who called herself merely "Mrs. Wellings" on the return and worked at a cardboard box factory. Another son, George Wellings, aged 9, also lived there. Mrs. Wellings, who had two other children living elsewhere, was from Blackfriars. She did not give a place of birth for her sons.

On 20 July 1915 a Thomas Henry Wellings enlisted in the 21st Battalion of the London Regiment. He was 16 but lied and gave his age as 19 and two months. He was found out and discharged but the Army was impressed with his good military character. "Could have made a good soldier if of the required military age," was written in his file.

Wellings's discharge papers give a portrait of a skinny teenager: a fresh complexion, grey eyes, light brown hair, 5 feet 6 inches, with a 36-inch chest, but under 8 stone. His physical development was judged to be only "fair". He gave his address as 2 Thorncroft Street, a few streets away from Camellia Street. If this is a correct identification he must have re-enlisted.

T. F. WELLINGTON

Thomas Frederick Wellington, killed in action on 2 July 1915, aged 26.
Driver, Royal Engineers, L.Z. Cable Section, Service no. 70152.
Remembered at Ypres (Menin Gate) Memorial, Belgium.

On 10 August 1915, less than a month after Thomas Frederick Wellington, a Driver, was killed in action at Ypres, the Royal Engineers Records Office wrote to his bereaved mother, Rose Cockman: "Special information has been received... He was killed in action 2/7/15 and was buried behind Signal Station at Zillebeke, approx: Square L.22.D Map Belgium Sheet 28. 1/40,000." But somehow Wellington's remains were lost, and he is remembered instead on the panels of the Menin Gate Memorial to the missing of Ypres.

The Records Officer's letter crossed with one of Mrs. Cockman's own in which she asked about the whereabouts of her son's will and small-book (a pocket-sized book containing an abbreviated record of service, as well as instructions for cleaning equipment and uniform, notes on field cooking, Army rules and regulations). These were not in his custody, the officer told Mrs. Cockman in a letter sent the following day. However, Wellington's personal effects were sent on. As well as the usual watch, pipe, diary, letters, handkerchiefs, gloves, and so on, they included a holdall containing a razor, two toothbrushes, a lather brush, shaving soap and a "housewife" (a small sewing kit for making repairs to uniforms). Plus his driver's licence.

Wellington's Army career was solid, with no conduct issues. He started out in the London Army Troops of the Royal Engineers. He stayed 139 days and was discharged "in consequence of joining [the] regular army." He transferred to the London Signals Training Centre and from there on 16 December 1914 went to Houghton Regis, Bedfordshire, where the Electrical Signalling Branch of the School of Military Engineering was based. He went to France on 26 December.

Thomas Frederick Wellington, 5 feet 6 or 8 inches tall (depending on who was doing the measuring – both heights are given in his records), weighed over 10½ stone, with a 39-inch chest, was judged of "good" physical development. He had a fair complexion, dark grey eyes and light brown hair.

In civilian life he had a varied career: from "ticket printer" in 1911, to engineer's photographer when joining the Army in 1914. He also described himself as a draughtsman. The 1911 census shows Thomas Wellington, then 21 and working as a ticket printer, living with his mother, step-father, and siblings and step-siblings at 15 Horace Street (this street is now disappeared), Stockwell. Charles Booth, in his poverty map of 1886–1903 described Horace Street as "poor and crowded".

Thomas's mother, Rose, 44, from Torrington, Essex, had married Ernest Cockman, 39, a timber carman from Wandsworth, in about 1894. She had at least two children from her previous marriage: Thomas, and Rose Wellington, 10, both born in Southwark. At the time of his death, Thomas had eight siblings.

J. WELLS

Not identified.

C. G. WHEELER

Clarence George Wheeler, died of wounds on 4 April 1917, aged 24.

Driver, Royal Field Artillery, "A" Bty. 162nd Bde., Service no. L/21895. Remembered at Faubourg d'Amiens Cemetery, Arras, Pas de Calais, France.

In 1911 Clarence George Wheeler, 18, was a grocer's assistant. He lived with his parents, George Henry Wheeler, 46, a glass cutter from Sevenoaks, Kent, and Fanny Wheeler, 48, from Canterbury, Kent, in four rooms at 35 Holland Street (now Caldwell Street), Stockwell, as well as his four siblings. Clarence was born in Stepney, east London.

A. V. O. WHITE

Not identified.

F. H. WHITE

Not identified.

H. I. WHITE

Henry Ingham White, died of wounds on 15 August 1917, aged 30.
Rifleman, London Regiment, 16th Bn. (Queen's Westminster Rifles),
Service no. 550898. Remembered at Lijssenthoek Military Cemetery,
Poperinge, West-Vlaanderen, Belgium.

The 1911 census shows that Henry Ingham White, 22, was one of two sons
of William George White, 57, and Emma White, 52. Henry and his brother
William lived with their parents at 11 Stirling Road, Stockwell, where they
shared seven rooms. Both Williams worked in a bag and luggage shop,
William senior as manager and William junior as secretary, while Henry
was a fancy leather worker. Henry enlisted at Westminster.

W. H. WHITE

William Henry White, killed in action on 27 May 1918, aged 19.
Private, Leicestershire Regiment, 8th Bn., Service no. 41697; formerly
Royal West Surrey Regiment. Remembered at Soissons Memorial,
Aisne, France.

William Henry White, a private in the Leicestershire Regiment, was in
England until 3 May 1916, when he sailed for Le Havre. The records show
that he returned to London on 22 August 1916 and was admitted to the
3rd London General Hospital at Wandsworth, where he was treated for
trench fever. This disease, variously known as Wolhynia fever, shin bone
fever, quintan fever or five-day fever, is caused by an organism transmitted
by body lice.

Soldiers serving on the front line lived in squalid, damp and cold conditions. In the fire trench – that is, the foremost of the three zig-zag trenches,
the others being the support trench and the reserve trench – soldiers
frequently lived among dead bodies and faeces. These were ideal conditions for rats and flies, and for transmitting dysentery and lice. In the
freezing cold, men huddled together for warmth, enabling lice to pass from
one person to the next. Even when not in the fire trench, the men stayed
close to one another because they were not allowed to light fires as these
would attract shelling or, later in the war, attack by enemy aircraft.

Opportunities for bathing and washing clothes were limited. The aim
was to take a bath every 10 days when away from the front line but this was
not always possible. Therefore, soldiers suffered almost permanent lice

infestations, especially in the seams of their uniforms. The usual method for killing lice was to run a candle up and down the seams or to pick them off by hand. Lice eggs attached to body hair were killed using a paste of naphthalene. From 1915 to 1918 between one-fifth and one-third of all British troops reported ill had trench fever, and it is estimated that 97 per cent of men, including officers, had lice.

Trench fever was an unpleasant disease. Symptoms came on suddenly and included high fever, severe headache, painful eyeballs, soreness of the muscles of the legs and back and hyper-sensitivity of the shins. The patient could relapse frequently and recovery usually took about a month. Even so, White's 47 days in hospital were probably a welcome respite from service on the front.

White, a messenger in civilian life, claimed to be just over 19 when he enlisted on 13 August 1915, although he was probably only 16. His file does not indicate that his deception was discovered. He was 5 feet 4 inches tall, with a 38-inch chest and a scar on the middle finger of his right hand. His physical development was judged to be "good."

White went missing on 27 May 1918 and was later declared dead.

In 1911 White lived with his parents and three siblings in four rooms at 8 Rattray Road, Brixton. His father, William Henry White, 40, an assistant in a bootmaker's shop, was born in South Lambeth; his mother, Matilda White, 33, was from Battersea.

E. F. WHITING

Ernest Frank Whiting, died of wounds on 14 October 1917, aged 26.

Private, East Surrey Regiment, 8th Bn., Service no 25607. Remembered at Dozinghem Military Cemetery, Poperinge, West-Vlaanderen, Belgium.

In 1911 Ernest Frank Whiting, 20, a law clerk, lived at 25 Durand Gardens, Stockwell with his parents, Edward Whiting, 60, a joiner, and Susannah Whiting, 57, both from Dover, Kent, and four siblings plus a brother-in-law, a niece and a boarder. Whiting enlisted in Dorking, Surrey.

S. F. WHITING

Stanley Franklin Whiting, died of illness on 27 January 1918, aged about 20.

Aircraftman 1st Class, Royal Naval Air Service, H.M.S. *President II*, Service no. F/13871. Remembered at Wandsworth (Streatham) Cemetery, Garratt Lane, Tooting, south-west London.

In 1911 Clapham-born Stanley Franklin Whiting was 13 and living in a six-roomed house at 85 Larkhall Lane, Stockwell where his family had lived since at least 1901. His father, Benjamin Franklin Whiting, 40, was a corn and coal merchant, born in Battersea; his mother, Augusta Whiting, 39, was from Biggleswade, Bedfordshire. Stanley had one sibling and the family had a live-in domestic servant.

C. L. WHITTINGHAM

Claude Lionel Whittingham, killed in action on 31 July 1917, aged 19.

Private, Hertfordshire Regiment, Service no. 269729; formerly Essex Regiment. Remembered at Ypres (Menin Gate) Memorial, Belgium. Brother of *Horace John Baker Whittingham*.

Claude Lionel Whittingham enlisted at Camberwell on 10 December 1914 and was attached to the 1st London General Hospital of the Royal Army Medical Corps (the military extension of St. Batholomew's Hospital). The hospital was stationed in buildings requisitioned from St. Gabriel's College, a residential training college for women teachers, on Cormont Road, Myatts Fields. Myatts Fields Park was closed to the public until 1921, due to its use as a hospital.

By September 1915 Whittingham was serving on the H.M.H.S *Aquitania*, which was built as a luxury liner but which had been converted to a hospital ship. With 4,182 beds, the *Aquitania* was the largest of 71 hospital ships used during the First World War. Whittingham served as an orderly until March 1916, when he joined the war effort in Gallipoli. We do not know what Whittingham's role was in this theatre of war but he may have continued to serve in some capacity on the *Aquitania*. He returned to England on 7 May 1916.

On 19 July, while based in England, Whittingham requested a transfer to the 3/5th London Field Artillery Brigade "for the purpose of serving abroad". It is not clear from the records what happened to this request. In any event, Whittingham was transferred first to the Essex Regiment and, on 9 September, to the Hertfordshires. He was posted to France on 4 November and listed as missing in action on 31 July 1917. A short time later he was presumed dead.

In civilian life Whittingham was a grocer's clerk. When he joined up he was described as 5 feet 6 inches, 9 stone, with a 35½ inch chest, a fair complexion, with grey eyes and "reddish" hair. By the time he transferred to the Hertfordshires he had grown three inches in both height and chest. His military character was described as "very good".

The 1911 census shows Claude Whittingham as a 13-year-old living at 28 Angell Road, Brixton, with his parents, Manchester-born John Whittingham, 48, an apartment housekeeper, and Alice Whittingham, 48, from Bermondsey, and five siblings (including 17-year-old Horace Whittingham, a junior commercial clerk, who is also on the Memorial) and six boarders, among them an Irish producer of plays and a pair of music-hall artists.

H. J. WHITTINGHAM

Horace John Baker Whittingham, died of wounds on 28 April 1918, aged 24.

Corporal, Tank Corps, 1st Bn., Service no. 76274; formerly Royal Fusiliers. Remembered at Marissel French National Cemetery (near Beauvais), Oise, France. Brother of *Claude Lionel Whittingham*.

H. C. WICKENS

Henry Charles Wickens, died of illness on 22 October 1918, aged 29.

Driver, Royal Field Artillery, "C" Bty., 342nd Bde., Service no. 238091. Remembered at Brookwood Military Cemetery, near Pirbright, Woking, Surrey.

After volunteering in 1914 and completing his training, Henry Charles Wickens served with "C" battery. He became seriously ill (the details are unknown) and died in the military hospital at Millbank, London in 1918.

In 1911 Henry Charles Wickens, then aged 22, was an assistant in a fish shop. He lived with his parents, Alfred Wickens, 49, who worked for a jam maker and was born in Camberwell, and Harriett Wickens, 47, place of birth is unknown. Henry was one of three children (the other two lived elsewhere) and the family occupied three rooms at 123 Wandsworth Road.

A. E. WICKES
Not identified.

H. W. WILD

Herbert William Wild, killed in action on 15 September 1916, aged 27.

Rifleman, London Regiment, 21st Bn. (First Surrey Rifles), Service no. 4023. Remembered at Warlencourt British Cemetery, Pas de Calais, France. Brother of *Reuben Edward Wild.*

Herbert John Wild's attempts to find out what happened to his two sons, Herbert William Wild and Reuben Edward Wild, and the whereabouts of Reuben's body have survived in the archive. Wild's letters are business-like and to the point, but nonetheless they make difficult reading. His sense of frustration with the lack of information coming from the Army and his grief for his boys bubble just below the surface.

Four of the five Wild boys, Herbert, John, Reuben and Edward, served in the war. Cicero, aged only eight in 1914, was too young.

The first sign of trouble was in October 1915. Annie Wild, their mother, wrote to the Army authorities enquiring about Reuben: "Could you give me any information concerning my son who I have not heard from for 3 weeks." The Army, it appears, had not yet told his family that he was missing in action at the Battle of Loos. The letter is annotated "No report on hand." The Wilds, however, persisted in trying to find answers.

In 10 September 1916, nearly a year after Reuben died, Herbert John wrote, "In answer to your letter regarding my son's death on 25/9/15, will you kindly inform me of how he met his death and also the name of the place." He was anxious also about proving to the insurance company that his son was dead as there was no death certificate. In fact, there were in the file two reports on the circumstances of Reuben's death. One includes a transcript of a statement given by Rifleman McMeahon:

> Wild is another chum of mine and he [went] missing 25/9/15. I asked a man called [Private] C. Taylor whose number I forget but he is in C [Company] 11 Platoon and he told me he saw [Private] Wild wounded in the shoulder in the second line of German trenches at the Railway at Ypres and he asked him to go back with him but he would not. The Capt. called one of them to go back with him so Taylor went on to the third line with the Capt. and left Wild in the trench. I understand they were driven back to the 2nd line where [Private] Wild was wounded but he has been missing ever since.

There was another report, from Private J. Taylor: "Wild was a short fair [man] about 19. He had no moustache. I saw him dead in the trench killed by a bomb. There was no time to bury him."

The files do not record whether this information was passed on to the family. On 3 April 1920, however, after receiving Reuben's medals, Herbert John, wrote: "I had four sons serving in the Great War. Two of them sacrificed their lives and I have never received any good information as to where they were killed or buried." This letter, badly damaged and illegible in parts, includes the words, "I intend to go to Belgium or France... If you would kindly... the name of the place... son R. Wild was last seen alive I shall be grateful to you. [...] My other son was killed in the Battle of the Somme 1916... several times by the Graves Commission but up to now I have not received any."

The "other son" was Herbert William Wild, who was killed in action on 15 September 1916, nearly a year after Reuben's disappearance. He was married to Polly Lily May Wild and had a baby daughter, Ivy May, born on 6 February 1916.

A note in Herbert William's file says that his personal effects were posted in February 1917 but in November his grieving father wrote: "My daughter in law [Polly] informs me that she has received no effects of her Husband the late Rifleman H. W. Wild... who has been dead 14 months. All she has received is his identification disc. I myself have the official information of where he was buried... If he was buried [and it was] possible to recover his identification disc it must also be possible to recover any other personal effects. I have lost two sons in this war and have two others serving... I have nothing at all to prove the other son's death [Reuben] as he was reported missing after the Battle of Loos."

In civilian life, Herbert William was an oil and calorman (selling fuel to householders), living at 34 Crawshay Road (now disappeared, this was adjacent to Eythorne Road, on the east side of Brixton Road). He stood 5 feet 2½ inches tall and his chest measured 39 inches. His physical development was deemed to be "good." After the war, his widow was awarded 18s. 9d. a week. She and her daughter lived at 64 Robsart Street, Stockwell.

At 5 feet 3 inches, Reuben Wild was a little taller than his brother. He weighed 8 stone and had a 36-inch chest and his physical development was also judged to be "good." As there are no Service records for Reuben, his occupation is unknown (the 1911 census describes him as an errand boy). Herbert John Wild, was a gas slot meter collector from Lambeth; Annie was from Southwark. In 1911 the family lived at 24 Halstead Street, Brixton.

R. E. WILD

Reuben Edward Wild, died of wounds on 25 September 1915, aged 20.

Rifleman, King's Royal Rifle Corps, "C" Coy. 9th Bn., Service no. R/6573. Remembered at Ypres (Menin Gate) Memorial, Belgium. Brother of *Herbert William Wild.*

J. WILKIN

John Wilkin, killed in action on 16 August 1916, aged 24.

Private, Royal Fusiliers, 12th Bn., Service no. 17677. Remembered at Thiepval Memorial, Somme, France.

John Wilkin enlisted in Southwark in June 1915, and in September was sent to the front. He saw action in the Battle of Loos and died in August 1916, during the first Battle of the Somme. He lived at 26 Wyvil Road, off South Lambeth Road.

The 1911 census includes only one John Wilkin in Lambeth, a 19-year-old flour mill labourer who was one of 13 children of flour mill worker Robert Wilkin, 45, and Annie Amelia Wilkin, 46, who then lived at 48 Commercial Road, Waterloo.

H. WILLIAMS
Not identified.

H. WILLIAMS
Not identified.

S. WILLIAMS
Not identified.

W. J. WILLIAMS

William John Williams, died on 8 August 1917, aged 30.

Rifleman, King's Royal Rifle Corps, "D" Coy. 11th Bn., Service no. R/19181. Remembered at Ypres (Menin Gate) Memorial, Belgium.

William John Williams was born in Vauxhall and lived in Lambeth. He enlisted in Piccadilly, central London. His parents, James and Henrietta Williams, lived at 36 Kenchester Street (now disappeared, replaced by Kenchester Close), near Wilcox Road.

S. H. WILLIAMSON

Not identified.

A. WILLIS

Not identified.

S. F. WILLIS

Stanley Frank Willis, died on 13 August 1917.

Rifleman, London Regiment, 1/9th Bn. (Queen Victoria's Rifles), Service no. 415208 ; formerly 7th London Regiment. Remembered at Ypres (Menin Gate) Memorial, Belgium.

Stanley Frank Willis was born in Clapham and lived in Stockwell. He enlisted in Camberwell.

B. H. WINTER

Bertram Horace Winter, killed in action on 11 April 1917, aged 27.

Rifleman, Rifle Brigade, 13th Bn., Service no. S/15614. Remembered at Arras Memorial, Pas de Calais, France.

Milkman and former butcher Bertram Horace Winter signed up at the Whitehall recruiting office on 15 February 1916. He served just over nine months before dying at Arras on 11 April 1917.

Winter initially joined the 3rd Battalion, but was transferred to the 13th in July 1916, and was appointed unpaid Corporal in November. He stood 5 feet 4½ inches tall, with a 37-inch chest, and weighed a little over 8½ stone. His physical development was judged to be "good."

Bertram's widowed mother Augusta was named as next of kin. She lived at 25 Viceroy Road, South Lambeth. The 1911 census shows that Winter was working as a butcher's assistant. He lived at 147 Larkhall Lane, over the shop, with butcher Albert Henry and his wife Lydia Eliza Henry, both 41, a childless couple.

In 1911, Bertram's parents, William Charles Winter, 59, a paper hanger and house decorator, and his wife Augusta Winter, 58, both Lambeth-born, lived at 31 Courland Grove, Stockwell. They had seven children, four living at home, and had lived at this address since at least 1901.

E. E. WINTER

Edward Ernest Winter, died of wounds on 24 August 1916, aged 34.

Lance Corporal, King's Royal Rifle Corps, 8th Bn., Service no. R/14491. Remembered at Thiepval Memorial, Somme, France.

It was easy to find Edward Ernest Winter in the standard sources of information, *Soldiers Died in the Great War 1914–1919*, the Commonwealth War Graves Commission database and the *National Roll of the Great War*.

However, Winter did not seem to exist in the 1911 census. I doubted that he was related to Bertram Horace Winter, as I had not seen the name Edward in any of the census returns for that family (and indeed that proved to be the case). However, before I gave up looking, I searched the 1911 census for 49 Kimberley Road, Stockwell, the address quoted in the *National Roll of the Great War*, to see if Edward was living at that address before the war. But there was no trace of him: the house was occupied by the Gibsons and the Weingartners.

Then I serched for Winter in the British Army World War I Service records. I was lucky – his file had survived. What's more, it contained a surprise. Edward Ernest Winter gave his next of kin as his mother, Mrs. S. E. Weingartner of 49 Kimberley Road. He had, it appeared, changed his name. Thousands of families with German origins did this after the war started. Although the German community was deeply knitted into the social fabric of Britain, particularly in cities where many worked in baking, confectionery and hairdressing, some felt under threat from local animosity. (Edward's father Charles Weingartner, who died at some point between 1891 and 1901, was not German but from Vienna, Austria.)

By the time Edward attested on 12 July 1915 (he volunteered in August 1914, according *The National Roll of Honour*), south London had already experienced bitter anti-German riots. In October 1914 there was a wave of protests against businesses and buildings believed to be German-owned, and this was followed by widespread aggression after 1 May 1915 when the passenger ship *Lusitania* was attacked by the Germans without warning and sank within minutes. While some Stockwell families with German-sounding names were confident enough to keep them (including those of Leonard Erdbeer, Bertie Hoft, Henry Lippold and Ernest Oehring, who are all on the Memorial), it seems that the Weingartners were not.

Edward Winter's family was deeply concerned about his welfare. On 29 September 1916, about a month after he was deemed to have died, his sister Lina, who had changed her name to Vera, was desperate for news of him. "The last I heard from him was the 11th of August... I heard through a friend [illegible] he had been wounded," she wrote to the Army authorities. On the day she wrote, the Army issued a form letter stating that Edward was missing. Vera wrote again in October. "Can you give me any news respecting L/Cpl. E. Winter... I may mention he has been wounded and missing since August 21st 16. Anxiously awaiting any news." Finally, there is a short, resigned note. By then the family can have had no expectations that he would be found: "I suppose there is still no further news of L/Cpl E. Winter."

The National Roll of Honour sums up Edward's war career: Having volunteered in August 1914, he was drafted to France in January 1915 and took part in the fighting at Neuve Chapelle, Hill 60, Ypres, Festubert, Vermeiles, Vimy Ridge and the Somme. He was reported missing on the Somme on 24 August 1916, and was presumed to have been killed in action.

From the Service records an image of Edward emerges: he was 5 feet 4½ inches tall with a 39-inch chest; there was a small mole in the middle of his back; he said his civilian job was "gas meter tester".

In 1911 Edward was a boarder at 54 Penton Place, Newington, near Elephant and Castle, where he lived with Henry Burnett, 69, a jewel case maker, and his wife Martha Ann Burnett, 65, and Martha's daughter Florence Emily Bousted, 39. At that time he was employed as a clerk. His mother, Sarah Ellen Weingartner, 68, from Marcham, Berkshire, lived with three of her seven children, including Lina/Vera at 49 Kimberley Road, Stockwell, where they occupied five rooms.

W. H. WILSON

Not identified.

S. C. WITHEY

Sidney Charles Withey, killed in action on 8 December 1917,
aged about 22.

Serjeant, London Regiment, 2/13th Bn. (Kensington), Service no. 490673.
Remembered at Jerusalem War Cemetery, Israel and at St. Andrew's
Church, Landor Road, Stockwell.

Insurance clerk Sidney Charles Withey lived at 14 Dalyell Road, Brixton
with his parents and six siblings. His father, Wiliam Henry Withey, 46,
was a travelling salesman for grocery products, born in Yeovil, Somerset.
His mother, Louisa Emily, 45, was from Camden Town, north London. The
family occupied six rooms and had lived at this address since at least 1901.
Withey enlisted in Kensington.

W. G. E. WOODARD

William George Edwin Woodard, died of wounds on 12 August 1918,
aged 55.

Lance Corporal, Army Service Corps, 364th Mechanical Transport Coy.,
Service no M2/079669. Remembered at Les Baraques Military Cemetery,
Sangatte, France.

William George Edwin Woodard, who died aged 55, is the oldest of the men
on the Memorial whose age at death I have been able to identify. The 1911
census shows that he was born in about 1864 and worked as a taxi driver.
His address was 16 Canterbury Road, Brixton, which he shared with his wife,
Helena Sylvia Woodard, then 49, originally from Holborn, central London;
sons William Woodard, 23, a taxi driver, and Frederick Woodard, 21, an
assistant in a grocer's shop; mother-in-law Elizabeth Robshaw, 78, from
Witham, Essex; May Robshaw, 21, an assistant in a draper's shop; cousin
Frederick Robshaw, 33, a bookbinder's assistant; and Dorothy Sherry, 22,
a grocer's shop assistant. Another of William and Helena's children lived
elsewhere. The family occupied seven rooms. In 1901 the Woodard family
lived at 39 Chester Street, north Lambeth.

H. J. R. WOODCOCK

Henry James Robert Woodcock, killed in action on 9 September 1916, aged 21.

Private, London Regiment, 1/14th Bn. (London Scottish), Service no. 6951. Remembered at Serre Road Cemetery No. 2, Somme, France.

The Service history file for Henry James Robert Woodcock contains few details. Woodcock enlisted in the Territorial Force on 28 February 1916 and was posted on the same day.

The 1911 census shows Henry, aged 16, was one of eight children of charwoman (cleaner) Eliza Woodcock, 41, from Donhead St. Mary, Wiltshire. He lived with his family at 125 Lavender Hill, Battersea, and worked as a book assistant. Henry's father, also called Henry, 44, from Gorleston, Norfolk, was described on the 1901 census as a "master bookseller". However, in 1911 he was a patient in the Wandsworth Union Infirmary on St. John's Hill, Battersea.

T. J. WOODLEY

Thomas James Woodley, killed in action on 15 June 1918, aged 29.

Private, Oxford and Bucks Light Infantry, 1/4th Bn., Service no. 203597; formerly 2725, Royal Buckinghamshire Hussars. Remembered at Boscon British Cemetery, near Asiago, Italy and at St. Andrew's Church, Landor Road, Stockwell.

Printer's labourer Thomas James Woodley, aged 23 in 1911, lived at 6 Edithna Street, Stockwell, where his family occupied six rooms. The other members of the household were his widowed mother, Rosa Ann Woodley, 55, from Southwark, and five siblings. Woodley married Ethel Worby at St. Andrew's Church on 14 December 1916. She later gave her address as 14 Glenelg Road, Acre Lane, Brixton.

A. WORBY

Arthur Worby, died on 16 November 1918, aged about 20.

Private, The Queen's Own Royal West Surrey Regiment, Service no. G/61093. Remembered at Lambeth Cemetery, Screen Wall, Blackshaw Road, Tooting, south-west London.

In 1911, Arthur Worby, aged 12, lived at 76 Crimsworth Road, near Wandsworth Road. His father, widower John Worby, 53, was an Army pensioner from Cambridge. There were five siblings on the census return, their places of birth possibly reflecting their father's Army career. Emma Worby, 24, was born in Chatham, Kent; Jessie Worby, 20, a laundress, was born in Port Royal, Jamaica; John Worby, 15, an errand boy, was born in Dublin, Ireland; Frank William Worby, 16, an errand boy, was born in Middlesbrough; Arthur Worby, 12, was born in South Lambeth. Arthur's one-year-old nephew, Arthur Worby Gridner, was present on the night of the census.

T.I. WORLEY

Thomas Isaac Worley, died of wounds on 8 December 1917, aged 34.

Private, London Regiment, 1/19th Bn. (St. Pancras), Service no. 613802. Remembered at Etaples Military Cemetery, Pas de Calais, France.

In 1911 Thomas Isaac Worley, then 27, was an auctioneer's clerk. He lived at 47 Lansdowne Gardens, Stockwell with his parents, Isaac Brames Worley, 56, a cook from Pimlico, and Margaret Worley, 53, from Coventry, and an elder brother. The family shared nine rooms. Another sibling lived elsewhere.

F. WORTHY

Frank Worthy, killed in action on 15 September 1916, aged 19.

Rifleman, London Regiment, "D" Coy. 1/21st Bn. (First Surrey Rifles), Service no. 4785. Remembered at Thiepval Memorial, Somme, France.

In 1911 Frank Worthy was a 14-year-old schoolboy. He lived at 5 Addison Place, Brixton (now part of Normandy Road) with his parents, Alfred James Worthy, 45, a sign writer for the council, and Matilda Clara Worthy, 37, both born in Lambeth. Frank had two siblings. The family occupied four rooms. Worthy enlisted in Lambeth.

J. T. WOTTON

John Thomas Wotton, died on 6 March 1917, aged 29.

Corporal, East Surrey Regiment, 13th Bn., Service no. 13413.
Remembered at Abbeville Community Cemetery Extension, Somme, France.

In 1911 John Thomas Wotton, then 22, was working as a potman and barman at the Wirtemberg Arms, at 165 Wirtemberg Street, Clapham. The street was renamed Stonhouse Street in 1919 – and the pub has likewise been renamed The Stonhouse. In 1913, aged 24, Wotton married Annie Lillian Ellis, 26, at St. Andrew's Church, Landor Road. He gave his address as 65 Cottage Grove, Stockwell.

A. G. WRIGHT

Arthur George Wright, died of wounds on 9 August 1916, aged 20.

Private, London Regiment, 2nd Bn. (Royal Fusiliers), Service no. 1633.
Remembered at Warlincourt Halte British Cemetery, Saulty, Pas de Calais, France.

Arthur George Wright was born in Lambeth and enlisted in Westminster; he lived in Lambeth. After the war, his father, Arthur John Wright, gave his address as 34 Thorncroft Street, Wandsworth Road.

F. WYBREW

Frank Wybrew, killed in action on 18 September 1916, aged 23.

Private, West Yorkshire Regiment (Prince of Wales's Own), 1st Bn., Service no. 10622. Remembered at Thiepval Memorial, Somme, France, and at St. Andrew's Church, Landor Road, Stockwell.

Frank Wybrew was baptised at St. Andrew's Church, Landor Road, Stockwell on 14 May 1893, the son of William Joseph Wybrew, a saddler, and Rosa Wybrew. They gave their address as 65 Andalus Road, Stockwell. I have not been able to find Frank Wybrew in the 1911 census.

C. J. YOUNG

Charles John Young, killed in action on 21 March 1918, aged 20.

Private, Essex Regiment, 11th Bn., Service no. 42404; formerly Northamptonshire Regiment. Remembered at Beaumetz-les-Cambrai Military Cemetery No. 1, Pas de Calais, France.

The 1911 census shows Charles John Young, as a 12-year-old schoolboy living at 21 Camellia Street, Stockwell. His widowed mother, Elizabeth Young, 44, was born in Germany and made her living as a charwoman (cleaner). There were six siblings and the family lived in two rooms. Elizabeth later lived at 97 Hartington Road, South Lambeth.

The index

NAMES

There are some errors in the names on the Memorial (transposed initials and spelling errors) and some names are not in strict alphabetical order. For the book, I have corrected the order and noted the mistakes I have found.

DIED

In some cases, *Soldiers Died in the Great War 1914–1919* gives information on how servicemen died. The usual descriptions are "Died", "Died of wounds" and "Killed in action". In many cases, the cause of death was not recorded or was not known (these were listed simply as "Died").

SERVICE

I have given rank, regiment and service number as provided by the Commonwealth War Graves Commission (CWGC). Where a soldier or sailor is not listed by the CWGC I have used details in *Soldiers Died in the Great War 1914–1919.* In a few cases, details are taken directly from Army Service records. *Abbreviations*: Battalion *Bn.;* Company *Coy.;* Battery *Bty*.

REMEMBRANCE

I have not distinguished between burial or other forms of remembrance. This overcomes the difficulty of inaccuracies over whether or not a body was found and buried.

MEDALS

I have not listed campaign or standard issue medals, but where I am aware that a man has been awarded a Military Cross or a Military Medal or similar I have noted this.

THE CENSUSES

Occupation: Most of the occupations are taken from the census (some are from Service and Pension records where they exist). *Accommodation*: The 1911 census returns give number of rooms occupied per dwelling. This does not include "scullery, landing, lobby, closet, or bathroom."

Research

The starting point of this project was, of course, the Memorial itself and the 574 names on it. My primary source was the information available online (both free and paid-for). I also used archives and libraries, books, local newspapers, maps and – most important and utterly invaluable – information and photos provided by the families.

MILITARY RECORDS
The first place to look for information on war casualties is the Commonwealth War Graves Commission (CWGC) database, which is available free at www.cwgc.org. The database has information on surname and initials; first names, if known; service number; rank; regiment; company; battalion or division; age at death; date of death; additional information (for example, next of kin's name, home town, address); cemetery or memorial details; nationality. However, many entries are incomplete.

I also consulted *Soldiers Died in the Great War 1914–1919* which is available in print in two separate publications for officers and other ranks and online (paid-for) as a combination of both. In many cases, information on birthplace, place of residence and place of enlistment is included, and this helped me to identify many of the names that were not in the CWGC database or were otherwise difficult to find.

For a few names, I found short biographies in the publications *The National Roll of the Great War 1914–1918* and *De Ruvigny's Roll of Honour 1914–18*. Both are available online (paid-for). Information on some of the naval casualites is available on the *Royal Naval Division Records 1914–1919* (again, available online). I also made some use of the Medal Roll, regimental histories and official war diaries.

The best free resource for information about the fate of the men is the collection of Service and Pension records held in the National Archive at Kew. Records for the men are available there on microfilm.

However, because I was trying to find out about the lives of hundreds of men, it was convenient to use the paid-for service at www.ancestry.co.uk. The original records were severely damaged during the Second World War when the building where they were housed was hit by a bomb. Some were destroyed completely, others were badly fire- and water-damaged.

Furthermore, the microfilm files are in some disarray. Many are mis-labelled or in the wrong order.

The records relating to officers are held as paper originals at the National Archives. You can order digital files (paid-for) to be sent to your email inbox or visit in person (free).

OTHER MEMORIALS

The tiled memorial inside St. Andrew's Church in Landor Road, where 35 of the Stockwell men are also listed with their first names and dates of death, helped me make identifications that had previously eluded me. Contemporary reports in *The South London Press* listed men who were named on temporary (and now lost) wooden war shrines at St. Mark's, Kennington, St. Michael's, Stockwell, and St. Anne's, South Lambeth Road.

THE CENSUS

The 1911 census provides a snapshot of life for the men just three years before the outbreak of war. This census was the first in which the house-holder completed the return him or herself. Currently, the 1911 census is available only at www.findmypast.co.uk (paid-for). Earlier censuses are available on a variety of websites.

MAPS

The 1938 Geographers' edition of the London A-Z, compiled before the Second World War bombing of London, was useful for tracing the location of long-gone streets, as were Godfrey's Old Ordnance Survey Maps, especially the 1913 editions for Stockwell & Camberwell, Kennington & Walworth and Battersea & Clapham.

In addition, Charles Booth's Poverty map, created in 1898, available free online at booth.lse.ac.uk, revealed information about the demographics of the area through a unique system of colour-coding.

NEWSPAPERS

The South London Press carried comprehensive coverage of the war and its impact on South London, including a weekly page devoted to lists of casual-ties (wounded, missing and killed) and extensive coverage of the service of local schools, workplaces and regiments. *The Brixton Free Press* had excel-lent coverage in the first months of the war and details of the riots of 1915. Both publications reported in detail on the unveiling of the Memorial on 3 May 1922.

Websites

Commonwealth War Graves Commission
www.cwgc.org

National Archives
www.nationalarchives.gov.uk

British Library Newspapers
www.bl.uk

Lambeth Archive
www.lambeth.gov.uk

Imperial War Museum
www.iwm.org.uk

UK National Inventory of War Memorials
www.ukniwm.org.uk

War Memorials Trust
www.warmemorials.org

Roll of Honour
A volunteer-driven project to record all the names on war memorials
www.roll-of-honour.com

World War One Document Archive
www.gwpda.org

The Long, Long Trail
Web resource focusing on the British Army in the First World War.
www.1914-1918.net

First World War
www.firstworldwar.com

The Heritage of the Great War
Dutch site dedicated to the events and consequences of the War.
www.greatwar.nl

World War One Photos
www.ww1photos.com

Acknowledgements

This book would not have been possible without the help and encouragement of the families of the men on the Memorial. Foremost among these is Sheila Dartnell, whose great-uncle Christopher is on the Memorial. Sheila has been tireless in her efforts to protect the names on the Memorial. Other relatives who contacted me include cousins Avril Heron and Clare Stone, who gave me information about the Rance brothers; Patricia Pearson, who told me about Guy Pearson; Ray Coleman who gave me his grandfather Frederick Parker's story; Daniel Desaleux, who mapped out his family for me after I contacted him on Facebook; Peter Brasier, who gave me Harold Hill's family background; Colin Charman, who gave me access to his family tree; Mike Barnes, who put me straight on the identity of A. H. Barnes; Sue and Ron Falder, who sent me letters and a photo written by Jesse Goff; Brenda Wilkinson, for information about Arthur Edward Blacker and John James Renton; Helen Carn, who contacted me about Charles Henry Charnock; Andy McIlvenna, who identified Albert Marjeram; the family of Albert Curtis for their help; Glynis Park, who told me about Horace Stilwell; Norman Routledge, who provided information on Arthur Routledge; Sue McCullough, who wrote to me about Joseph Terrett; Alan Humphries at the Department for Business, Innovation and Skills for information on Frederick Marlow and John Strachan Kelly; Peter Joslin for information on the Joslin family; Paul Ley, who told me of the fortunes of his tailor grandfather Samuel Levy after the war. Also, thanks to Roger Francis, who talked to me about his stone-carver grandfather Frederick Francis. Special thanks go to Peter Munt-Davies, who told me the story of his researches into Harry Hill and proof-read the manuscript for me. Thanks also to the staff of Lambeth Archives and the British Library, and to Ross Davies, Ginny Dougary and Amanda Conquy for their professional insights.

The contributions of Lloyd Clater of Sharpedge, who designed the cover, and of book designer Zara Frith for her advice and assistance with the layout are immeasurable.

Lastly, I must pay tribute to my family: my partner Tim Clifford, who used his legendary editing skills on the manuscript, and patiently put up with my almost permanent attachment to my laptop, and, of course, my two long-suffering daughters Lily and Izzy.

Credits

Amendments

Send amendments and additions to naomi_klein@elefantbooks.com. Corrections will appear on www.stockwellwarmemorial.co.uk.